Practical Project Management

Practical Project Management
Tips, Tactics, and Tools

Harvey A. Levine

JOHN WILEY & SONS, INC.

Copyright © 2002 by Harvey A. Levine. All rights reserved.

Published by John Wiley & Sons, Inc., New York.
Published simultaneously in Canada.

Library of Congress Cataloging-in-Publication Data:

Levine, Harvey A.
    Practical project management : tips, tactics, and tools / Harvey A.
    Levine.
        p.   cm.
    Includes bibliographical references and index.
        ISBN 0-471-20303-3 (alk. paper)
    1. Project management.   I. Title.
    HD69 .P75 L484   2002
    658.4'04—dc21   2002003007

Printed in the United States of America.

10 9 8 7 6 5 4 3 2

CONTENTS

ACKNOWLEDGMENTS

Project Management has often been called the "accidental profession." That designation has come about due to the preponderance of PM practitioners who have found their way to this field, not through a structured education or career strategy, but rather as a side trip from their planned careers. My side trip has lasted some 40 years and, thanks to many whom I have met along the way, the side trip has become a journey of discovery and fulfillment. This book records much of what I have learned and disseminated during that trip. Therefore, it is only fair that I express my gratitude not only to the direct contributors to this material, but also to those who helped to pave the way.

It was way back in 1962 that Adelaide Oppenheim offered me the opportunity to change careers and try my hand at planning and scheduling at GE's Knolls Atomic Power Laboratory. Adelaide encouraged personal growth and enlisted us soldiers to spread the word about the benefits of structured planning and control of projects. Later, moving on to GE's commercial operations, I was afforded the opportunity to bring the benefits of project management to several divisions of this conglomerate. Along the way, Jack Gido encouraged me to present my first technical paper, which eventually led to my emergence as a writer and educator, as well as stimulating me to get involved in the Project Management Institute. After the support of many led to opportunities to teach at Rensselaer Polytechnic Institute, to publish a book for Osborne/McGraw-Hill, and to be elected President and Chairman of the Project Management Institute (all in 1985–1986), I was further encouraged to leave the comfort of the corporation and to strike out on my own. The apprehension associated with such a decision was eased by Joel Koppelman, President of Primavera Systems, who became my first client and a supporter for the next 15 years. Joel was the first of dozens of leaders in the project management tools and services industry that extended a friendly hand and allowed me to become an active member of their community. I wish that I could name all of these people who became an important part of my life, but they would number in the hundreds. But I will single out Roger Meade, CEO of Scitor Corporation, for his faith and support for a decade and a half.

A special attribute of this profession, which has been so endearing to me, has been the willingness of my fellow practitioners to share their ideas and wisdom with each other. People like David Cleland, Harold Kerzner, Francis Webster, Max Wideman, Bill Duncan, Paul Dinsmore, who through their publications, seminars, and support for the development of a body of knowledge in the field of project management, have helped PM to become a recognized and respected profession. I am honored to have been in their company and to have had them as my colleagues.

Much of what is presented in this book is based on work that I have prepared during the past decade, based on my experiences in the field. There were a few areas for which I reached out to others for the benefit of their insight and expertise. I offer my gratitude to the following colleagues, who responded to my invitation to participate in this project: Lois Zells, Patrick Durbin, Wendy Wheeler, Brad Holtz, Richard Hayden, Nancy Allen, Matt Light, and Ted Tzirimis. My thanks also to some of the consulting firms that provided reports and data, including Gartner Group, SPEX, KPMG Consultants, PricewaterhouseCoopers, LLC, and Project Partners, LLC.

To the many hundreds of people with whom I have had professional contact through the years (you know who you are), I thank you for the enrichment that you provided and for the opportunity that you extended for me to share my knowledge and ideas with you. You are all clearly contributors to this book.

Harvey A. Levine

April 2002

PREFACE

It was the first Sunday in April 1986, when the *New York Times* reviewed my first book *Project Management Using Microcomputers*. What struck me the most in that review was the reviewer's description of project management as *arcane*. I had to look the word up and found it to be a synonym for *mysterious*. To be *arcane* is to "be beyond one's powers to discover, understand, or explain," says my thesaurus.

Well, perhaps it was arcane in the mid-1980s. But that's not quite true as we enter the twenty-first century. Projects, and project management, are garnering much more attention, today. And while it might not be appropriate to describe project management as arcane or mysterious, there are many people who would still claim that it is "beyond one's powers to discover, understand, or explain."

So here we find the main purpose of this book. Here we strive to uncover the mysteries of project management. We explain basic, practical aspects of project management and hopefully bring to our readers a new understanding of the value, purpose, and skills of this important discipline.

Project Management as a Discipline

Perhaps the most important thing to note is that project management is, indeed, a discipline of its own. It has its own terminology, its own body of knowledge, its own set of skills and practices. One might not need a degree in project management to practice this discipline. But you cannot just have someone wave a magic wand in your direction and bestow these capabilities upon you. As obvious as this might appear, there are far too many instances where this is exactly what happens. A senior manager *declares* that Jack is going to manage projects, with all the knowledge and skills required of that discipline. No way!

Some 40 years ago, I had the good fortune of making a career change, from engineering to project management. Starting with basic planning and scheduling, I learned and practiced practical skills in project management, eventually reaching into all aspects of the discipline. For 24 years, these skills were first honed for my own use, and then used to develop and implement project management capabilities and systems in several divisions of the General Electric Company. Since 1986, as founder and principal of The Project Knowledge Group, I have had the opportunity to share my project management expertise with hundreds of clients—and to learn from them as I came to understand their challenges.

A unique and beneficial aspect of this consultancy is that half of my clients were firms that were in the process of developing a project management capability and implementing a computer-based project management practice. The other half were firms that were developers and vendors of the tools used in managing projects. With this balanced involvement, I found myself to be acting as a bridge between the vendor and user communities.

I continually fed insights to the vendor community about what the users felt that they needed. And I was able to bring to the users, the latest developments in PM tool concepts. Through all of this, I was able to learn what impediments lay in the way of the successful adoption of project management in the field, and was able to develop practical applications of essential project management concepts to smooth the way around, over, and through these impediments.

These were wonderful experiences. Challenges, leading to discoveries and solutions to aid in making project management work. What I learned is, as they say, enough to fill a book. So here it is.

Why Read a Book about Project Management?

Sure! You've heard it all before. "It's a jungle out there!" So many traps befall the typical project. Things can go drastically wrong at every turn and there are dangers lurking behind every rock.

You probably accepted your project based on a set of good assumptions—most of which will prove to be in error before the project is over. Is there anything that you can do that can minimize what can go wrong? And when they go wrong, is there anything that you can do to minimize the damages?

That's what practical project management is about. You'll make your plans. Things won't happen as planned. But you'll know what is happening. You'll be able to evaluate alternative strategies. With some heroic effort, you will bring the job in on time, under budget, and with the full committed scope.

There have been numerous studies that report an excess of project failures—failures that resulted in extensive consequences. Projects failed, and when these projects were tied to the future health of the enterprise, the sponsoring businesses also failed. True, the potential for project failure is large. But the potential for project success is just as available.

Projects are essential for most businesses. The failure to execute projects successfully will prevent most businesses to grow and prosper in an ever-changing and challenging environment. The question isn't whether to engage in project work. The issue is how do we promote project success?

Projects fail. And when we evaluate the failures, we often find that the project never had a chance. We find that the failure was in the basic inability to specify, plan, and manage projects. So we decide to implement a computer-based project management capability.

And still projects fail. And when the failures occur, we look around for somewhere to place the blame. Frankly, we can often find the culprit by looking in the mirror. *For the most part, the failures in implementing project management can be traced back to this simple misconception: that we can take shortcuts with project management—that we can treat it casually and unprofessionally—and still have it work.*

Success, in any endeavor, doesn't just happen. It requires a serious and time-consuming effort to develop the proper organization and to populate it with the best prepared resources available. It requires the top-down development of an enterprise-wide culture, complete with the practices that are necessary to carry out the firm's mission. It requires that the firm understand the technology associated with the products and that it invest in the machinery to effectively execute the technology, using the accepted practices.

The business of projects deserves no less than this. It requires commitment, leadership, resources, skills, practices, and tools. And all of this must be brought into an environment that recognizes the importance of project management as a means of achieving the firm's mission.

We hope that you will find this book to be a useful guide in achieving these goals.

The Scope of This Book

Project management is a many-faceted discipline. It will usually involve project scoping, task planning and scheduling, resource planning and workforce management, budgeting and cost control, risk and contingency management, change management, and project closeout. And while we are doing this, we will need to apply skills in maintaining quality, avoiding scope creep, and managing extensive and sensitive communication, with numerous stakeholders, in widespread locations.

If this were not enough to intimidate even the most stalwart soul, we then throw in the challenge of learning to use new computer-based tools. We claim that these tools are necessary for efficient and effective project management, and will help us to do the job. But the challenge to learn to use and effectively apply such new tools, at a time when most new users are involved in some kind of crisis management (we are rarely asked to learn and implement project management at our leisure) can be disabling, at the least. If you have been to this place, I can understand and feel your pain.

All of these skills that are specific to project management must be applied by individuals who also are endowed with the more traditional management skills: (1) the ability to lead and work with others; (2) the ability to converse with technical experts in their applied field; (3) the ability to interface with operations, finance, and human resources personnel; (4) the ability to participate in strategic and operational planning; (5) the ability to mentor, negotiate, and make decisions. While we don't cover most of these skills in this book, we don't ignore the fact that these skills are necessary components of the Project Manager's toolkit.

While the breadth of project management is indeed wide, the subject really isn't that complex. Failures in project management are more likely to come from trying to take excessive shortcuts than from not mastering the requisite knowledge. There are basic requirements, including those for (1) organizing for project management, (2) management support, and (3) documenting and communication. These are no different from the requirements for any other discipline.

In this book, we outline and discuss these basic requirements, so that your organization can recognize the commitments that must be made to successfully implement project management. We introduce shortcuts that *do* work—because they are designed to facilitate good project management practices, rather than circumvent them. We cover the wide spectrum of project management, although you will have the option of studying each area as you identify a need. We will guide you to the appropriate sections.

Our Style and Conventions

We aim at keeping the style and language of the book as casual as possible. Yes, there will be the usual new terms and alphabet soup. But the general approach is a one-to-one sharing of knowledge and insights.

The whole idea is to present the practical aspects of project management. In some cases, we offer suggestions on straightforward ways of accomplishing some of the essential components of project management. We point these out to you as *Tips*. Many of these will be optional functions, to be performed if needed for your specific applications. In other areas, we point the way to common misconceptions—things to avoid. We'll note these as *Traps*.

Many of the discussions will involve the use of project management software. These are the tools of the trade. We talk about the features and functions to look for in the tools, but no tool evaluations are included and no specific tool recommendations are made.

Last, we try to prevail upon the reader to do the right thing. We point the way to the things that organizations must do to give project management a chance to succeed. All in all, we provide the benefit of 40 years of project management practice, updated to meet the needs and environment of this new century, and expanded to be applicable to emerging industries that, heretofore, were not considered to be the center of project management activity.

How to Use This Book

This book may be used as a complete guide to practical project management—reading each of the sections in the order that they appear. However, it is more likely that most readers will either be looking first for the essentials needed to get a feeling for and the requisite knowledge to get started in project management. Yet others may be looking for some of the finer points of this discipline.

To this end, we have identified four categories for use in classifying the chapters according to their primary value to the end user. These categories are

PM 101 These are essential to understanding the basics of project management. Newcomers to the field are urged to read these chapters, in the order that they appear. Others are invited to review selected chapters in this category to refresh their understanding of these topics.

Missives with a Message   These are in the style of editorials, either urging the reader to buy into the concepts and philosophy presented, or to be aware of important ideas. Some of these chapters provide insight into popular misconceptions or identify dangers associated with certain actions (or inaction). In many instances, the reader may wish to use one or more of these chapters to help convince others of their own position on matters of importance, such as: organizing for project management, or dealing with risk.

Finer Points   These chapters contain discussion of some of the finer points of practical project management. They assume a working knowledge of the basics, and an interest in understanding some of the important, but less apparent, aspects of the discipline. Understanding the finer points will help the reader advance from a novice PM practitioner to an expert in practical project management.

Off the Beaten Path   There is a softer side of project management. This includes issues dealing with people and organizations. If you are committed to providing the best environment for people to contribute to project success, you will want to read these important chapters.

Deliberate Redundancy

There are several topics in this book that have more than one appropriate chapter in which to appear. Although to repeat this material would be redundant, to leave pieces out because they appear elsewhere would weaken the subject chapter. Also, with the assumption that some chapters will be skipped, or read later, we can't be certain where you will come across the material first.

Therefore, we have deliberately repeated some of the material in more than one chapter, feeling that it was important to retain continuity and flow, without sending you all around the book to find referenced passages. Rereading these parts, as they are placed in each appropriate chapter, will help you to get the full impact of the subject and to reinforce the message.

Enjoy.

Harvey A. Levine

April 2002

SECTION 1

SETTING UP THE PROJECT MANAGEMENT OPERATION

Project management doesn't just happen. Successful project management is the result of a structured and determined effort to develop practices and skills within an organization that has been deliberately designed to support project work and the management of that work. There are almost unlimited options as to how to achieve this. One option that does not exist, however, is to engage in project work without setting up some kind of projects operation.

There is no option to engage in project work in the absence of a set of project management practices. These practices must be developed specifically for your organization and circumstances, and must be communicated and implemented throughout the operation. Neither is there an option to manage such project work in the absence of the skills needed to address all of the many facets of this discipline. Project objectives get achieved because there are skilled people who can define the objectives, and can plan and direct work to satisfy the objectives.

So the most important step toward project management maturity is to set up a project management operation that can best develop and utilize skilled personnel and direct their efforts, via a set of project management practices, supported and directed by an enlightened senior management.

Section 1 shows the way to set up the project management operation. We start with a general definition of projects and project management (1.1). We then discuss the general aspects of organizing for project management (1.2). We present a case for the Central Project Office and a Chief Project Officer (1.3). Then, we outline the steps to implement a computer-based project management capability (1.4).

CHAPTER 1.1

ABOUT PROJECTS AND
PROJECT MANAGEMENT

Here's a familiar scene. It is played out daily, across the world. The firm finds itself with a "project." It "assigns" the project to one or more project leaders. Other people are asked to contribute to the project. The work starts. Responding to an inquiry from a senior level person, the project leader reports, "We're not sure where we're going, but we're making good time." The boss asks, "Where's the plan?" Leader responds, "Who has time to plan? We are already in over our heads." Leader continues, "Where are all the people whom I was promised?" Boss asks, "Where is the project charter? And, besides, without the plan how do we know what you need and when?"

Well, you can fill in the rest. It goes on and on and gets worse and worse. The firm is not set up to work on projects. Roles are not clear. Procedures are nonexistent. Senior management expects that projects will be staffed and managed, but has not provided any mechanism or protocols. They fail to realize that executing and managing projects is not the same as normal daily operations. Meeting deadlines, working with increased risk, using people who normally work in different departments, working to stay within defined budgets, controlling scope creep—these are special characteristics of the projects' environment. It's not "business as usual."

The firm must take steps to organize for projects. This does not mean that there must be a projectized organization. Nor does it mean that any resulting organization is intended to be permanent. But something must be done to expand from a straight functional orientation. And something must be done to add new skills and to support cross-disciplinary teams.

Just what are these special characteristics that make projects different, and that require special skills to manage? Let's look at a generally accepted definition of project management, prefaced with a definition of a project.

A Project Is

- A group of tasks, performed in a definable time period, in order to meet a specific set of objectives.
- It is likely to be a one-time program.
- It has a life cycle, with a specific start and end.
- It has a workscope that can be categorized into definable tasks.
- It has a budget.
- It is likely to require the use of multiple resources. Many of these resources may be scarce and may have to be shared with others.
- It may require the establishment of a special organization, or the crossing of traditional organizational boundaries.

With the definition, above, we should start to see why we need a different set of practices to manage projects. Here we are managing specific tasks and resources against a time-oriented set of objectives. The budgets are associated with defined work, within a specified time frame. Resources are often led by people to whom they do not report. It's not so much what we manage that is so different, but rather the way that we manage and the measurement and control practices involved in this task. There are many areas of project management, but the eight below are the major components.

What We Manage

- Workscope.
- Time.
- Resources.
- Costs.
- Quality.
- Communication.
- Risk.
- Contracts and Procurement.

The workscope definition is key to the project management function. Without a precise and complete definition of the work, there is no foundation for the management of time, resources, and costs. There are several techniques that have been recognized to aid in the process of workscope definition. Best known is the WBS (Work Breakdown Structure). See Chapter 2.2. We also strongly advise that traditional strategic planning techniques be applied at the project initiation stage (see Chapter 2.1).

Standard routines have been established for the planning and control of schedules, resources, and costs. Usually, we use computers and project management software to aid in these tasks. Such computer-aided tools are strongly recommended, both for efficiency and standardization. Computers also aid in and improve upon project management communications. In fact, seven of the eight key project management functions, listed previously, can be substantially aided by the use of computer tools. Quality, although perhaps not directly aided by computers, is likely to have a better chance when a project is run effectively using computer tools. And it is a well-accepted doctrine that standardization is an essential element of a quality program.

Typical Planning and Control Functions

The whole process of defining the work and developing and tracking schedules, resources, and costs falls under the general heading of Planning and Control. There is a natural sequence to the steps of this function, as follows.

The Planning Phase

- **Establish the Project Objectives**
  Wait! Don't turn on your computer just yet. There's some front-end work to do, first. Resist the tendency to start scheduling the work until you define it. Preface the workscope definition by performing a strategic analysis of the project. See Project Initiation Techniques in Chapter 2.1, for a discussion of project objectives and constraints and other start-up tasks.
- **Define the Work**
  As noted earlier, the workscope definition is the foundation of a project plan. If you can't define the work, you can't schedule it, you can't assign and evaluate resources, and you can't define a valid project budget. Use the WBS (Work Breakdown Structure) technique to break the project down into smaller, outlined segments, until you get to work packages and tasks that specifically define the work to be done. See Project Initiation Techniques, in Chapter 2.1, for an introduction to the WBS. Also see Do You

Weebis?, in Chapter 2.2, for important commentary on Work Breakdown Structures.

- **Determine the Work Timing**

  Now that you have a list of defined project tasks, you can work on the schedule. Estimate the task durations and define the links between tasks (precedence relationships). This is the place to use the computer. Let your Critical Path Method (CPM) software calculate a tentative schedule, based on estimated task durations and precedence information.

- **Establish Resource Availability and Resource Requirements**

  The first-cut schedule is probably not realistic. It assumes that there are unlimited resources available to do the work. Probably not on your job! So now we need to do two additional things. First, define the resources expected to be available. Who are they? What are their classifications? How many are there? When will they be available? Also, assign a cost rate to each resource, so we can let the computer generate a resource-driven cost estimate for each task.

  Then, go back to your task list and schedule, and assign resources to the tasks. You may want to designate some tasks as resource-driven. In this case, the computer will calculate the task duration, on the basis of the defined effort (resource quantities and rate of use).

  At this point, your computer will provide an illustration (resource histogram or table) of the loads for each resource for each time period. We call this resource *aggregation*. If the histogram shows periods where the resource demand exceeds the defined availability, you have choice of manually adjusting resource assignments, or using the automatic resource leveling features of your CPM software. The result of a resource-adjusted schedule is the first cut of your project resource loading plan, or your Resource Baseline.

Trap Warning! Most automatic resource leveling routines are not very efficient, leaving periods of unassigned resources where there is work that can be done. See Chapter 4.3 for further discussion on computer-based resource scheduling.

- **Establish the Cost Baseline**

  If you have established cost rates for your resources, you are now in a position to develop a cost baseline, or Task Budget. You may have to add fixed (nonresource) cost to some tasks. The computer will calculate the estimated cost for each task, and roll it up to various levels of your WBS. Also, because the work is now scheduled, you will have a time-phased budget, usually called a Cash Flow Plan or Project Expenditure Plan. This will become a valuable baseline for tracking project performance, later.

Setting the Baseline

- **Evaluate the Baseline Plan**
  So now we have a baseline schedule, and a baseline resource loading plan, and a baseline budget. What are the chances that this first pass will meet all of your project objectives and constraints? Probably, the computed project end date will be unacceptable. We can usually do something about that. Perhaps the resource demand is impracticably uneven, or has peak loads that cannot be supported. We'll probably need to tweak it a little.

- **Optimize the Baseline Plan**
  Now is the time to consider alternatives. If time is a problem, look at overlapping or expediting some of the tasks. This is where we really begin to see the computer pay dividends. We can easily do what-ifs. Let the computer point out the critical path. The *critical path* is the series of tasks, in the CPM schedule, that will cause an extension to the project if there is a delay in any of these zero float activities. This is the first place to look for overlapping or expediting options.

  If resource loading is a problem, you'll want to consider such options as outsourcing or resource substitution. Time, resource, and cost conflict resolution can also involve applying overtime, changing priorities, and even scope reduction.

- **Freeze the Baseline Plan**
  Once you have developed an integrated plan that you can support, you'll want to set the baseline. This will allow you to measure schedule and cost performance during the execution of the project.

  Figure 1.1a shows the traditional sequence of planning activities leading to the baseline plan.

The Tracking Phase

- **Change Control**
  During the tracking phase, we will manage the workscope, the schedule, the resources, and the costs. Remember that the baseline that we recently established is like the abominable snowman. It is a myth, and it melts under pressure!

Figure 1.1a   Flow Diagram:
Steps toward Developing the Baseline Plan

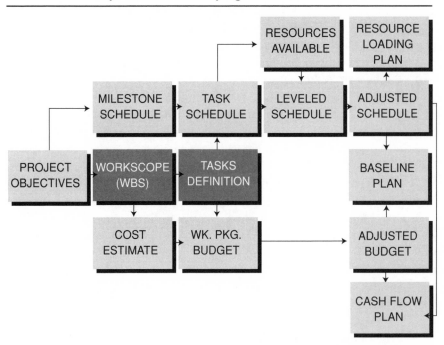

Scope change is a natural situation in projects. This is only a problem if it is not managed. Then it becomes scope creep, a really nasty situation. It is essential to establish a method of change control. When changes are introduced into the workscope, you must define the specific tasks that will be added, changed, or deleted, and the effect of these changes on time, resources, and costs. One rule to follow is that the working budget is always a task budget. The total project cost is the sum of the budgets for each task (plus contingency and margin). The task budget does not get adjusted unless there is a defined change in the task list. See Chapter 7.1 for Change Control and Scope Management.

- **Track Work Progress**
  If you follow the defined process up to this point, you should derive significant benefits from your planning investment. From here on out, the process requires extreme diligence, to continue the payoff. It is fair to say that there are those who will not want to make the commitment to track the work in detail, or to track all of the project elements. For instance, you

may want to track the work accomplished, against the schedule (that's not too hard), and pass up detailed resource and cost tracking. While complete project tracking and control involves the tracking of work, resources, and costs, there will be many situations where this level of effort cannot be supported (due to lack of expertise or resources) or cannot be fully justified. That is a management decision—not something that we can make for you. But here's what it involves.

Tracking the actual work consists of noting when a task has started and when it has been completed. Actual dates should be recorded. When a task has started, but not completed (in progress), we need to note the percent complete, and any adjustment to the remaining duration.

If you are going to do Earned Value analysis, you will need these measurements. The percent complete times the budget will give you the earned value (also known as BCWP—Budgeted Cost of Work Performed). You can compare the work accomplished (BCWP) to the planned work (BCWS—Budgeted Cost of Work Scheduled) to calculate the Schedule Variance (SV). The SV is an excellent indicator of project progress—much better than the popular (but perhaps overused) Total Float (or Total Slack). Keep a trend curve of the SV. If it starts out below target, look for improvement in future updates. Project managers who ignore increasingly negative Schedule Variance get what they deserve when the projects come in late.

- **Track Resource and Cost Actuals**
  This is the hard part. If resources and costs are tracked at a different level of detail from the project CPM plan, then it is almost impossible to match the tracking data to the plan data. If you're going to use time sheets and invoices, you will have to set up charging buckets to match the CPM tasks. Easier said than done—but much easier to do at the initiation of the planning process than in midstream.

  There are two benefits to doing this tracking, if you can. The first is that you will be able to measure the actuals against the plan—to evaluate performance and facilitate replanning. The second is that you will be able to collect a project history. This is the only way that you can eventually validate your earlier estimates and improve upon them for future projects.

- **Compare to Baseline**
  We already discussed the Schedule Variance measurements. These compare the amount of work accomplished to the amount of work that was scheduled to be done. One application for SV is in motivating subcontractors to intensify their project efforts when confronted with a down-spiraling SV curve. There are many others.

  If you're tracking cost actuals, you can also get a cost variance (CV). The actual cost (ACWP—Actual Cost of Work Performed) is compared to the earned value (BCWP) to compute the CV. You'll find extensive coverage of earned value analysis and performance management in Section 8.

- **Evaluate Performance**

  Use your actuals measurements to track SV and CV and to analyze when progress does not support the plan. Using WBS frameworks, you can analyze the data at a high level. Where an out-of-tolerance condition exists, drill down to the details to find the source of the anomaly.

  The data can be analyzed in tabular or graphic formats. The data can be produced either directly from the CPM program, or data can be exported to other applications for eventual presentation. The latter option allows for combining data from multiple sources or for adding special formatting or notation.

  Figure 1.1b illustrates a Cost/Schedule Status Report. Figure 1.1c compares BCWS, BCWP, and ACWP. Figure 1.1d shows cost (CPI) and schedule (SPI) performance trends.

- **Forecast, Analyze, and Recommend Corrective Action**

  There's no sense in collecting all of these data, analyzing, and evaluating, unless you're going to do something about the results. Use these data to fore-

Figure 1.1b   CSSR Report

Project Workbench – evtes102.aca – [Cost Schedule Status Report [CSSR]]

File   Edit   View   Setup   Operations   Window   Help

Phase One

Sort by Category

Task Name	BCWS	BCWP	ACWP	SV	CV	BAC	EAC	VAC
Phase One								
Wk Pkg A								
Task 1	200.0	200.0	250.0	.0	−50.0	200.0	250.0	−50.0
Task 2	120.0	80.0	100.0	−40.0	−20.0	200.0	220.0	−20.0
Task 3	120.0	40.0	40.0	−80.0	.0	200.0	200.0	.0
Wk Pkg B								
Task 10	200.0	200.0	200.0	.0	.0	200.0	200.0	.0
Task 11	120.0	160.0	80.0	40.0	80.0	200.0	120.0	80.0
Phase X								
Task 20	500.0	500.0	500.0	.0	.0	500.0	500.0	.0
Task 21	.0	.0	.0	.0	.0	500.0	500.0	.0
Phase Y								
Task Y	300.0	300.0	300.0	.0	.0	500.0	500.0	.0
Phase Z								
Task 30	500.0	.0	.0	−500.0	.0	500.0	500.0	.0
Task 31	200.0	.0	.0	−200.0	.0	200.0	200.0	.0
Task 32	100.0	.0	.0	−100.0	.0	100.0	100.0	.0
Task 33	100.0	.0	.0	−100.0	.0	100.0	100.0	.0

<F8> Modify <Inc> – Insert <Del> – Delete

Figure 1.1c   Earned Value Performance Chart

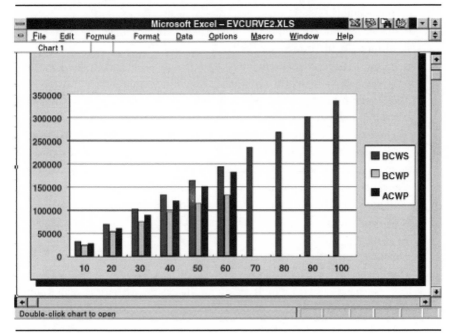

Figure 1.1d   Schedule and Cost Performance Trends (SPI–CPI)

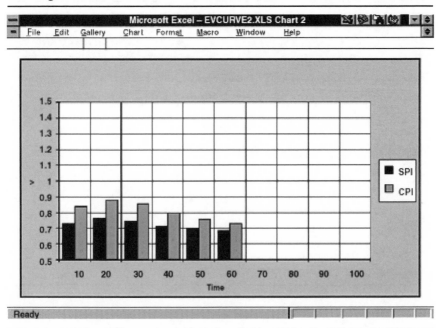

cast against key project milestones and to effect corrective action, where indicated. Establish interim milestones and trigger points. The latter are key events that occur (with adequate lead time) when there is still a window of opportunity to take corrective action or to adopt alternative strategies, when things are not going as planned.

Top management usually wants to know two key pieces of information: When is the project going to be completed? What is it going to cost? Using your computer-based ability to evaluate project performance and forecast these key items, you are in position to provide a precise and intelligent management report. You can present the forecast schedule and costs, compared to the targets. You can include a trend curve and analysis, and can focus in on trouble areas, using the drill-down capabilities. And you can report on pending corrective action and the expected effect of these alternatives (using what-if analyses).

Figure 1.1e shows the typical activities associated with change management and for tracking a project that is in progress.

Figure 1.1e   Flow Diagram: Tracking Steps

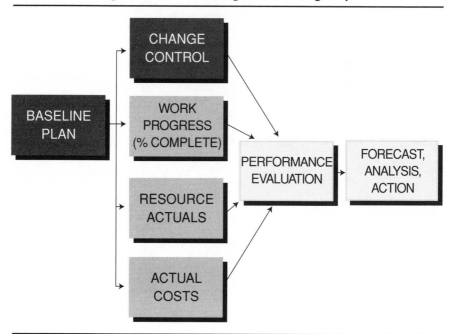

Summary

The functions involved in planning and control of projects, as previously described, are just a part of the scope of project management. Add to this some of the soft skills, such as managing resources who report to other managers, using temporary or outsourced personnel, communicating with a wide span of involved or concerned individuals, on several levels, and satisfying multiple stakeholders, the task becomes rather large and specialized.

Each of the functions is discussed in detail later in this book. For now, we wish to consider the implications of these challenges on the organization, and address issues in organizing for project management. These are addressed in the following chapter.

CHAPTER 1.2

ORGANIZING FOR PROJECT MANAGEMENT

We can devote an entire book, let alone just a chapter, to discuss how to effectively organize for managing projects. For much of the past century, organizational design concepts were fairly stagnant. We essentially derived all organizations from the basic Functional Organization design. The key arguments revolved around whether a highly centralized Functional Organization or a decentralized Functional Organization was better. Then, starting in the 1950s, revolutionary organizational design concepts emerged, about every two decades.

In the 1950s, it was the Project Organization that received a lot of attention, as a better way to address the needs of managing large projects. In the 1970s, much was written about the next revolution (or revelation): the Matrix Organization. The movement away from rigid structures, blossoming in the 1980s, gave way to the proliferation of Teams in the 1990s.

Much has been written about these three traditional organizational types: Functional, Project, and Matrix. In the past couple of decades, even more has been written about emerging, less-structured ways of leading project-oriented work. We hear of the adhocracy and teamocracy, as movements away from the more conventional bureaucratic approach toward project management.

There is considerable and justifiable support for organizational methods that facilitate the sharing of resources and the softening of traditional boundaries. Although not without some disadvantages, you will find that the Matrix and Team concepts are best suited for situations where the firm is engaged in multiple projects, of various sizes and duration.

We can only present an overview of these organizational concepts here. In order to best understand the options available to us, we start off with a description of the classic organizational types, followed with discussion on emerging variations.

Basic Organizational Structures

There are three classic organizational structures available for dealing with projects. These are:

1. The Functional Organization.
2. The Project Organization.
3. The Matrix Organization.

The Functional Organization

The Functional Organization is the granddaddy of them all. It is the traditional organization for performing ongoing work. Its focus is on operational discipline. It is best for routine work and the maintenance of standards. See Figure 1.2a.

A pure Functional Organization is a poor model for the execution of projects. The typical functional manager is measured and rewarded for running an effective functional operation. These measurements would usually include (1) hiring and developing personnel having the skills to execute the work expected of that function, (2) career development, (3) development and auditing of functional standards, (4) minimizing unapplied and lost time. While these are all important, and are required even in a highly projectized environment, none of these are consistent with project performance.

Usually, in a pure Functional Organization, projects are assigned in one of two ways. In the first mode, a project is assigned to a specific functional manager. For instance, a project that has a high degree of manufacturing content might be assigned to the Manager of Manufacturing. That manager has the responsibility to coordinate contributions from the other disciplines. In the second mode, the responsibility for managing the project is passed from functional manager to functional manager as the concentration of effort shifts to different disciplines. For instance, the project responsibility might start off in the hands of the marketing manager while the project objectives and scope are being developed, get passed on to the engineering manager during the conceptual phase, then on to the design manager during detailed design, on to the manufacturing manager

Figure 1.2a The Functional Organization

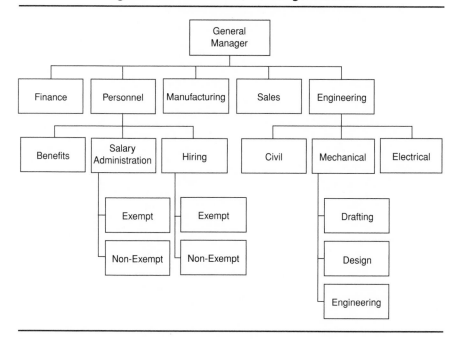

during fabrication, and then back to the Manager of Marketing to be delivered to the client.

I won't say that these models can't work. But there are several potential impediments. A really big one is the lack of recognition, measurement, and reward for project performance. When you read the position guides for these managers, there is nothing even remotely suggestive of a project management responsibility. People tend to work to meet expressed management objectives. If project performance isn't one of them, where is the motivation to focus on the project objective as compared to the functional objectives? And even if these managers did aspire to superior project performance, where did they get the skills to manage projects?

Then there are the conflicts. Let's say that the Manager of Engineering is supporting five projects. He is the project manager for one of the five, and is supporting the other four. When there is contention for scarce resources, guess which project gets first choice?

If the firm insists on maintaining a pure Functional Organization, as it moves into a growing projects environment, effort must be put into obtaining and growing project management skills. Job descriptions, measurements, and rewards must be altered. And senior management must motivate a culture change to accommodate a shifting focus on projects.

The Project Organization

The Project Organization is a specialized organization for executing projects. It was designed for isolated, one-of-a kind work, with a strong focus on the project. In the case of major projects, a separate project organization is established specifically for a single project. The organization's lifespan is equal to the lifespan of the project. The Project Organization makes less efficient use of resources. It is a poor model for technology transfer. See Figure 1.2b.

The Project Organization first came into being for major aerospace and defense type projects. In fact, many of these projects required the establishment of a dedicated organization prior to submitting a bid. If the project was not awarded to the firm, the newly created staff was disbanded. In the Project Organization, staff buildups would occur to match the peaking of effort in each discipline, followed by a decline in personnel as the peak was passed. New people were

Figure 1.2b   The Project Organization

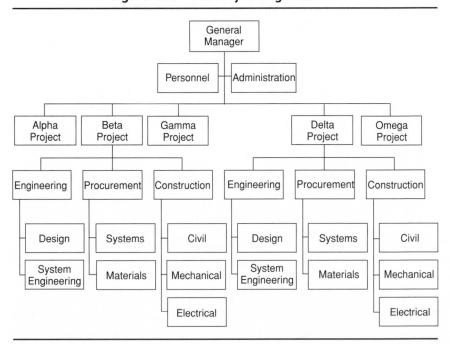

brought on board and had to be indoctrinated into the ways of doing things in that particular project group. And by the time that they became a cohesive team, they were let go.

However, there was no doubt about where the focus was. There was no conflict. There was only the one job. But because there was only the one job, resources might sometimes be out of work to do. It is close to impossible to plan and execute work so that the demand for resources is exactly level. But with dedicated resources, there is no place to put the underutilized people during the slack periods.

The Matrix Organization

Recognizing the limitations of both the classic Functional Organization and the pure Project Organization, it is understandable that a new type of organization would emerge. The Matrix Organization, which gained popularity in the 1970s, offers the best-of-both-worlds solution—but not without problems. See Figure 1.2c.

These problems might involve leadership, communication, understanding roles and expectations, and personal rewards. Individuals report to (at least) two managers—solid line to the functional manager and dotted line to the project manager. This can lead to confusion, conflict, and ambiguity. Most of the potential problems involve people, and can be avoided with good orientation and lead-

Figure 1.2c The Matrix Organization

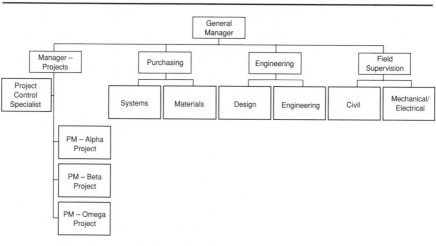

ership. Senior management must understand the concept of Matrix Management and maintain sufficient involvement to make it work.

Beyond these dangers, however, the Matrix model represents the most practical organization for the firm that is continually involved on multiple, overlapping projects. The functional managers are responsible for maintaining adequate levels of staffing and developing or acquiring skills as needed to support incoming project work. They also maintain technical standards, and assure that the group is up to speed on the latest developments in the discipline. They oversee the assignments of personnel to projects, and provide for evaluation and career development of their personnel.

The functional specialists are assigned to one or more projects, based on the current needs of the project. Efficient utilization of resources is achieved due to staggered peaking of resource needs as the projects move through their various phases. In an engineering/design project, the engineering group will move on to the next development project, as the designers move in to execute the design (obviously, with a degree of overlap). In a software development project, the systems designers might move on to the next development project, as the programmers move in from another project.

Knowledge and technology gained from one assignment is immediately available to the next project that is worked on. The functional specialists form a temporary team, focusing on the project objectives, while maintaining a functional discipline.

At the same time, all the benefits attributed to the Project Organization remain available to the Matrix Organization. Via the Projects function, we provide projects standards, develop project management practices, and maintain a strong focus on bringing the project to a successful conclusion, to the satisfaction of all the stakeholders. Professional project managers and project support personnel are developed and assigned to projects. The project function assures the availability of skilled projects personnel and provides for personnel evaluation and career development. The Projects function develops the PM standards and oversees their application to the various projects.

As I said earlier, this is the best of both worlds, under most conditions that involve projects.

Trap   All of a sudden, we see companies attempting to implement project management by putting a copy of Microsoft Project on everyone's desk, and asking functional managers or self-directing teams to be responsible for achieving project success. This is a perilous approach. Managing projects re-

quires special knowledge and skills. So does the effective utilization of project management software. You wouldn't think
of asking your Human Resources manager to design a hydro-
electric plant. Nor should you ask your Manager of Electrical
Engineering to be responsible for project management.

If we review some of the key things that we ask of project managers, the requirement to have specialists for this function should become apparent.

Tasks and Responsibilities for Project Managers

- Get all key players on the project team.
- Manage task interfaces.
- Assure clear identification of task completion.
- Assure communication of task completion.
- Manage responsibility interfaces.
- Question blurry responsibilities.
- Clarify delegation levels.
- Balance the needs of project, client, organization.
- Identify stakeholders and their definition of project success.
- Balance project objectives with other objectives.
- Act as a catalyst, and when necessary, a devil's advocate.
- Promote effective communication and wide participation in decision making.
- Manage conflicts. Conflict and aggressiveness are necessary elements in an adhocracy. Management's job is to channel them toward productive ends.
- Bring conflicts to an early resolution. Do not sweep them under the rug. They won't go away.

Role of the Project Manager

In short, the project manager has a very special role, which requires very special
talents. The project manager acts as an integrator. The project manager channels
conflict and aggressiveness. The project manager pays attention to the stakeholders. The project manager creates a structure for project planning and control.
The project manager initiates practices to minimize possible failure. The project
manager makes sure that risks have been evaluated and that risk mitigation plans
have been prepared. The most effective project organization will have a Manager
of Projects, who will be responsible for the firm's project management standards
and practices, and the project management personnel. In the pure Project Orga-

nization, the Manager of Projects is the chief honcho. In the Matrix Organization, the Manager of Projects shares overall leadership with the functional managers.

Tip   You can't leave project management to chance. If you're going to be serious about managing projects, then project management must become a way of life in the organization. Furthermore, support for project management cannot be voluntary. It must be a condition of employment. Top management must see to this by providing substantive, visible support, via directives, staffing, and recognition.

Teams

The Matrix Organization configuration provides the built-in flexibility to deal with most project situations. However, long before the Matrix Organization configuration was documented, firms had found ways to address the needs of special situations. We used to call this solution *task forces*. This term seems to have fallen out of favor lately, having been replaced by *cross-functional teams*. The team approach, regardless of what term you choose to use, calls for pulling strategic resources out from affected functional groups, for the purpose of meeting a critical challenge, usually under difficult schedule conditions. Teams have been used for numerous applications, but the project application is a natural for the team approach.

Team members may be assigned either part or full time to the project. The team may pick its own leader, or the leader may be appointed by senior management. Teams can be very effective for both short- and long-term projects.

There are several potential problems in implementing the team approach. One is the potential for conflicts. Because this is a less structured mode of operation, there can be maneuvering for power and influence. Because the team members do not report to the team leader, there can be resistance to accepting the direction of the leader or the will of the team.

Of major concern is the possibility of a lack of project leadership skills. If the firm is a traditional functional organization, and there are no people with developed project management skills, the team will be missing a vital resource for success.

An excellent text on teams has been written by Cleland (David I. Cleland. *Strategic Management of Teams*, John Wiley & Sons, 1996). Here, Cleland states: Teams are the common denominator of organizational change—a medium for cross-functional and cross-organizational integration of resources to accomplish a specific purpose.

What we have seen in the past decade has been both the recognition of teams as an organizational option and the formal attention given to the team approach by senior management so that the traditional motivational and reward strategies of the firm can be redesigned to cover team activities. For instance, Cleland quotes the following from the 1993 Annual Report of the General Electric Company: "The use of teams at GE has brought about major changes in training, performance appraisal, and compensation systems—for example, '360-degree appraisals,' in which peers and those above and below an individual evaluate performance. Employees are paid on the basis of the skills they attain rather than just the work they perform."

Unfortunately, this vision has not been universally shared. Several organizations retain individual measurement and reward systems that fail to recognize a person's contributions to project success and the growth in potential gained from exposure to new learning and experiences. This would be counterindicated in this age where we have begun to seriously count knowledge and our human resources on the asset side of the ledger sheet. Some organizations have also been slow to break down the rigid boundaries that impede the application of the team concept.

When organizing for projects, you need to be prepared to make changes to the organizational structure and to make cultural changes that will allow the structural changes to be effective.

Changing Attitudes and Culture

For the contemporary enterprise that is heavily engaged in projects, the options come down to some kind of matrix or team operation. Yet, moving in that direction will not assure success. This kind of change also requires changes in attitudes—changes in the entire organizational culture. In this regard, there is no choice. Failure to bring about the operational and attitudinal changes that will allow the matrix or team approaches to work will lead to failure of the projects themselves, and possibly failure of the entire enterprise.

This is easier said than done. The changes at the individual contributor level are not that difficult. But at the managerial level, it's a different story. In the Matrix Organization, it calls for a sharing of responsibility and leadership between the project manager and the functional managers. In the team environment, it calls for a diminished role for the managers with transference of many leadership functions to the team members. This control, inherent in the more traditional organizational styles, is hard to surrender.

For the individual contributors, the common issues are career development, recognition, and reward. In the older, more tightly structured organizational systems, there was always a direct, solid-line link between the individual contributor and the manager. The manager was entrusted with the responsibility to define expectations, make the periodic measurements, and meter out rewards. The manager was also expected to provide for personal development and career opportunities.

While this subordinate dependency upon a single boss was not always the healthiest arrangement, at least the individual contributor knew whom he reported to and what was being measured. And there was some continuity.

There is no reason why these individual contributor needs cannot be supported in the matrix and team modes. But it is more complicated because it would require the involvement of multiple managers. More and more measurements (evaluations) are being made on a peer-to-peer basis. However, the system has to be administered at the managerial level.

Who Knows What, and Where Are They?

Another potential hurdle is maintaining an inventory of skills. In the matrix and team modes, there must be a fresh database containing information about the firm's human resources, their skills, their availability, their experience, their location, and so on. This need has been recognized by the increased availability and sophistication of what has come to be called *workforce management software*. For the firms that have very uneven resource demands, these software systems are being used to hold data about temporary resources (outsourcing) as well as internal resources. Some of these programs are even linked to outsourcing suppliers so that they can respond to demand forecasts and bid on the opportunities.

Benefits of Teams

We have already stipulated that some type of matrix or team approach is necessary for the success of a project-oriented enterprise. This is to imply that there are usually improved results from adopting these models. Benefits of the Matrix Organization are discussed previously. Although the preceding paragraphs warned of many potential stumbling blocks for the team approach, the potential benefits, when implemented successfully, are many in number. For instance, Cleland lists the following positive results, from studies done on team implementations.

- Productivity increases.
- Quality improvements.
- Cost reductions.
- Earlier commercialization.
- Improved supplier relationships.
- Enhanced customer satisfaction.

- Changed management systems.
- Cultural enhancements.
- Employee satisfaction.
- Creativity and innovation.
- Strategic initiatives.
- Stakeholder image.
- After-sales service improvements.
- Development of management potential.
- Development of leadership potential.
- Reduction of parochialism and provincialism.
- Improved product, service, and process development.
- Greater use of knowledge, skills, and attitudes.
- Organizational design changes.
- Profitability increases.
- Ability of teams to make and execute managerial decisions.

As I look at this list, I see some items that I would call inputs to the teaming process rather than a result. Nevertheless, we can expect most of these benefits to be realized from the successful implementation of a team model. Wearing my projects hat, I would have at the top of this list project success. What we should expect is improved project performance, including less schedule slippage, less cost overruns, more efficient utilization of resources, and (as noted earlier) improved quality and stakeholder satisfaction.

CHAPTER 1.3

DOES YOUR COMPANY NEED A CPO?

(Author's Note: This chapter is an editorial presenting a case for the Central Project Office and a Chief Project Officer. Containing many of the important points made in the previous chapter on organizing for project management, it may be used as a position paper to forward the concept of the Project Organization.)

Project management is one of the fastest growing, most widely recognized trends of the past decade. Its recent popularity can be seen in many quarters. More than 50 percent annual growth in membership in the Project Management Institute is just one sign of this popular movement. Similar growth can be seen in project management certification candidates, formal project management educational programs, project management websites, and project management articles. The growth in opportunities for project management trainers and consultants has certainly been appreciated by this author, a 40-year consultant/practitioner of project management. Nevertheless, this has been accompanied by increasing frustration about the way that project management is being implemented in those organizations that have recently come to embrace this discipline.

Below are a few simple questions. Answer them truthfully. Then think about the answers.

- Is your company running without a CEO?
- To whom do your engineers report?
- Do you have an accounting or finance function? To whom do they report?

Even in this day of flat organizations and multidisciplinary teams, almost all of you will have replied that your organization does have a CEO. Your engineers report to an Engineering Manager, and there is a Chief Financial Officer (or similar title) heading the finance function and watching out for the firm's financial health and objectives.

Is this bucking the trend? Or does it still make irrefutable sense to maintain hierarchical structures within our organizations? Without defined leaders in these important functions, who will define the department's mission? Who will set the standards? Where will the leadership and mentoring come from?

You won't find many organizations without structured functions for Information Systems (IS), Human Resources, Marketing and Sales, Procurement, and so on (where applicable). Yet, there is one vastly important function, in many organizations, that has been declared exempt (wrongly) from this rule. That is the project management function.

Most of our organizations have discovered the impact of projects on the success of the enterprise, and have acknowledged "project management" as a distinct and valuable discipline. What they have yet to recognize is the importance of implementing project management under the same structures and centralization that has become the paradigm for most other disciplines.

As an emerging discipline, it is even more essential that we provide structured leadership for project management than any other function in the enterprise. Through this centralized leadership, we can meet so many important needs that would not be served without the project office function. The Project Office (PO) addresses these needs:

- It creates a cadre of people skilled in the art and science of project management.
- These people view their jobs totally as project management, eliminating the conflict with other responsibilities. Measurements (and rewards) can be developed more along the lines of critical project success factors.
- These people reside outside the individual technical functions, removing home territory biases.
- The PO becomes a repository for project experience, models, and standards—to be shared with all the project leaders.
- The PO maintains awareness of the "big picture," seeing the whole project and all the projects.

Therefore, the PO is more readily able to monitor trends and see global problems. The PO is in a better position to provide information and reports to senior management, and to make recommendations to resolve conflicts and problems.

The Gartner Group (among others) has documented the justification for the

Project Office (or the Project Management Competency Center). They cite four classes of services that can be provided by such a group, in an IS organization:

1. *Project Management Services*—trainer, consultant, and practitioner of PM practices and techniques.
2. *Methods, Processes, and Metrics*—guardian of corporate methodology and standards, estimating guidelines and metrics. Emphasis is on sharing and exchange rather than corporate edicts.
3. *Best-Practice Brokerage*—Documents successes and blunders. Searches outside the enterprise for best practices worthy of adopting internally.
4. *Reuse*—of project plan templates, estimates, and so on.

If our projects are to be successful, we must create an environment that will recognize project leadership as a separate and distinct discipline. It must provide a structured organization to house these essential skills and to foster the development of standards and expertise. Through the project office, we:

- Clarify the role of projects and project management in the enterprise.
- Establish a standard project management methodology, including tools and communication.
- Develop forms and templates to facilitate the development of project estimates, plans, and reports.
- Provide for training in project management and project management tools.
- Provide guidance and mentoring.
- Develop a cadre of trained and competent project managers and project control specialists.
- Audit the implementation of project management in the enterprise and provide assistance in complying with standard project management practices.
- Perform a watchdog role to assure that good project management practices are being applied.
- Gather project experience and data for use in future projects and to improve project management methods.
- Provide a neutral, centralized office for planning, negotiating, and analyzing projects, and for reporting throughout the enterprise.
- Provide a central, customer-focused office to care for the concerns of the client/sponsor.

If you do not embrace the Project Office concept, then examine what you are doing now for project management and ask if you are supporting all the important functions listed above.

The implementation of a computer-based project management capability imposes a need for special skills. It is often assumed (erroneously) that all managers and senior practitioners possess these skills. In the typical IS organization, we tend to designate people such as Senior Systems Analysts as Project Leaders, assuming that they will capably undertake the role of work manager, resource manager, and project manager. Yet, this overlooks several impeding conditions.

1. Project management skills are weak or nonexistent.
2. The Project Leader views self as a technical leader and concentrates on management of the technical content of the work. Furthermore, the measurements (and rewards) may be more aligned with technical success and management of resources (which are more easily and visibly measured than "project" success).
3. The Project Leader is embedded in a functional unit, while the work crosses functional boundaries. It is difficult to eliminate or overcome biases, or for the Project Leader to convince other functions to put aside high priority work for their projects.

Similar theory exists in engineering, manufacturing, and other types of organizations. Just change the job titles.

It has been my experience that a computer-based project management capability cannot be developed and implemented by committee (unless that committee is operating under the leadership and direction of a recognized project management function). The implementation of a computer-based project management capability involves five phases: (1) Methods (practices), (2) Tool Selection, (3) Training, (4) Implementation, and (5) Audit. (See Chapter 1.4.) All of this must be accomplished under the direction and coordination of the Project Office.

When we recognize the role of the Project Manager (vis-à-vis the Functional Manager) we can readily see why this takes a special set of skills and conditions. Here again (we noted these in the previous chapter) are some of the *Key Things That a Project Manager Must Do*.

- Get all key players on the project team.
- Manage task interfaces.
- Clearly identify task completion.
- Communicate task completion.
- Manage responsibility interfaces.
- Question blurry responsibilities.
- Clarify delegation levels.
- Balance needs of Project, Client, Organization.

- Identify stakeholders and their definition of project success.
- Balance project objectives with other objectives.
- Act as a catalyst, and when necessary, a devil's advocate.
- Promote effective communication and wide participation in decision making.
- Manage conflicts.

Obviously, we cannot take it for granted that any senior person or even any manager will have the skills and temperament for project management. Some of these skills can be learned, but many important qualifications are embedded in a person's personality. Unless we recognize that project management is a distinct discipline, requiring a special set of skills and capabilities, we cannot expect to implement a successful project management function in the enterprise. And until we recognize that these skills must be located in a structured function, with dedicated and empowered leadership, any project management skills that are available will flounder like a ship without a rudder.

So it is that we must add to the cadre of "chiefs" to which we entrust the success of the enterprise. We must add a Chief Project Officer (CPO), to support all the functions discussed above, and to lead the organization in meeting its project portfolio objectives.

As we closed the twentieth century, we saw the spread of the chief philosophy to the centralization of corporate technology. Recently, in a survey of Chief Technology Officers, the CTOs were asked: What keeps you awake at night? At the top of the list was "completing projects on time."

Call it a Project Office. Call it a Project Management Competency Center. Call it Project Mentoring. The name does not matter. However, development of a separate, recognized, structured organization with personnel skilled in project management is essential to having a successful project management function, and in turn, bringing your projects to a successful completion. For most of us, project success equates to success of the enterprise. Can we afford to do less?

CHAPTER 1.4

Implementing a Computer-based Project Management Capability

When I think of project management, I see two major components: The ART of project management, and the PROCESS of project management. The latter component, the process, involves considerable data, measurements, analysis, and communication. For this, most people will rely on one or more computer-based tools. Most of the processes involved in managing projects cannot be handled efficiently without the aid of project management software. So we must assume that the process of organizing for project management will include the selection of project management tools.

The process for selecting and applying project management software has changed over the past four decades. Like almost everything else in this technological society, the changes during the past few years have been more rapid and extensive than ever before. We are seeing changes in who uses such software, in how the software is designed, and in the environment in which it is used.

While these changes are influencing how we go about selecting the proper tools to use in supporting project management, we continue to have to address the larger process of how to best implement a computer-based project management capability within the firm. This process has not changed a great deal. While many newcomers to the world of project management try to take shortcuts, we have found that these attempts have failed unless a solid foundation has been put in place for the project management process.

The specification, evaluation, and selection of project management software is a key component of the process of implementing a computer-based project management capability. Much can be and has been written about this subject, and often, the reader is left with as much confusion as existed before the research started. The marketplace is loaded with products to assist in project management—products that change so quickly that the vendors have abandoned hard-copy documentation in favor of electronic media.

Moreover, this process of specifying, evaluating, and selecting project management software is only one part of the larger process of implementing a computer-based project management capability. For this implementation to be successful, we must apply four additional steps. The five components of this process are:

1. Methods.
2. Tools (Software Selection).
3. Training.
4. Implementation Plan.
5. Audit Process.

In this chapter, we provide overall guidance through the entire five-step process, based on actual, successful implementations. In the tools overview, we introduce a new, simplified, balanced approach toward software selection, recognizing the latest application of such tools and the popular configurations that are available in today's market. A detailed discussion of this modified approach appears in Chapter 12.1, A Simplified and Balanced Approach to PM Software Selection.

Methods

The Methods phase must precede the tools selection phase. The tools are required to automate and facilitate the application of your project management methodology. Therefore, you have to define this methodology first. By *methodology* we mean, "how do you manage projects?" This includes how you are organized to handle projects, as well as what practices are in place to manage projects.

If you do not yet have such practices in place, this is the time to address these issues, rather than after you have selected the tools. Specifically, I prescribe that you outline the entire PM process, creating manual forms for all of the practices, data, and reports that you will need for the process. Later, in the Tools phase, you will replace the manual forms and reports with your software-generated forms. These may be hard copies, screen forms, or both.

Start by holding workshops and brainstorming the desired PM processes. Review your current methodology. Assess the adequacy of your current methods. Consider the corporate culture and the system users. We can describe *Processes* as the steps that employees follow to accomplish a result. *Culture* is defined as their attitudes and behavior. Naturally, both must be considered.

Identify the project stakeholders and get them involved in the process. Project stakeholders may include The Project Manager, The Functional Managers, The Project Sponsor, Top Management, The Doers, The Client, and Regulatory Agencies. Don't forget the staff functions, such as Finance, Training, Systems, and Personnel.

Ask the team: What do you manage? What are project sizes, data volume, update frequency? Who are the system users? What is your computer environment? Is this environment changing?

All of this should lead to the determination and documentation of your preferred PM process. Now you can move on to determining your PM software needs and developing the selection criteria.

Software Selection

I think that I have seen just about every possible approach toward software selection. I have seen teams of more than 50 people formed and spend 2 years in a structured selection process. A selection specification was developed that would dwarf the typical phone book. Vendors were called in for presentations. Shortlist products were tested. Selection candidates were approved by several levels of management. Perhaps a bit of overkill?

On the other extreme, I have seen PM software selected by the edict of a single individual, based on something that he had read, without any knowledge of the product or the application. I guess that I'd rather have the overkill.

I have seen a selection team review dozens of candidates, against an extensive selection specification, and then reject the lot of them in favor of developing an in-house tool. Not something that I would recommend. The firm's talents can be better put to use for other tasks that would contribute to the firm's mission. The firm's mission is not "to develop project management tools."

Again, on the other extreme, I have seen the selection process completely short-circuited when a complimentary copy of Microsoft Project mysteriously appeared on a desk. "Why bother looking at anything else" was the result.

I cannot recommend any of these approaches. Nevertheless, I can prescribe a middle-of-the-road solution.

A Simplified and Balanced Approach to PM Software Selection

The selection of project management software should be a team effort. Normally, the team would consist of from three to six key players, relying on contributions from all stakeholders. The team needn't find consensus among all of the stakeholders. However, their inputs should be sought and valued, and they should be made to know that their inputs count.

Trap   It is a basic tenet of human behavior to wish to be included in decisions that affect you. It is usually very difficult to include all such stakeholders in the entire decision process, and it is virtually impossible to satisfy the desires of all the stakeholders. But it is also a general behavioral response that, if contacted and included in the discussions that lead to the decisions, these individuals would be more likely to accept the eventual determination.

Furthermore, this same human behaviorism tends to make people oppose and reject decisions that were made without their inputs or consideration. Therefore, to avoid unnecessary opposition to your PM software selection decisions, you should openly seek wide discussion and communication of the process.

Selection should be made based on the large picture. Consider connectivity to other systems. Consider both current and future needs. Avoid political decisions, such as choosing a product because you would have less risk of criticism if the solution failed. Look for ways to bridge the normal chasm between the projects and the operations functions.

Don't concentrate too much on software cost. Most tool solutions represent but a miniscule part of the costs of doing projects. However, do consider life-cycle costs. How much will it cost to operate the system, say for five years, including software, hardware upgrades, and training?

Don't get caught up in little details. Look more at what you need to accomplish with the software, rather than at the feature set.

There will need to be a balance between the expanse of features and ease-of-use. But here are two things to note about this. First, due to differences in product design, some products will be easier to use than others, even when having similar functional attributes. Second, expect all PM software products to be complex. They will not be as easy-to-learn or easy-to-use as word processing or spreadsheet tools because the typical user will have to learn many new things about planning and control in addition to learning the new tool itself.

The Four Key Categories

If we are to look more at what we need to accomplish with the software, rather than at the feature set, we should consider these four important areas:

1. The User Interface.
2. Data Management.
3. The Scheduling Engine.
4. Multi-user Access and Communication.

If we can satisfy all four categories, we are likely to have a product that we can use effectively as part of a computer-based project management system. If any one of these areas is unduly weak, we can expect failure of the entire system.

For a detailed discussion of these four key areas of PM Software Selection, please read Chapter 12.1.

Training

Now that we have taken care of the first two phases, Methods and Tools, we can move on to the third key element preceding the implementation itself. This is personnel training. There are two distinct training categories:

- Project Management Training.
- PM Software Training.

General PM training is the most important. You can be certain that the results from use of the tools by unknowledgeable individuals will be detrimental to your success. Everyone involved in contributing to project success should be trained in the basic concepts of project management. It is an error to assume that everyone inherently understands project management, and it is unfair to expect these people to perform successfully in this area without the benefit of such training.

A formal program should be made available to a wide audience, encompassing a wide scope of topics and skills of value to both project and functional performers participating in projects. This program should define the firm's policies and expectations for the management of projects. It should also make it clear that project management is a *way of life* in the firm, and that support for the program is a *condition of employment*.

Tip   Get your corporate training function involved. First, they will have skills and resources available to support your training needs. Second, they will resent you if you do not ask them to participate, and perhaps get in the way.

Detailed PM training, including use of the tools, should vary according to the role of the individual. For instance, I first like to divide the user community into two types: *In-ses* and *Out-ses*. The In-ses are people who feed information into the system. The Out-ses are people who use and respond to information from the system. This first group of people must understand the basics of planning and control. If you are using critical path scheduling, they must understand what really happens when you say that task A is a predecessor to task B. My experience has been that untrained people will describe their project to the system and be completely astonished by the result because they did not understand what the tool did with their inputs.

The Out-ses also need to understand how the resulting information was determined. However, my biggest concern is that they often don't know how to interpret and respond to the information. It is important to remember that reports are not issued just to provide status. They are issued so that problems can be identified and that corrective action can be taken. Therefore, we need to train these people to read the reports, how to identify an out of tolerance condition, and how to respond to such situations.

When implementing the system, you will want to identify all recipients of the outputs and determine what they need to know. Then, design custom outputs for each one that presents the story that will help them to carry out their specific project responsibility. Once these reports are designed, tutor these individuals to get the response that you need. You cannot take it for granted that the reader will know what to look for and how best to respond so as to remedy any problems. In each case, we need to look at what each participant needs to know to be effective in his or her project management role. You need to ask: "Who needs to know what?"

Finally, to bring a professional demeanor to the PM process, think about implementing a PM certification program, either internally or by sponsoring attendance at an educational institution. Also, consider promoting PM certification via the Project Management Institute's PMP program.

Tip Today's project-centric organizations are promoting excellence in project management and are finding ways to recognize project management excellence within their organization structure. This can encompass design of the positions and/or salary recognition. A company-sponsored education program is an essential part of such a program.

Implementation Plan

Now that we've defined our PM methodology, selected tools, and trained personnel, it's time to look at how the new process will be implemented. It is imperative to develop an *Implementation Plan*. There are several components to this plan, including:

- Directive.
- Procedure.
- Plan.
- Kick-off Program.

First, you'll need a *Directive*, from senior management, establishing project management as a way of life in the firm, and support for project management as a condition of employment.

Next, develop a set of *Procedures*, defining the implementation process. Remember, the implementation of your computer-based project management capability is, in itself, a project. Treat it like one, and use this opportunity to test and improve your process.

Follow this with an Implementation *Plan*, showing the steps of implementation and a schedule for their accomplishment. It is not necessary to implement the full project management process at once, across the firm. It is best to select pilot projects for implementation. That gives people and the processes time to come up to speed. The practices can then be fine-tuned as we learn from our initial experiences.

Start things off with a *Kick-off Program*. You're looking for procedural and cultural change when you implement project management. You need to make a big deal out of it. You need to draw attention to the program and its importance. You need to make certain that people know that top management is serious about this. Introduce the Directive, the Procedures, and the Implementation Plan with a formal program.

The Audit Process

You can't initiate a program and expect that things are just going to happen. There needs to be an *Audit Process*. Therefore, you need to develop a procedure for monitoring the implementation plan. The audit process makes sure that the directive and procedures are clear and are being followed. Responsible Managers are designated to conduct the audit, on an ongoing basis. They will provide assistance in getting people up to speed, and, if necessary, call people to task for not supporting the program.

Trap Don't fall into the trap of letting people think that the Audit Process is a Big Brother Is Watching thing. Although a component of this program is to monitor the progress and support for the implementation of the PM process, it is much more than that. Emphasis should be put on mentoring. The objective is to make the new PM program successful, not to find fault with those who have trouble with it. When the audit team finds someone that is not supporting the new practices,

Figure 1.4a   PM Implementation Plan

#	Task Name
1	**METHODS**
2	Sponsor's Request
3	Clarify Mission
4	Clarify Organization
5	Establish Methodology
6	Prepare Procedures
7	**TOOLS**
8	Perform Needs Analysis
9	Prepare Spec
10	Evaluate Software
11	Select PM Software
12	Prep PMS Procedures & Models
13	Develop Integration Procedures
14	**TRAINING**
15	Perform Needs Analysis
16	Develop PM Training
17	Develop PMS Training
18	Develop Exec Overview
19	Develop Certification Program
20	**IMPLEMENTATION PLAN**
21	Issue Directive
22	Develop Impl. Plan
23	Issue PM Procedures & Practices
24	Conduct Kick-off Program
25	**AUDIT PROCESS**
26	Issue Directive
27	Develop Audit Procedure
28	Assign Audit Responsibility

Timeline header: 2nd Quarter, 3rd Quarter; months 0M, 1M, 2M, 3M, 4M, 5M; weeks 0w, 1w, 2w, 3w, 4w, 5w, 6w, 7w, 8w, 9w, 10w, 11w, 12w, 13w, 14w, 15w, 16w, 17w, 18w, 19w, 20w, 21w, 22w, 23w, 24w, 25 they should ask how they could help. Frequently, that is all that is needed to bring that person around. Do what you can do to remove the intimidation factor, from either use of the practices and tools, or from being monitored.

Final Comments

We highly recommend that you take a balanced approach toward the selection of project management software. Furthermore, to enhance success with these new tools, we recommend that you adopt a formal, five-step process toward the implementation of your computer-based project management capability. Methods, Tool Selection, Training, Implementation Planning, and Implementation Auditing are all essential elements of the process.

The Gantt chart (Figure 1.4a) illustrates a typical PM Implementation Plan. The timing is not as important as the phases and steps.

SECTION 2

GETTING STARTED

If there is one section of this book that we can call the most important, this is the one. Here we discuss how to get the project off on the right footing. Here we point out several common errors that contribute to project failure.

We continue our discussion of project organization and project teams, relating these items to the project initiation process. We introduce the concept of the Project Charter, as a means of authorizing and defining the project. We promote the concept of Strategic Planning, as an important process in project initiation. In addition to showing the way to properly initiate a project, we provide examples of how things can go awry.

In Project Initiation Techniques (Chapter 2.1) we cover the three primary concerns for getting the project off the ground. First, there is the need to establish the project team, and to get them (the entire team) involved at the earliest stages of the project. Second there is the need to look at objectives, constraints, issues, opportunities, threats, and stakeholders—the traditional components of strategic planning—here applied to the project as if it were a business opportunity (which, of course, it is).

And finally, there is the need to establish structures to facilitate the building of the plan and schedule. These include Work Breakdown Structures, Organizational Breakdown Structures, Budgeting Structures, and Project Milestone Schedules. We introduce these structures in Chapter 2.1, and discuss the finer points in Chapter 2.2, Do You Weebis? Clarifying WBS, OBS, and RBS.

Most projects have a project life cycle (PLC). The PLC typically forms the basis for one of the work breakdown structures. Using the PLC as a WBS offers several advantages. These are discussed in Chapter 2.3.

The use of WBS type hierarchical structures does more than just facilitate the development of the plan. They also provide a basis for sorting, selecting (filtering), and summarizing all the project data.

There are several things that we want to accomplish by having a set of project initiation techniques. The first is to address the problem with overcoming inertia. It is important and helpful to have a mechanism and templates to facilitate the initiation of the project. The more that we have in the way of guides and guidelines, the easier it is to get started.

Another is to help funnel the early project efforts toward the project objectives. The opposite of procrastination in project initiation is to move too quickly. All too often we find that we "don't know where we're going, but we're making good time." This will backfire, and have a deleterious effect on project success.

Project charters, team building, strategic planning, structure building, all help us to get off to a good start.

CHAPTER 2.1

PROJECT INITIATION TECHNIQUES

Getting Started

Perhaps the hardest part of the project planning process is getting started. Certainly, overcoming inertia will usually contribute to the problem. And then there's always the problem of getting some relief from your other duties. But, the major cause of difficulty and procrastination is the *lack of a framework* for engaging in the process and developing the plan itself.

To start with, you will want to address the crucial identification of project objectives, constraints, and stakeholders. Then you will need to move on to organizing for the project and development of the project team. This team will participate in the development of a strategy for achieving the project objectives, and the clarification of the role of the various project stakeholders. The team will then proceed to the development of a framework for the work scope, timing, and budgeting aspects of the project. These will include Work Breakdown Structures (WBS), Organizational Breakdown Structures (OBS), structures for cost accounting, and Project Milestone Schedules.

It is not unusual to seriously falter at this project initiation stage. We don't quite know where and how to start. Some project managers will put the process off until it's too late to develop a plan of their own choosing, getting stuck, instead, with a plan that is by now doomed to failure from the start. Other project managers attempt to produce a quick schedule, or a resource plan, or an expenditure plan (budget), or perhaps all three. What they soon find out is that they don't have all the answers that they need, and that their plans are full of holes. That is, indeed, the nature of the beast. In most cases, the project planning process starts off with a set of assumptions, and the project planning process is used to validate these assumptions. Rather than putting off the planning process until the missing pieces are found, the smart project manager uses the process to help generate the missing data.

Obviously, there is a lot of front end work that must be executed prior to establishing the project schedule, resource plan, and budget. And, contrary to popular thought, a good deal of this effort does not involve the use of the computer. At this point, the project manager would do well to consider the following course of action:

- Examine the objectives for this project and the various constraints that impact upon these objectives.
- Identify the project stakeholders and how they, too, will impinge upon those objectives.
- Develop a project strategy that will support the project objectives and stakeholders, while meeting the various constraints.
- Put together a project team and other required resources, and evaluate what limits they impose on the execution of the project within time and budget constraints.
- Eventually, the PM has to implement a planning and control procedure that can support the needs of the project while being able to be supported by the project team.

Defining Project Objectives

A project plan is a *blueprint* of how one intends to achieve the objectives of a project. In several aspects, it is not that different from a building drawing. To prepare such a drawing, the architect must focus on the purpose and use of the building, amass conceptual data, develop outlines, and conduct certain technical and cost inquiries. Once prepared and approved by the owner, the drawing serves as the guide for the construction of the building. We can view a project plan in a similar light.

It naturally follows, therefore, that the very first item of order, in this planning process, is to make sure that the project objectives are perfectly clear and are defined in terms that can be used to develop the project plan. An inseparable part of this process is the identification of the constraints associated with the project.

The project objectives typically cover a number of elements, for example, time objectives, budget objectives, technical objectives, and scope objectives. Let's consider, for instance, a banking group that has decided to develop a new computer-based transaction processing system.

- *Technical objectives*—such as volume of transactions, turnaround time, ease-of-use, and error handling.
- *Timing objectives*—such as initial implementation of the system, system cutover, and operator training.
- *Budget objectives*—such as total system cost, operating cost ($ per transaction), and equipment costs.
- *Scope guidelines*—such as type of transactions to be processed, equipment to be used, locations involved, communications, and training.

All of these must be clearly identified before the project planning can commence in earnest.

Constraints would include:

- Time constraints.
- Technology constraints.
- Personnel constraints.
- Cultural constraints.
- Money constraints.

These too, must be clearly identified at the outset.

Tip Although often omitted from the project process, there should be a formal project authorization practice. This is best instituted by means of a *Project Charter* document. The Project Charter should contain much of the early description of project content, objectives, and budget. It is both a starting point for the project initiation process and the basis for the strategic planning and plan validation that takes place at this time. It specifies the project sponsor, the intended benefits and benefactors, and the source of funding. The lack of a Project Charter will potentially lead to conflict and confusion.

Developing the Project Strategy

Once the project manager has outlined the objectives and considered the constraints for the project, it's time to initiate the development of the project strategy.

A project strategy is simply *how* the project objectives are going to be attained. If the term "strategy" hints at a more involved process than you might expect, that is intentional. It is not enough to choose a course of action to achieve project objectives. That course of action must be tested for its likelihood of success. The set of processes that have been developed, within the discipline of Strategic Planning, are equally applicable to the process of developing the strategy for a project.

Stakeholders

First, it will be advisable for the project manager to identify all of the project stakeholders. Who are the people who will have an impact on project success, either positive or negative? Or, stated differently, who are the people who can make or break the project? For starters, don't forget the owners of the enterprise. They probably have the most to gain or lose from this project. The project manager and the owners will have to evaluate whether the objectives of this project are consistent with the general mission of the enterprise. Will attainment of the project objectives enhance and be in harmony with the primary purpose of the business? Will implementation of the project represent an improved utilization of the business' financial, human, and physical resources? Will the successful completion of the project improve the position of the company in its overall business objectives?

There are two very important reasons for obtaining yes answers to these questions. The first is to check for a proper fit with the other business of the company. The lack of such a fit will often place the company's resources in disarray, exacting a toll on both the new project and the other company business. The second is that, without this required fit, the project manager is unlikely to obtain the required support of his superiors. Without sponsorship in high places, a project will eventually fail for lack of support in critical situations.

This evaluation will be the first of many instances where the project team will be required to determine whether to continue the project, to make significant adjustments to objectives and strategy, or to abandon it.

Tip   At every stage of a project, the team must consider and evaluate the worth of the project. This includes consideration of project termination as an option. It is during the project initiation phase that assumptions are first tested and validated. On occasion, things are learned about constraints, costs, risks, and so on that could affect the perceived worth of the project, or put the project at odds with the overall mission or operational objectives of the firm. It is best to deal with these observations honestly and promptly, rather than to hope that they will go away. The potential damage will increase with the delay of facing the truth.

Other stakeholders would include the project sponsor, key project participants, company clients and prospective clients, regulatory agencies, suppliers and subcontractors, users of the project product; essentially anyone who can have an impact on the success of the project, or who might be involved in the determination of the project success.

Opportunities, Threats, and Issues

In the traditional business strategic planning process, the next function is to attempt to identify significant opportunities, threats, and issues. This same process should be applied to a project. Any project involves risk. An early evaluation of potential threats will help the project team to prepare to deal with these and to minimize their impact. Any project involves opportunity. While the key opportunities are usually part of the original project purpose and justification, an evaluation of potential secondary opportunities may uncover additional benefits to the company and the project participants. An attempt to identify all issues that may impact on the project, to list them, and to discuss them with the project stakeholders should promote knowledge of and sensitivity to the issues and prevent them from having a severe negative impact on the project.

Involving the Project Team

The strategic planning process, as well as the project planning process, is not a one-person process. At this time, the project team must be identified and assembled. While it certainly is possible that the strategy that develops may impact upon the makeup of the project team, some of the key players should be involved in generating the data for the strategy development and analysis, and in developing the project strategy. At a later point in the process, a strategy and project plan will have to be adopted. It is most important that the project team understand the strategy and support it. The more that people participate in the development of a plan, the more likely they are to support it. This buy-off of the strategy is a key to success of the project.

Of all the phases of the project initiation process, it is the act of dealing with strategies, stakeholders, and the organization that will have the greatest impact on project success. Ideally, many of these issues will have been addressed while the project was first being considered or proposed. Once the project has been officially authorized or awarded, it may be too late to do much about some of these issues. Unfortunately, projects often come into being without full consideration of these issues. Regardless of the level of attention given to this area in the pre-project stages, the sage project manager will repeat the process at the initiation of the project. The following is an expansion on some of the strategic and organizational concerns that should be addressed.

Strategy and Organizational Culture

Most projects exist within the larger sphere of an existing, ongoing business. They are accomplished by people who generally are part of this business and are part of its organization and culture. Yet many organizations treat projects as though they took place in a different, separate environment from that of the organization. When this happens, project managers, and their senior managers, tend either to ignore or to independently change key practices that are crucial to maintaining the organization's essential structure, culture, and business strategy.

Clearly, there are important differences between managing a project and the day-to-day operations of a business. But when the project unfolds independently or outside an organization's mainstream operations and culture, it can often have an adverse impact on the integrity of the business. In many industries, project objectives are virtually synonymous with an organization's business goals. In such instances, the success of key projects may have a major impact on the ability of the business to continue to be competitive, even to survive.

Therefore, organizations that apply traditional strategic planning practices to a project must focus on integrating the project into the organization and its culture. This requires analyses of several project constituencies—the project sponsor, other project stakeholders, the organization in which the project unfolds, and the project team—as well as of the strategic planning process itself.

Stakeholder Analysis

How do we align the project objectives with the goals and expectations of the stakeholders, so as to minimize the potential for conflicts that could adversely affect the project's success? One way to do this is to expand our view of project success.

The traditional view of project success is to accomplish all of the schedule, budget, and technical objectives as planned. Couldn't we also define project success as "accomplishing the goals of everyone who has a stake in the project"? If so, then the stakeholder analysis must ask:

- Who are the project stakeholders?
- What do they want?
- How can they impact success?
- How can they be satisfied?

Carrying this thesis further, we might say that project success is determined by:

- The power and influence of the project stakeholders.
- The difficulty and risk involved in the stakeholder's goals.
- The talent and resources available to accomplish these goals.
- The perceptions of the stakeholders of what was actually accomplished.[1]

Organizing for Project Management

If you are in the business of doing projects, then your company has probably modified its organizational structure to help it to respond to the demands of the projects environment. Your firm, like most, has probably migrated from a primarily *functional* or *line* type of organizational structure to the currently ubiquitous *matrix* format. Conceptually, the matrix approach implies that the responsibility for achieving project objectives will be shared equally by the functional and project managers. All too often, the company makes these organizational changes in a vacuum, giving little attention to the corporate culture, and with insensitivity to the corporate resources. As a result, these changes fall far short of achieving the objectives, and, in fact, become an actual impediment to effective project implementation and success.

The matrix management structure is available as a practical solution to bringing a projects capability into an ongoing business. It is difficult to dispute the premise that a matrix organizational approach will probably be best for most situations. We must be careful, however, to avoid two problems that are common to the establishment of the matrix structure.

One problem is that the new organization will often address and change areas of responsibility, but will fail to change the methods of measurement and reward. If people are asked to perform to new standards, but are measured and rewarded according to the old structure, the behavior and performance changes that are supposed to occur from the reorganization will not happen. Human nature dictates that most of us will perform so as to support the measurement and reward practices. If project and line supervisors are asked to perform on a shared basis, but continue to be measured and rewarded on the basis of individual performance to old and different standards, can we expect to achieve our objectives?

---

[1]Tuman, John, Jr. "Success Modeling: A Technique for Building a Winning Project Team," *1986 Proceedings*, Project Management Institute, Drexel Hill, PA.

The second problem in moving to a matrix mode is that the role of the functional or line manager is often diminished, in the new organization. Or at least, the line managers perceive their role to be diminished in relation to that of the project manager. Yet the real importance and contribution of the line manager can never be underestimated or undervalued. The resources and the standards essential to the successful completion of most projects are controlled by these key contributors, and their importance to this success must be clearly identified, acknowledged, and rewarded.

In short, a diagram of an organization, matrix, or otherwise, should not be mistaken for the organization itself. An organization is a living, working organism. The organization chart is similar to a bar chart. It doesn't get the work done; it only shows how the organization might work. Lots of things can break down between the diagramming of an organization and its successful implementation.

Bringing a successful project management capability into an organization requires significant change, but does not require a total dismantling of existing cultures. Like any other change, it should retain what works, fix what's broken, and recognize that the very people involved in these changes must buy into the new practices, if they are to succeed.

Role of the Project Team

If we acknowledge the importance of both project and line management, then there is little need to define a set of rules and responsibilities for the project team. Each member of the team must respect what the other members bring to the project. Each member must also remember that they are supposed to contribute to the attainment of the project objectives, as well as their individual, functional measurement.

A frequent cause of project problems is the lack of project team participation in making decisions. The case history on the opposite page exemplifies this.

The message here should be clear. Project team members should neither overstep their bounds nor ignore the responsible contribution of the others. When there is a problem or a decision to be made, the project manager, and the others involved, would be wise to seek the widest participation possible in the solution. This approach not only increases the potential for the best solution, but also gets the other team members to buy into that solution.

Developing Sub-Project Strategies

The concept of strategic planning can be applied at several levels of the project. Up to now, we have been looking at project-level strategies. Eventually, we will move from our top-level objectives to the next level (the deliverable end items), and then

CASE HISTORY

The Project

The design and installation of a new factory steam supply.

The Incident

The field superintendent calls the project manager to report a problem with the boiler installation. There is an unexpected interference of the water inlet piping with some adjacent crane rails. The superintendent recommends a quick field fix by moving a 90 degree bend, that is currently six feet out from the inlet nozzle, to two feet out, to avoid the interference. The project manager, wishing to respond quickly, approves the change, without involving other disciplines.

The Problem

Some time later, when the system is put into operation, the operating engineer reports seemingly erroneous water flow readings. The problem is reported to the design engineer, who eventually finds out about the piping change. It seems that no one bothered to discuss the piping change with the design engineer. If they had, they would have been told that the six-foot run of pipe, at the inlet, was required for the flow instrumentation to function properly. *Now*, the project manager wants Engineering/Design to fix the problem.

on to the work package detail and to the individual activities themselves. At the intermediate levels, the project team must develop a strategy and plan. They start with a set of givens or assumptions. Then, for each of the key areas, they look at the objectives, the current situation, the favored plan, constraints, and alternatives.

Let's look at how this approach might be implemented. In this hypothetical situation, the Clinton County Community College (CCCC) is engaged in a project to upgrade their athletic facilities. Their overall objective is to increase the school prestige and revenue by elevating the school sports program to a higher competition division. This requires an expansion of the CCCC stadium and the supporting infrastructure. One of the key project areas (deliverable end items) is the athletic field parking lot. The project team develops a planning worksheet.

DESIGN AND PLANNING—PARKING LOT

Design Objectives
- Provide parking for 3,000 vehicles.
- 1,000 of that capacity to be paved.
- 1,000 to be gravel based (for later paving).
- Remainder to be overflow on grass field.

Budget Objectives
- Costs to be charged to capital improvement budget—not to exceed $250,000 for all infrastructure items.

Timing Objectives
- Complete repaving before annual homecoming football game. Do not interfere with any other scheduled games.

Current Facilities
- Paved parking for 1,000 cars. Needs repaving.
- Adjacent level field for 1,000 cars. Dirt base.
- Additional adjacent field (undeveloped), available for 1,000 cars.

Favored Plan
- Repave existing 1,000-car lot.

      Area = 270,000 sq. ft.
      Cost = $0.40 per sq. ft.
            = $108,000

- Improve old overflow area with gravel base.

      Area = 270,000 sq. ft.

      Costs
        Gravel: 3,400 tons of #1 crushed gravel @ $6/ton = $20,400
        Trucking @ $30/ 25 ton load = $4,080
        Spread and compact = $13,500
        Total cost = $37,980

- Clear and grade new overflow area.

      Area = 270,000 sq. ft.
      Cost = $6,000

- Paint stripes in paved area.

      Quantity = 20,000 linear ft.
        Cost = $5,000

(Continued)

DESIGN AND PLANNING—PARKING LOT *(CONTINUED)*

Constraints

- Planning Board approval.
- Funding approval.
- Timing interface with football games and other events at the stadium.

Strategic Considerations and Alternatives

- If repaving/curing of paved lot cannot be completed prior to the homecoming weekend, consider completing gravel placement in old overflow lot plus grading of new overflow lot, and using these for homecoming parking.
- If insufficient funding is available for all infrastructure items, hold off on repaving old lot.

This is just one illustration of the kind of orderly, strategy-oriented thinking that should be employed in developing a project plan. In many instances, this sub-project strategic planning is part of the pre-project estimating function. On the other hand, there may be times that the project team would not have this level of detail available at the initial planning stages. You have to work with what you have, and make assumptions for the rest. Eventually all of the data will have to be confirmed. And at all times, this planning should be tested for consistency with the overall project objectives, the overall business objectives, and the criteria for project success.

Creating a Project Framework

We have repeatedly noted that a key factor in getting a project off the ground is the development of a structured approach toward identifying the work scope and timing for the work. It is easy to be overwhelmed by just the mass of the project. Furthermore, most project estimates and proposals are not prepared in a format that lends itself to easy conversion to a project plan. Although a definition of the project work scope may be present in the pre-contract documents, it will almost always require a major restructuring in order to turn these data into a pragmatic project plan. Another aspect of this project initiation phase is bringing the pre-project plan up to date. The pre-project documentation will define the project "as proposed." In the development of the latest project plan, these data will have to reflect the definition of the project "as sold." These are often not the same.

A major component of the front-end work required to effectively plan and initiate a project is the development of a framework for the project model. This framework or structuring of the project is important to the development of a complete and organized project plan. It is also essential to permit the sorting, selecting, grouping, and summarization of the project data, which, in turn, are essential to support recognized management-by-exception techniques and reporting to the various stakeholders.

If we define the process of project planning and control as the integration of the project work scope, timing, resource usage, and cost, then we will need to develop a structured base for each of these.

- **Work Scope**—a top-down hierarchical model, called a *Work Breakdown Structure (WBS)*. And, perhaps, an alternate hierarchical model, by responsibility or performer, called an *Organizational Breakdown Structure (OBS)*.
- **Timing**—a *Project Milestone Schedule*.
- **Resources and Cost**—a set of *Resource Codes and Cost Accounts*, used to facilitate selection, sorting, summarization, and interrogation of resource and cost data. Sometimes called *Resource Breakdown Structure* and *Cost/Budget Breakdown Structure*.

Work Breakdown Structure

The first step is usually to define the work breakdown structure (WBS), as this is the framework for the project work scope. If you cannot define the work scope, then you cannot define the schedule, resources, or budget for the project. The WBS first helps with this (work scope) definition, and then becomes the framework for the identification of the details of the project. The WBS is an organization chart for the project work. If you were to draw a typical project WBS, it would look just like a typical business organization chart. At the top would be a single box, for the project. Under that would be the main divisions of the project. A popular term for this level is *project deliverables*. The WBS can also be depicted in an outline form.

The approach works for any type of project. For instance, if your project is a prototype bomber for the Air Force, the WBS, at the deliverables level, might look like this.

AIR FORCE PROTOTYPE BOMBER PROJECT

Aircraft Structure
Propulsion Systems
Aircraft Control Systems
Armaments Systems

If your project is the development of a new product, the WBS might start off like this.

ALMONDS AND MOLASSES CEREAL PROJECT

Product Formulation
Lab Testing
Pre-production
Test Marketing
Package Design
Advertising Program
Sales & Distribution Program
Certification/Regulation
Production Engineering
Production Facilities

The deliverables section gives us our first level of project definition, and a framework for further structuring. Each of these items can usually be traced back to a basic project objective. Each of these items can usually be assigned to a specific responsible individual, for accountability. The development of the WBS continues in increasing levels of detail. Returning to the bomber project, we can expand the first item of the WBS as follows:

1		**AIR FORCE PROTOTYPE BOMBER PROJECT**
1.1		Aircraft Structure
	1.1.1	Fuselage
	1.1.1.1	Cowling
	1.1.1.2	Cockpit
	1.1.1.3	Body
	1.1.2	Wings
	1.1.2.1	Fixed portion
	1.1.2.2	Trim portions
	1.1.3	Tail
	1.1.3.1	Fixed portion
	1.1.3.2	Trim portions
	1.1.4	Landing Gear
	1.1.4.1	Main landing gear
	1.1.4.2	Nose landing gear

Thus far, we have illustrated the WBS in an outline format. Figure 2.1a shows more of the Air Force Prototype Bomber WBS, in the alternate organization chart.

Eventually, each of the lower items can be subdivided even further, into work packages and individual activities. A hierarchical numbering system can be used to imbed the WBS into the activity identification code. There is rarely an ideal work breakdown structure for a given project. The important thing to keep in mind is to develop a framework that truly is indicative of how the project itself is structured and how the participants are likely to follow its execution.

Note that with this numbering system, your project management software system should permit you to use these codes to select specific portions of the project, to group activities within a common code, to sort activities by that code, and to summarize certain activity data at higher levels. A few products feature an outlining function, which allows you to develop your project activity details in an outline form. Other programs provide user code fields for this purpose. Most provide both formats. The outliner format offers greater simplicity but is usually limited to a single WBS type framework. User code fields—which may range from 2 to 20 code fields, depending on the product—offer greater flexibility and the ability to have more than one WBS.

Why would anyone want to have more than one WBS? The answer is to sup-

Figure 2.1a   Work Breakdown Structure—Air Force Bomber

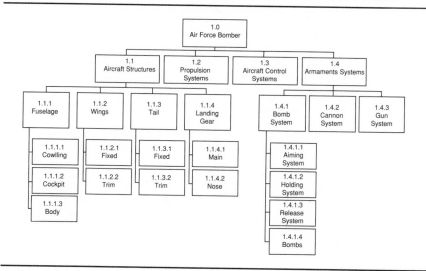

port the information needs of all the stakeholders. The deliverables-oriented WBS may be a handy way for the project manager to group the work. But the functional or line managers may want to look at it from a responsibility-oriented point of view. To facilitate this, we often develop a second framework, called the Organizational Breakdown Structure (OBS). Using the OBS, we can assign codes by responsible manager or department. Additional activity coding schemes can be used to assign physical locations, project phases, priority codes, budget divisions, and so on. Each of these codes can be used to sort and select activities, and for grouping and summarization.

The WBS and other structures, established in a coding scheme or an outliner, allow for the efficient and effective display and reporting of vast amounts of project data, to the various interested parties. Also, once established, the WBS can be used as a checklist for additional project work that may be similar to an earlier project.

Project Milestone Schedule

The development of the WBS and other structures does not necessarily occur all at once. During the project initiation process, the WBS is initiated and developed down to some intermediate level. At that time, it is also advisable to develop a timing framework for the project.

The WBS is a framework for the definition of the project work scope. Another framework is the Project Milestone Schedule (PMS). The PMS is a framework for the timing of the project, and provides a structure for the project detailed schedule. Again, we face the question of where to start. And again we will note that the development of the schedule is an iterative process. We may initiate that process when the top levels of the WBS are developed, and continue to increase the level of detail, as we define the project in greater detail. Continuing the schedule development, we will then integrate the schedule data with expected resource constraints. Finally, we will attempt to optimize the schedule by balancing timing, resources, and other constraints, until we accept the schedule as part of a baseline plan.

The Project Milestone Schedule, as the framework and first part of this scheduling process, is a vehicle for recording the time constraints, time objectives, and other givens pertaining to the schedule. Therefore, the process for developing the PMS is as follows:

1. *Start with the key dates that you already know.* These may be a given project start date, a target or contractual project end date, and interim milestone dates.
2. *Note any special time-based constraints:* a plant shutdown, a critical design review, a company board meeting, a trade show commitment, and any contract commitment dates.
3. *Add any internal interim milestone dates and preliminary high-level time frames:* target starts and completions for various phases, resource-based timing objectives, arbitrary time dividing elements, weather-dictated factors, known or typical time cycles for major components or effort-driven work.

The Project Milestone Schedule provides guidance by defining the time windows into which the task scheduling will attempt to fit. Figure 2.1b is an example of a Project Milestone Schedule for a turnkey power plant project.

Resource and Cost Frameworks

Up to this point, we have been talking about work scope and timing structures for activities. In a project management database, each activity may have one or more resource or cost elements associated with it. There will be people associated with the project that will be more interested in an aggregation of resource and cost information than in the activity view. This is achieved by assigning resource codes to each resource (or each task) and defining a cost account structure to the system.

Figure 2.1b   Project Milestone Schedule—Design–Construct Project

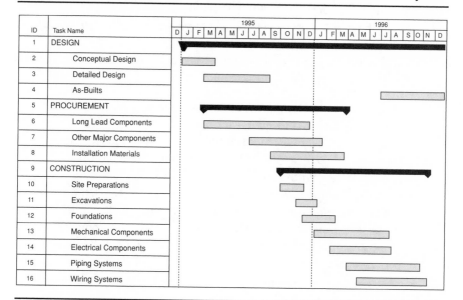

If possible, you will wish to set up a resource hierarchy, so that resources can be put into groups. Fortunately, most of the commercial project management software programs now support this feature, as well as some kind of cost account numbering system.

If you intend to use any performance measurement procedures, you will need to establish a structured basis for subdividing the project into collective elements that are meaningful to those people who are interested in the project performance results. Most programs provide at least one data field that can be used to define a code of accounts to the system.

Trap   Effective cost management, through the utilization of project management software systems, is an elusive objective. The integration of work measurement (schedule progress) and cost measurement, the main ingredients required for project performance measurement and control, is built into most project management software products. Yet the system users do not often achieve that potential. There are three significant causes of this failure:

1. Difficulty in synchronizing the timing for the progress measurements and the cost measurements.
2. Linking of the project management systems to the accounting systems.
3. The tendency to set up different measurement categories for the progress and the cost.

The latter two items can be addressed when we develop the activity and cost structures for our project. It is imperative that you identify and recognize the way that cost data will be collected for your project. If the project database is set up to one structure, and the cost data is being collected to a different structure, the integration of the two is obstructed. Useful project performance measurement requires the integration of the progress and cost data, which mandates the establishment of a common set of pigeonholes into which to funnel the experience data.

Effective Project Initiation: A Key Factor in Project Success

Getting started may be the hardest part of the project planning process. But the diligence applied at the initiation stage will almost certainly pay large dividends at the conclusion of the project. This is where we *build the foundation for the project.*

- We look at organization and culture and establish plans to work within the existing environment and the overall business strategy.
- We identify the project stakeholders and look at how they will measure success.
- We develop a project strategy that is fully consistent with the business and the stakeholders and addresses the opportunities, risks, and issues associated with the project.

These front-end activities are essential to the initiation of a project, regardless of the automated project management tools employed, if any.

- We develop a set of structures so that there is a framework for the project database.
- We use these structures as an aid to identifying the project work scope and in developing the baseline schedule and budget.

- Assuming that some kind of project management software is being used, we then use these same structures (the WBS, OBS, Project Milestone Schedule, Code of Accounts, etc.) to sort the data, to select sections of the data, to group the data, and to roll up activity, resource, and cost data to various summary levels.

No project is ever easy to manage, and no project management software system is a panacea. But we can be pretty certain that the application of automated project management tools will fail to deliver its potential without a decent framework. Without a proper foundation, of strategic thinking and organized structures, the project will crumble to the ground.

CHAPTER 2.2

DO YOU WEEBIS?
CLARIFYING WBS, OBS, AND RBS

Every discipline has its alphabet soup, abbreviations or acronyms for seemingly nonmistakable terms and functions. In project management, we have the WBS, OBS, and RBS, which, of course, everyone clearly understands. Right? It should only be that simple.

The truth is that these terms have been applied somewhat loosely within the project management community and by the popular project management software packages. Sometimes, new terms are introduced to replace the basic three, and even worse, these basic terms are being applied to functions that differ from the traditional concepts.

In some cases, this deviation may primarily be a careless application of the wrong term or willingness to stray from the traditional concept. In other, more deleterious cases, the misuse of the terms will make it appear that the product has capabilities that are not present. For instance, the availability of a data field that contains an activity tag number called WBS does not necessarily mean that the product has a true WBS capability.

Trap Any full WBS-type function (including OBS or RBS) must be able to facilitate data summarization and reporting by these codes, to any level. Using WBS codes solely for sorting and selecting (filters) does not constitute a WBS function.

Outlines and Other Frameworks

Fearing that many of us need something more simple and visual than WBS type structures, several project management software developers, especially at the low end, focus on an Outline mode. This provides a practical and very readable method of defining and displaying a hierarchical relationship of individual tasks within a larger project (and everyone knows what an outline is). It works, but with limitations. The biggest constraint is that the outline provides only one project hierarchy, when there may be several. For instance, the project manager may wish to view the project using a work breakdown based on the phases of the project, or geographical divisions, or perhaps deliverables. A functional manager is often more interested in an outline that reflects the organizational structure, such as division, department, section, discipline. The corporate comptroller may wish to segment and interrogate the data based on a code of accounts. So you can see that a single outline may not do the job for everyone.

Not to worry! Many of the project management packages provide multiple code fields for this multiple outline function. Some confusion has been generated by this expansion of outline fields. In an attempt to expand upon the hierarchical capabilities of the software, and to create some standard terminology, the market has produced a set of new terms and formats. However, these are anything but standard.

In order to facilitate frameworks for project plans (a very useful function), we have created the Work Breakdown Structure (WBS), the Organization Breakdown Structure (OBS), and the Resource Breakdown Structure (RBS). One of my clients referred to them as the Weebis, Obis, and Reebis (which, once you stop laughing, is easier to say). But! These terms, as they are being used, do not always mean the same thing.

What to Look For

Ordinarily, we would expect the outliner function to provide a summarization capability. That is, we expect the project data to be able to be rolled-up to the various outline levels. This is almost universally true, for all outliners. We would expect similar capabilities from a WBS. But, look out! Occasionally, you will come across a WBS function wherein the WBS numbers are used solely as IDs, rather than summarization points. In this case, the term WBS is really misapplied, as the field is nothing more than an auxiliary code field. You will run into this situation primarily in a few low-end products, where the outline based products are trying to appear to have WBS functionality.

A larger problem is the varied use of the term OBS (see definitions). It can mean two very different things. In fact, I once found the terms to be used quite differently in two products being distributed by the same project management software vendor.

To set the stage for a clarification of these terms, and their use, it is important to establish a clear understanding of a basic premise of project data. Two basic areas are defined and managed. One is the work itself, consisting of the project(s) and the tasks that are to be accomplished within the project. The other is the resources that are going to accomplish the work. It is very important to recognize this distinction. All project management software is based on this protocol. There is task information, and there is resource (and cost) information. We need to make the distinction between frameworks for the work (tasks) and frameworks for the resource data.

Definitions

- The **Outline,** for those programs using this mode as the primary (or only) framework, is always a work (task) framework.
- The **WBS** is fairly clear cut. It is essentially the same thing as the Outline. It is the primary hierarchy for the *tasks* within a project. It applies to the work, as opposed to the resources. When there are multiple WBSs, they are merely additional codes applied to the list of tasks to facilitate multiple sorts, filters, and summarization hierarchies.
- The **RBS** applies to the *resources*. It provides a basis for defining a parent group for each resource (perhaps all resources within a specific discipline). For instance, we might have Tom, Joan, and Iris, who are mechanical designers. The parent category would be Mechanical Engineering and Design, which, in turn, is a part of the Corporate Engineering and Design Function.
- The problem child in this alphabet soup is the **OBS.** Sometimes, it is set up to be the exact same function as the RBS. In other words, it is an RBS that is called an OBS. Other times it is set up to be a second variation of the WBS (as we noted, it is quite normal for there to be several WBS-type hierarchies). There is certainly a significant difference in these two concepts, as the RBS should be used only for the resource data, whereas the OBS (according to the most popular accepted practice) is intended solely for task data.

Last, about these definitions, I will again state that a true WBS, OBS, or RBS must be able to facilitate data summarization and reporting by these codes, to any level. Using WBS codes for sorting and selecting does not constitute a WBS function. Having a data field to designate a group for resources (even if called RBS or Resource Outline) is not an RBS if it does not allow you to look at resource assignment data, at any level of the coding structure.

Clarifying the Concepts: WBS, OBS, and RBS

The following summary is offered as an attempt to clarify the concepts of WBS, OBS, and RBS.

Common Characteristics

WBS, OBS, and RBS:

- Provide a logical breakdown of a project into successive levels showing increasing detail.
- Are composed of elements related in such a manner that each element is associated with one and only one higher level element.
- The elements can be progressively summarized upward to present the time spans, or resource and cost total for the next higher level element, and ultimately for the project.

Differentiating Characteristics

At the lowest levels of detail, in the project database, the codes are associated:

- With activity records, for the *WBS*.
- With activity records, for the *OBS*.
- With resource assignment records, for the *RBS*.

The Logic of the Breakdown Structure

- *WBS* is generally based on deliverables, sometimes within phases of a project.
- *OBS* is generally based on organizational entities.
- *RBS* is generally based on
   Common resource usage wherever used in the project, for example, all electricians
   Common types of work wherever appearing in the project, for example, all concrete placement or
   Used to differentiate between work to be expensed versus capitalized

In many programs, the term *Cost Account* is substituted for RBS. If the Cost Account function provides a means of defining a code structure at the assignment level, it is the functional equivalent of an RBS (rather than a WBS or OBS).

Usage Characteristics

- *WBS*—to accumulate all timing, resource data, and costs associated with a project as incurred in performing each activity in the project. It is important for scope management as well as analyzing earned value.
- *OBS*—to accumulate all timing, resource data, and costs in a project for which an organizational entity is responsible and relate them to the administrative budgeting process of the organization.
- *RBS*—to aggregate all timing, resource data, and costs in a manner required for control by trade, skill, or profession or by expense versus capitalization accounts.

CHAPTER 2.3

PROJECT LIFE CYCLES

While we're talking about structures, we should discuss project life cycles. Certainly, the project life cycle is a primary project structure. We can use the project life cycle as one of our work breakdown structures—essentially a phase-oriented WBS.

There is a tendency to look at the project life cycle as a standard cycle for all projects. But this is clearly wrong. Within each industry and application area, there is at least one project life cycle that is tailored to the nature of the work in that area. Recognizing and using the project life cycle structure is important to identifying and organizing the work associated with the project.

Some Typical Project Life Cycle Models

The phases of a project—the project life cycle—can take many shapes. To illustrate this, we need only to look at some of the work done by the Project Management Institute (PMI). Several members of the PMI have contributed to the development of standards and guidelines as part of the Project Management Body of Knowledge (PMBOK®). Below are a few typical life cycles, as presented in *A Guide to the Project Management Body of Knowledge (PMBOK® Guide)*.

- **For Defense Acquisition**
  Determination of Mission Needs (ends with Concept Studies Approved).
  Concept Exploration and Definition (ends with Concept Demonstration Approval).
  Demonstration and Validation (ends with Development Approval).
  Engineering and Manufacturing Development (ends with Production Approval).
  Production and Deployment (overlaps with Operations and Support).
  Operations and Support.
- **For Construction**
  Feasibility.
  Planning and Design.
  Production.
  Turnover and Start-up.
- **For Pharmaceuticals**
  Discovery and Screening.
  Preclinical Development.
  Registration Workup.
  Postsubmission Activity.
- **For Software Development** (A spiral model of four cycles with four phases in each)
  Proof of concept cycle.
  First build cycle.
  Second build cycle.
  Final build cycle.
  Each cycle has four components: Identify, Design, Construct, and Evaluate.

Certainly, anyone who has worked within these application areas can recognize the applicability of these project life cycles to some of the projects in these areas, while justifying modifications to these project life cycles for other projects. Without arguing the exact correctness of any of the above project life cycle illustrations, we can submit that it is valuable to identify an appropriate project life cycle for any project and to use that structure as one of the bases for developing the plan.

Where Do Proposals Fit In?

A problem that has always bothered me is how the proposal phase fits in (if there is one). When there is a proposal phase, some planning and budgeting (and risk assessment, etc.) are performed at that phase and then again at inception. When a proposal is not involved, these activities take place during the earliest phases. The problem here again is that it's difficult to define a one-size-fits-all approach.

A Generic Project Life Cycle—Example 1

Ignoring my own earlier advice to avoid defining a typical project life cycle, here is one of two variations on a framework that I like to use, when an application-specific, phase-based project life cycle does not exist.

- Pre-Project (Estimating, Proposal, Feasibility).
- Strategic Planning and Project Initiation.
- Implementation Planning.
- Implementation/Execution.
- Termination/Closure.

A Generic Project Life Cycle—Example 2

For the second variation, I have added lists of common activities within each phase and listed some of the system support requirements that are associated with each phase. These are just for guidance and should not be considered either as complete or as a standard.

Concept (Pre-project or Proposal) Phase

Every project begins with a concept. For traditional contract projects, this phase might include identifying a new opportunity, developing a proposal, and negotiating a contract. Overhead projects, or projects that result in new assets (capital projects), could begin by recognizing a need or issue, evaluating potential solutions, estimating resource requirements, determining a plan of action, and developing a project plan.

Activities in Concept Phase
- Identify new opportunity.
- Assess and develop new opportunity.
- Prepare project proposal, resource requirements, and budgets, and for contract projects: price.
- For contract projects: negotiate contract terms and conditions.
- Identify Objectives and Constraints.
- Identify Milestones.
- Perform Risk Evaluation.

System Support Requirements in the Concept Phase
During this phase you need system support for:

- Planning.
- Estimating.
- Risk Analysis.

Inception (Initiation or Start-up) Phase

When you have decided to continue with the project, your project enters the inception phase. Milestones in this phase are commonly marked by the awarding of a contract or the funding of a project budget. If you were collecting the costs of all of your proposed projects in one large pool, you would now create a project specifically for managing the approved initiative and optionally transfer the costs already accrued from the pool to the new project. You can even include the costs of planning the project on the project itself.

Activities in Inception Phase

- Award Contract or Release Project.
- Update and Validate Objectives, Constraints, Milestones, Risks.
- Expand Project Scope Specification, down to Work Packages and Tasks.
- Prepare Risk Mitigation Plan.
- Establish structures for Planning and Budgeting (CBS, WBS, OBS, Cost Accts.).
- Prepare Schedule.
- Prepare Resource Plan.
- Prepare Budget.
- Establish Baseline.

System Support Requirements in the Inception Phase

- Risk Management.
- Database with multiple hierarchical coding structures.
- Scheduling.*
- Resource Planning.*
- Budgeting.*

Production (Execution or Implementation) Phase

Now your project is ready to go into the production phase. This is the part of the life cycle most commonly associated with project control. In this phase, you fol-

---

*The last three items must be able to support variable time distribution structures.

low progress on the job, updating schedules and resource plans. You collect actual hours and costs, and for contract projects, you generate revenue and create invoices. If you are using Earned Value techniques, you can convert the measured accomplishments to progress payment based billing.

Activities in the Production Phase

- Contract Administration.
- Scope Control (avoid scope creep).
- Change Control (approved changes to scope with audit trail of effect on schedule and budget).
- Work Statusing.
- Time Capture.
- Cost Capture.
- Replanning.
- Monitoring and Performance Evaluation.
- Progress Payments—Billing.

System Support Requirements in the Production Phase

In addition to items from earlier phases:

- Time Reporting (by project coding structures).
- Invoice assignment by project coding structures.
- Earned Value Analysis.
- Invoicing (based on accomplishment—other).
- Multiple Baselines (for replanning).

Closeout (Termination) Phase

This is the phase that we usually let get away. Everyone who has been on the project is either busy patting themselves on the back (for achieving project success), looking for new challenges, or running for cover (if the project has failed). In doing so, we lose a lot of valuable data and experience.

There is much to do to tidy up the loose ends, and to capture lessons learned and new technology and capabilities. A key benefit from doing projects and managing them well through to closeout is derived from technology transfer and the final project audit.

Activities in the Closeout Phase

- The Project Audit (This can also be performed at key stages during the project execution).

Why, What, When, Who.
Current status of project.
Forecasts.
Status of key items.
Risk assessment.
Info pertinent to other projects.
Recommendations.
* Post-Mortem (Evaluation).
    Scope Accomplished.
    Technical Objectives Met.
    Recommendations for other projects.
    Project Historical Data.
* Other Closeout Items.
    Final Measurements.   Sell Residuals.
    Punch List.   Transfer Residuals.
    Uncompleted tasks.   Toss Residuals.
    Special Closeout Tasks.   Document Transactions.
    Final Report.   Personnel Disposition and Reports.
    Client Acceptance.   Arrange for transfer or reassignment
    Client Acceptance   of dedicated resources.
        Documents.   Release assigned resources.
    Client Feedback.   Document performance.
    Testimonials.   "Atta-boy/atta-girl" letters.
    Assets Disposition.   Archives.

Using Project Life Cycles

If the project life cycle is a phase-oriented view of the project, then it stands to reason that we can and should use the project life cycle as one of the mechanisms to monitor the project progress against the project goals. Often, but not always, there is a definable set of deliverables associated with each phase. We should pause to review the project accomplishments, as each phase comes to completion. This is one of the times during the project when we look at the objectives and evaluate performance to date against these objectives. If the objectives are not being supported, should the strategy be changed? Should the project be terminated? Should the objectives be re-examined? If the project moves ahead, should new targets be examined and communicated? Should the stakeholders have an opportunity to re-evaluate their positions and to influence how the job goes forward?

This concept of phase-oriented progress review is gaining popularity, under the name of *phase-gate* or *stage-gate*. The end of a phase is treated as a gate. The project does not pass through the gate unless it is reviewed and progress is determined to be consistent with objectives.

Trap When we are reviewing the project progress, it is not enough to look for consistency with the project objectives. We need to look for harmony with the overall business objectives and the mission of the enterprise. A successful project that does not support the larger mission of the firm is like winning the battle but losing the war.

Another use of the project life cycle is as a basis for standard work breakdown structures. All projects having a similar project life cycle can have a default WBS, by phase. This can be used as a starting point for the development of the project workscope definition and the project plan.

Two of the most popular models for WBS are the phase model and the deliverables model. Perhaps the best is to combine the two. Develop the phase-based model, based on the project life cycle. Then add the next level, based on the deliverables within each phase. This allows you to have a standard WBS down to the phase level and then to modify the next level according to the specific deliverables for that project.

The phase-based WBS is a WBS that is time oriented. The default approach is to start with the assumption that each phase will be completed before the next phase starts. Normally, there will be exceptions to this rule. There will be work on items that will start before a preceding phase is completed. This is done with the knowledge and acceptance of a measured risk.

There will be times when the phase-by-phase timing of a project will extend the project completion date beyond an acceptable time. In these cases, the project team will look for opportunities to overlap or fast-track the work. In Chapter 2.1, we illustrate a Project Milestone Schedule for a turnkey power plant. If you look at Figure 2.1b, you will note that the first level of the schedule is based on project phases, and that these phases have been overlapped to reduce the overall project duration to 24 months. The first cut of this schedule, without overlapping, produced a project duration of 36 months.

Trap   A frequent mistake by novice project managers is to assume that the WBS has to be time oriented. This is not a requirement. In fact, it is preferable to ignore the element of
time when developing a WBS that is based on deliverables, organization structure, cost accounts, locations, and so on. The
exception is the WBS that is based on the project life cycle. This
one is time oriented—at least at the phase level.

But as a guide (with the above-noted exception), avoid developing a WBS that looks at items as they occur chronologi-
cally. That's what the critical path network is for.

See Chapters 2.1 and 2.2 for more on using WBS.

SECTION 3

SCHEDULING

To many people, project management is synonymous with scheduling. We know that project management is so much more than that. Nevertheless, it is scheduling that provides us with the foundation for many of the important functions that are part of the project management process. Without the definition of the workscope, and the scheduling of the work, we would not have a basis for planning the assignment of resources or for managing the cash flow. Furthermore, the timing of the work and the management of the project end date are two of the most watched and sensitive areas of most projects. So, without falling into a false sense that the schedule is everything, we must recognize that scheduling is a very critical component of the project management process.

In Section 2, we discuss the importance of defining and organizing the workscope, and the value of developing a Project Milestone Schedule. These are the initial steps toward the development of a detailed project schedule. It is certainly possible to develop the schedule without the use of the computer. But this would be folly. First of all, in the manual approach, every time that you made a change, you would have to redraft the schedule. Of course, you could use simple bar chart software to generate a manually calculated schedule. This avoids the complete redrafting of the schedule to incorporate changes. But it would not provide the benefits of task relationship planning—a key component of the *critical path method* (CPM).

With the use of CPM software, you can define the tasks, their durations, and their relationships and have the program generate a schedule. It is possible to impose your will on what the computer does, by defining constrained start dates, target end dates, interim milestones, concurrent work, and so forth. You can test for options and alternatives (what-ifs). You can use the work breakdown structure and other coding to select, sort, and summarize the schedule data. I could go on and on about how useful, even necessary, critical path software is. In the chapters that comprise this section, we discuss these benefits and talk about practical ways to use such tools.

It is unfortunate that many people wait until there is a project crisis before getting friendly with CPM tools. Then, under the pressure of the crisis, they fail to learn the few fundamentals that are necessary to utilize these tools effectively. Frankly, the initial use of these tools can be intimidating. The trick is to get introduced to them when not under extreme pressure, and to take the time to learn some of the basics. Another good idea is to have a resident CPM guru on the staff to mentor the others. Last, try to get into the use of CPM progressively, starting with a small project and with basic functions, and growing in both scope and functionality.

For every science (project management is both an art and a science) there is a set of fundamentals. These include basic assumptions, algorithms, formulae, terms, and protocols. The science of critical path scheduling is not exempt from this. Therefore, on the possibility that a few readers will not be well versed in these fundamentals, we have provided a CPM primer, in Chapter 3.1.

In the past decade, a variation of critical path scheduling, called **critical chain project management** (CCPM), has emerged as an alternative method to CPM. We choose not to take a position on this somewhat controversial subject, opting instead to present a balanced, objective discussion on CCPM vs. CPM, in Chapter 3.2. A major aspect of the CCPM approach is that of shared contingency. This is a concept that we can strongly support, and we illustrate several ways of achieving this objective.

We also present a very strong case for the importance of schedules and time compression, regardless of whether CPM or CCPM is used. Please read Chapter 3.4, to find clear evidence of the multitude of cost penalties due to projects stretching out longer than planned or necessary.

Schedules are built by defining tasks, estimating task durations, and defining task relationships. The hardest part is dealing with task durations. For most tasks, you could come up with a range of times that could be all over the place, and have no trouble justifying any of them. In Chapter 3.3, we provide a rationale for various approaches to estimating durations, and offer some guidance on assigning durations to tasks.

In keeping with the intent of this book to provide guidance for Practical Project Management (PPM), Chapter 3.5 offers several pages of tips on how to apply the basic tools of computer-based scheduling. Nothing fancy, but lots of very effective suggestions. These tips will help you to develop realistic schedules that reflect how you intend to do the job. You'll find that it is easier than you thought.

Again, this is an important section. The most visible component of the project plan is the schedule. The schedule is the basis for all the other aspects of the plan, including the resource loading plan and the budget. The schedule is also the basis for progress and performance measurement. Obviously, with a poorly developed schedule, it will be impossible for any other aspects of the plan to be very useful, and project control is equally encumbered.

Bad schedules are, unfortunately, fairly common. And the effects of bad schedules on project performance are terribly harmful. Poor schedules lead to confusion and inefficient assignment of resources. The project team looks to the schedule for guidance and gets discouraged when they cannot rely on that document. Eventually, alternate versions of the schedule appear from sources that are not satisfied with the official schedule, leading to even more confusion and desertion.

The development of a valid schedule is not that difficult. It takes some knowledge of scheduling conventions, and some patience to do it right the first time. All too often, we rush to get that first schedule out, eventually wasting way more time trying to fix the poor schedule later. We can't help you with having patience, but we can do something about the knowledge part. We do that with the next five chapters, on project scheduling.

CHAPTER 3.1

CRITICAL PATH SCHEDULING

Now here's a boring subject: *Critical Path Scheduling*! Many of you will be well-versed in the subject and can move on to more interesting topics. You can also find detailed discussion on critical path scheduling in many of the basic books on project management and in books and electronic notes distributed with all project management software products. For the PM 101 crowd, we include a brief discussion of critical path scheduling in this chapter.

The *Critical Path Method (CPM)* is the basis of almost any project schedule. Even if you do not use a computer for scheduling, you probably use CPM concepts—possibly without even realizing it. My advice is to obtain a good project management software system and to use the critical path scheduling capabilities effectively to develop and manage your project schedules. Therefore, our discussion on project scheduling will assume that you are utilizing computers for planning and control, and that you have critical path scheduling capabilities on these computers.

What is critical path scheduling? Basically, it is the process of determining when work can be done, by identifying the precedence relationships between the tasks. It seems simple enough. Yet, many people botch up this simple process and several totally ignore the critical path scheduling capabilities, even when using critical path scheduling tools. What a shame!

CPM Basics

Regardless of the method used to create a project schedule, the first step is always the same. You must identify the work to be scheduled before you can determine when the work will be done. There are many ways that you can work up to the point of developing the schedule. We recommended a few effective practices in Chapter 2.1, Project Initiation Techniques. We will assume that you will utilize these practices as we move to the next steps of developing the project schedule.

Reviewing these front-end steps:

- You will have identified the project objectives and constraints.
- You will have initiated strategic planning and performed a stakeholder analysis.
- You will have developed a set of frameworks for the workscope and timing.
- You'll use the WBS as a framework for identification of the project tasks.
- You'll use the Project Milestone Schedule as a framework to develop the detailed project schedule.

The next steps include:

- Creating a list of all the tasks to be performed.
- Estimating the probable duration of each task.
- Defining the precedence relationships between tasks.
- Identifying date constraints and imposed dates.

Let's look at each of these in greater detail.

Defining Tasks   A favored way of building the list of tasks is to use a work breakdown structure that is based on either deliverables or phases. Actually, where it is practical, I like to use a combined WBS, where the first level represents the phases (or project life cycle) and the next level represents the deliverables within each phase. The WBS is then developed down to lower levels, such as major components, subsets, or milestones within each deliverable, and then further, down to groups of tasks that I like to call work packages. A *work package* is a set of tasks, usually under the responsibility of a single party, that represents a minor deliverable or milestone. Each task will have a single party identified as the responsible owner. Tasks may have one or more resources assigned and may have budgets (later). Every task (like every project) has an identifiable start and finish.

Estimating Task Durations   There are several ways to assign a duration to each task. The most common is to just come up with an estimated time and establish that as the task duration. Depending on the type of work, these durations may be in days, weeks, hours, and so on. In each case, these are considered *elapsed times*. For example, a task that has been assigned a 10-day duration is expected to take 2 weeks (assuming a 5-day-a-week calendar). It does not necessarily mean that the task is worked on for all of these 10 days, or that it is a 10 man-day effort. Later, in our discussion of schedule risk, we introduce the concept of multiple duration estimates. But we'll leave these alone for now.

A second popular method of determining task durations is called *effort-driven*. With this method, we enter the total hours to be applied by each resource that is working on the task, as well as specifying the rate of effort. For example, a wall is built by two bricklayers, working full time, for a total of 80 hours. The task duration is calculated as 5 days (40 elapsed hours). If there are multiple resources and rates of effort, the task duration is determined by the longest assignment.

There are numerous variations and fine points that can be introduced here, but we proceed with our coverage of critical path scheduling using these two classic methods.

Task Precedence Relationships and Date Constraints   Scheduling, of course, is deciding when the work will be performed. In a few instances, this timing will be free of constraints. But this is the exception to the rule. It is more likely that the timing of the work will be influenced by one or more factors. These may include:

- A date committed by contract or other agreement.
- Dependencies on other tasks.
- Availability of required conditions (weather, space, permits, funding, etc.).
- Availability of materials.
- Availability of labor resources.

The critical path method allows the specification of any and all of these constraining and dependency conditions. The normal process calls for the identification of task dependencies, followed by the imposition of dates that will force the calculated timing to be overridden. Let's examine these options in greater detail.

Defining Dependencies   The default dependency is a Finish to Start (FS) relationship. That is, task B cannot start until task A is finished. However, conditions may exist where an overlap is possible. For instance, task B can start 2 days after task A starts. This is designated as a Start to Start (SS) relationship. There can also be instances where 2 tasks can start independently of each other, but the completion of one is dependent upon the completion of another. Here, you would use the Finish to Finish (FF) relationship. For instance, task B can finish 5 days after the completion of task A (FF-5). The duration of the delay (in this case, 5 days) is called the *lag*.

Tip A practical way of working with critical path scheduling is to start off by defining most relationships as default FS dependencies. Then, after the project schedule has been calculated, use the ability to overlap tasks to selectively compact the project duration. See Chapter 3.4 for discussion on the value of time compression and Chapter 3.5 for more tips on practical scheduling.

CPM: How It Works   There are several options for imposing date constraints on the schedule. In order to understand how these work, we have to pause a moment to review how critical path scheduling works.

After the project model has been defined to the computer (task definition, task durations, dependencies, and imposed date constraints), the computer makes a *forward pass* to determine the earliest start and finish of all tasks. Then, after determining the earliest project completion date, the computer makes a *backward pass* from that end date, to calculate the *latest* start and finish date of all tasks that would support the project end date.

The difference between the early dates and the late dates is called *total float* or *total slack*. The path through the critical path network that has the least amount of float or slack is called the *critical path*. If the user has not imposed a required end date on the project, the critical path would have a float/slack of zero. If a project end date is imposed that is earlier than the freely computed end date, there will be tasks that have negative float. The tasks having the largest amount of negative float are said to lie on the critical path.

Therefore, it can be noted that any tasks that lie on the critical path cannot be delayed without delaying the completion of the project.

Tip The terms *float* and *slack* are used interchangeably. They are the same. Float had been the common usage, until Microsoft introduced their scheduling products, which substituted slack for float.

The forward pass establishes a pair of early dates for each task. These are called *Early Start* and *Early Finish*. The backward pass establishes a pair of late dates. These are called the *Late Start* and *Late Finish*. The difference between the early dates and the late dates is the *total float*.

Tool Tip   Sometimes the user does not wish to publish the late dates or the float. This is controlled in the reporting process. In such situations, it is also popular to change the name of the early dates to something like *Scheduled Start* and *Scheduled Finish*, or perhaps just *Start* and *Finish*. Just about all programs allow the user to rename the standard calculated fields.

Also, at times, the user does not wish to calculate or publish the early dates. Instead they want to have the dates calculated and displayed as the latest dates. This would be equivalent to a just-in-time scheduling approach. Most products have an ALAP (as late as possible) calculation option that can be used to accomplish this. The default is the ASAP (as soon as possible) mode.

Date Constraints   Now that we understand how the CPM calculates schedule dates, we can understand how to use imposed dates and how they affect the schedule calculations. Of the several options to impose dates, the most popular of these is the Start No Earlier Than (SNET) or Finish No Later Than (FNLT).

The SNET dates are used to impose a task start date that may be later than the earliest start as determined by the computer. They may override the forward pass calculations. For example, the computer may determine that a ditch can be excavated starting on January 15 (based on completion of identified predecessors). However, your crew may not want to initiate any excavation work (in Montana) prior to March 15, due to the frigid weather. By imposing a SNET date of 3/15, the calculated early start of 1/15 is overridden. Note that if, for any reason, the predecessors slip out beyond the 3/15 date, the imposed date is now overridden by the naturally calculated date. This is why we call such an imposed date Start No Earlier Than, rather than Start On, which is a forced date that is not overridden by the calculations.

Trap   First time users of project management software often tend to overuse imposed dates, especially the Start On option. In an attempt to force the schedule to predetermined dates, this improper use of the Start On option creates two problems.

First, it prevents determination of a schedule that is based on defined dependencies. Second, it makes updating the schedule much more difficult, as the user must go in and manually change all of the imposed dates.

Often, this overuse of imposed Start On dates is motivated by a desire to avoid the effort of defining all the dependencies. Ironically, the result is not only a poorly developed schedule, but also vastly increased effort to maintain it.

Furthermore, one of the great benefits of project management software comes from using these tools to help develop a supportable schedule, based on defined work, dependencies, and available resources. Ignoring all of this to create a forced schedule may be easier to do and more politically acceptable. But if it is not supported by the facts, what good is it in the long run?

The Finish No Later Than (FNLT) constraint works in just the opposite manner from the SNET constraint. The FNLT date, when imposed, affects the calculation of the late dates. This can be best illustrated by an example. Let's say that the calculated schedule for construction of a house says that the roof can be completed as late as March 15 in order to meet the contract house completion date of June 30. We are in Iowa and the snow can be expected to make a substantial appearance by December 1. It is decided that it is important to have the roof up by that date in order to be able to work inside the house and to protect the materials. By imposing a FNLT date of 12/1 on the roof completion task, we then drive all other late dates to support that imposed constraint. The FNTL date does not have any effect on the early dates, which are computed during the forward pass.

Other Constraints   Some of the constraints on scheduling the work of the project may involve events and conditions that are not on the list of defined tasks. We may be waiting for the availability of the plot on which to erect the house. Or we need the building permit. Erection of the roof trusses may require the availability of a crane. Purchasing of the erection materials may be dependent upon the availability of funds. Placement of the windows may be constrained by completion and approval of the final construction drawings. Availability of the electricians may depend on completion of the electrical work on another building.

Actually, all of these constraints should be incorporated into the project schedule. For most of those in the preceding list, we would create a new task (which may have a zero duration) to note the constraint. We would enter a

SNET date on these "dummy" tasks and make them predecessors to the tasks that cannot be started until this constraint is satisfied. For instance, you may be able to survey and lay out the lot while waiting for the building permit. But the first excavation task would be constrained by a starter task called Obtain Building Permit. The duration would be zero. A SNET date would be imposed based on the expected permit date. This task would be defined as a Finish to Start predecessor to the excavation task. A zero-time task is often called an *event*, because it is a point in time.

Tip   Creating dummy tasks to note any of the above constraints is favorable over just imposing a SNET date on the affected task. There are two reasons for this. First, by using a distinct task, there is a specific, separate line item in which we can define the specific constraint. Second, there could be more than one such constraint for a task. We can use a separate constraint task for each.

Still More Constraints   Up to this point, we have allowed the schedule to be computed without considering the availability of *labor resources*. We have assumed that whatever resources are needed to support the work, when scheduled, would be available. Obviously, this is not a good assumption. Eventually, we will want to build a definition of available resources and to allow the program to consider the availability of resources while making an adjusted computation of the schedule. This is called *Resource Leveling*, or *Resource-Constrained Scheduling*, and will be discussed in detail in Section 4.

If we have defined the resources needed to perform the tasks, we can have the CPM program calculate the quantity of each resource required for each date. These quantities may be number of units of a resource (when using classes of resources, such as electricians) or may be number of hours per time period for named resources, such as Jack Smith, a systems designer. By executing this calculation of required resource quantities, we can see and evaluate the level of resources needed to support the schedule (prior to adjusting for resource limits). This process, of computing the required resources against time, is sometimes called *Resource Aggregation.*

Where the resource aggregation indicates that there is a significant period of time where resource needs will peak, you can use this as an early warning to either try to arrange for added resources, or to be prepared for significant schedule adjustments. More on this in Section 4.

Baselines   Do not expect to have an acceptable schedule after the first computation. Even without adjusting for resources, it is likely that there will have to be several iterations before the computed schedule satisfies the stakeholders and the key dates in the Project Milestone Schedule.

Once an acceptable schedule has been developed, it is customary to save the set of dates as a *Baseline Schedule*. This baseline represents a set of targets that will be used to compare progress as the work moves forward. Each task will gain a new pair of dates, usually called *Baseline Start* and *Baseline Finish*. Target Start and Finish are alternate headings.

Trick   It is often desirable to be able to save multiple baselines. The first is usually the initial or contract baseline. A second might be a set of negotiated revision dates. I usually reserve one baseline set for my last schedule computation. Then I can compare the next update to that baseline to analyze changes during the last period.

This completes our overview of critical path scheduling. We can go into considerably more detail, but this might add to the confusion. At this time, you know enough to be able to appreciate some of the issues associated with project scheduling, such as discussed in Chapters 3.2 (Critical Path, Critical Chain, and Uncertainty) and 3.4 (How Important Are Schedules and Time Compression?). In Chapter 3.5, Practical Scheduling, we look at ways to use these basic scheduling capabilities in a practical and effective manner.

CHAPTER 3.2

CRITICAL PATH, CRITICAL CHAIN, AND UNCERTAINTY
Exploring Concepts of Shared Contingency

In the 45 years that formal critical path scheduling has been around, all the popular protocols essentially dealt with uncertainty in a similar way. They addressed it (if at all) on a task by task basis. The original PERT method did have a formal mechanism for uncertainty, by providing for three task durations (optimistic, most likely, and pessimistic). Some of today's CPM programs have carried over this three-duration capability (see Chapter 6.3). For those that did not employ the three-duration approach, uncertainty was dealt with by sneaking in a bit of extra time in each task duration estimate.

There are several problems with this approach. In the case of the latter, haphazard approach, there was no consistency in the treatment of the schedule contingency allowance, and there was no documentation of what part of the duration was actual contingency. In all the approaches, the contingency (allowance for uncertainty) was doled out to each individual task, although the actual uncertainty would be better addressed on a group of tasks basis.

This situation has been explored by several individuals, and there is a growing interest in some emerging treatment of (what I call) *shared contingency*.

Trap Schedule contingency is a vital component of a successful project. However, this contingency must be clearly identified and managed. Inconsistent and unstructured padding of

84

time estimates, while a common practice, is not a good thing. There are better ways to allow for the uncertainty that exists in all projects.

Exploring Goldratt's Critical Chain Theory

Of all the emerging solutions for shared contingency, the one gaining the most attention is one presented in a very interesting book by Eliyahu Goldratt, called *Critical Chain* (North River Press, 1997). Eli Goldratt has been successful in using the fiction novel method to promote his hypothesis on the Theory of Constraints, via the subject book and two others: *The Goal* (1992), and *It's Not Luck* (1994).

There have been a plethora of papers, both in print and on websites, either extolling the benefits of the critical chain approach, or advising restraint in adopting this theory. The discussion tendered herein is entirely neutral, finding both praise and fault with aspects of theory and practice of Critical Chain Project Management (CCPM), as presented by Goldratt and supporting disciples.

As I shared my thoughts with two colleagues (both involved in developing software for project management), the question arose as to whether there were two separate camps. One said that you had to be a supporter of either CCPM or traditional CPM (TCPM), but couldn't straddle both philosophies. I choose to disagree. I am not ready to either abandon TCPM or adopt CCPM lock, stock, and barrel.

For example, looking at just one of the beliefs associated with the two camps, let's consider the rules for multitasking. In TCPM, it has become the accepted practice to assume that resources will, at times, move back and forth between concurrently scheduled tasks. In fact, we often find that such movement produces more efficient schedules and utilization of resources, and we have criticized software that does not support resource assignment splitting. Now Goldratt comes along to dispute that assumption. He says that multitasking is required only because we establish task durations that are longer than the actual time required to perform the tasks. He claims that multitasking is inherently inefficient. If we reduce the estimated task duration to match the real effort, says Goldratt, then we don't have to shift the resources. CCPM, therefore, deliberately disallows resource assignment splitting, claiming that it is a negative attribute rather than a preferred capability.

In brief, Goldratt's position is that project schedules are always too long due to the safety factors that are added to the task estimates. He claims that estimates are usually based on a 90 percent confidence factor (rather than 50%). In addition task durations are also padded unless the performer is assured that everything needed to do the task will be ready at the start of the task (which is usually not the case). To this, we generally add a collection factor whenever a group of tasks come together, providing some margin in case one of the tasks slips. Similarly, each level of management adds a safety allowance. Finally, on top of this, everyone knows that the total duration will not be accepted. They expect to be pushed for a 20 percent reduction, so they add 25 percent to the already inflated estimate.

Of course, inflated estimates are not news to our readers, and, likewise, Goldratt's solution, which merits our attention, is far from being original. In fact, I have written and taught similar concepts of schedule duration management, schedule risk, and contingency management for more than three decades. See *Risk Management for Dummies: Managing Schedule, Cost and Technical Risk and Contingency*, PM Network, Project Management Institute (October 1995 and April 1996), and in an updated version in Chapter 6.2 of this book.

Another interesting approach to dealing with contingency in schedules is presented by Bradford Eichhorn. See *Manage Contingencies, Reduce Risk: The PCA Technique*, in PM Network, Project Management Institute (October 1997). In the plan contingency allowance technique, Eichhorn supports my appeal for the specific identification and management of contingency.

The Shared Contingency Idea

Essentially, any of these solutions might be called *shared contingency* (my term). In the Goldratt approach, it is applied in several stages. First, he locates the critical path and reduces task durations to be consistent with a 50 percent probability rather than 90 percent. Half of the removed duration is added at the end of the path, as a *project buffer*.

Next, the *feeder paths* are located and treated in a similar manner, and half of the removed duration is added at the end of each feeder path, as a *feeder buffer*. The overall project schedule is reduced. Emphasis is placed on monitoring the project buffer and feeder buffers (for shrinkage), rather than managing the critical path.

For a more detailed description of the Critical Chain Project Management (CCPM) method, see the paper by Larry P. Leach, in June 1999 *Project Management Journal*, Project Management Institute.

Critiquing Goldratt's Concepts

In general, I agree with the concept of shared contingency, represented by the project buffer and feeder buffer method. But it has to be implemented on a case basis.

On the one hand, the problem (as described by Goldratt) is that the project schedule contingency is usually added to invisible task contingency—resulting in an unreasonably extended schedule, and relieving pressure to get jobs done in the shortest reasonable time. On the other hand, one has to be careful not to be overzealous in the reduction of contingency so as to put the project at risk for meeting contract required dates.

The concept of removing the contingency from individual tasks and placing it in project and feeder buffers makes a lot of sense and is highly recommended. It is a simple idea that can be easily applied. Goldratt omits discussion of tools to aid in the application of his methods. We will provide such advice later in this chapter. Goldratt goes on to state three policies associated with the basic concept. I have some serious reservations on these.

First, he suggests that we use *remaining duration* rather than *percent complete* to measure task status. This makes sense, but only if you are not employing earned value analysis techniques (which I almost always recommend). Remaining duration has always been a statusing option in most project management software.

He also states that "all we are concerned with is the critical path." But then, Goldratt goes on to contradict himself by discussing means of using feeder buffer analysis to manage the schedule. I prefer using EVA (BCWP vs. BCWS) to analyze work production (as discussed further in this chapter, and in Section 8). However, a formal application of Feeder Buffer analysis can be used as an alternative method.

I strongly disagree with Goldratt's policy that we eliminate management by *milestones*. Milestones are good for interim accomplishment (providing immediate recognition and reward). Some milestones are required interim targets. The use of selected milestones should be retained to supplement other measurements. I almost always develop a Project Milestone Schedule for initial top-down planning and as a guide for detailed planning.

Resource and Bottleneck Buffers

Up to this point, Goldratt deals with a scheduling model, wherein potential resource conflicts and limits are not considered . He goes on to addresses the complexity of resource constraints. He introduces *resource buffers* and directs that the critical path now must go through all tasks that involve simultaneous contention for scarce resources. He inserts resource buffers when work shifts to a new resource. These resource buffers are applied only to the critical chain, placed before critical tasks to alert resources of pending work. Goldratt acknowledges, at this point, that computer support is needed for analysis and determination of resource overloads and scheduling.

From what I can fathom from his discussion on resource constraints, some method such as the familiar resource leveling technique (see Chapter 4.1) must be employed. However, the use of resource buffers in the critical chain method does not insert actual resource contingency (no resources are assigned to the resource buffers), but rather just inserts a time contingency prior to the scheduled resource usage. This gives me cause for concern. If we acknowledge that we should assign the shortest reasonable duration to tasks and then add schedule contingency, then doesn't the same philosophy apply to resource effort? That is, if we reduce the task duration and associated resource effort to get the fat out, then surely we have to add some resource effort contingency to the plan. Otherwise, we go blindly into our projects thinking that we have budgeted enough resources and have no reserve to work from when the effort (as it surely will at times) exceeds the plan.

This, therefore, is a serious flaw in the critical chain theory. It effectively addresses risk and contingency for schedule, but ignores risk and contingency for resource effort and cost.

Other Goldratt Ideas

Goldratt correctly points out that people are often moved to inflate their task estimates because of the poor communication of the status of predecessor tasks, and when their task will start. Goldratt suggests that a regimen for monitoring and communication, that would provide for 10-day, 3-day, and 1-day advance notification, would alleviate this problem. This just makes good sense, no matter what the PM approach.

Finally, Goldratt teases us with some good thoughts on the cost benefits of improved schedule performance, but falls short of presenting a complete and cohesive treatise. Without saying as much, Goldratt starts to address what we are now calling Project Portfolio Management. In view of the current hoopla regarding this subject (see Chapter 9.1), I would like to see a follow-up on his points, specifically relating them to project portfolio management issues.

Disagreements and Fallacies

I have to admit to a chronic weakness—that of seeing both good and bad in almost anything. Hence, while I support the general concept of shared buffers, as forwarded by the Critical Chain Project Management method, I can't help but see numerous fallacies in some of the basic premises. What is especially disturbing are the inconsistencies and contradictions, some of which have been already noted.

A review of some of the earlier writings on CCPM and subsequent discussions with other consultants who have been engaged in research and dialog on traditional and critical chain methodologies has given rise to some interesting commentary.

For instance, we have a claim that "The critical chain plan effectively eliminates most resource contention before the project starts. CCPM specifies the critical chain, rather than the critical path, as the project constraint. This path includes resource dependencies, and does not change during project execution."

I have a problem believing that the multiproject resource environment is so stable as to support the long-range scheduling of resources, without modification. Are we to ignore the current trend toward project portfolio management and the pressure to adjust the project mix and priorities to support the strategic objectives of the enterprise? On the other hand, CCPM advocates argue that the buffers created within the plan will cover the most likely areas of adjustment.

I certainly can't accept as any revelation the following capability: "Defines the constraint for multiple projects as the constraining company resources. It links projects through this resource. . . ." Heck, I've been doing this since 1962.

CCPM advocates also cite several examples of corporate success in implementing CCPM. I don't doubt the results, but can we conclude, for certain, that these successes were the result of a shift from traditional project management to CCPM, or the result of adopting structured and practical PM practices in place of a nonproject management environment? There is a lot of good, practical sense in the Critical Chain, and Goldratt has an approach that can get the attention of people who may have been intimidated or turned off by earlier attempts to indoctrinate them in the value of good project management. But I can't see anything revolutionary in the CCPM approach. It is still fundamentally based on traditional critical path theory. The unique and valuable aspect of CCPM is its use of shared contingency, via the various buffers.

I would suggest that the improved results would be available to any organization that modifies its behavior and decides to take PM seriously.

Software for CCPM

Goldratt acknowledges that computer assistance is necessary to calculate the critical chain and to manipulate the various buffers. Here are two products that are available to support CCPM.

The first is *ProChain Project Scheduling*, from ProChain Solutions, Inc., (703) 490-8821 or www.prochain.com. ProChain sits on top of Microsoft Project, and is run from within MSP. Task Bars and ProChain Views are added to the MSP screen. ProChain will first Load Level, considering dependency and resource constraints. Next, it identifies the critical chain. The next steps create and insert the various buffers. Options are provided to set the parameters for the buffers and to override the automatic placement or computation. A Factor Durations option can be used to set a duration multiplier. For instance, you might want to use the Duration Factor to cut the task durations in half, and then set the buffer options to 50 percent of the path duration. In the brief test that I ran, I had to reduce the durations by about half to compensate for the added duration for all the buffers. Also, in this test, the project duration (after load leveling, but without buffers) was the same as when I invoked MSP's resource leveling function (which I would expect). However, the selected sequence of task execution was different.

If you don't wish to use separate software for CCPM, some of the functions can be achieved via creative use of traditional CPM software that has PERT (three-time-estimate) capabilities. This is available in Scitor's Project Scheduler as well as in MS Project (*version 98 and later*). Neither of these products will calculate and place buffers, but the PERT analysis can be used to estimate the time that should be allocated for schedule contingency.

Tool Tip Scitor's latest scheduling release, *Project Scheduler 8*, is the first traditional CPM program to offer support for CCPM as an available option within the basic product. PS8 offers a complete Critical Chain capability as a scheduling option within the basic program. The CCPM capability in PS8 has support for multiproject critical chain scheduling, based on project priorities and constrained by key resources (Drum Resources feature). Scitor can be reached at (408) 745-8300, or at www.scitor.com.

Planning and Tracking Issues

It must be obvious by now that the road to good schedules is strewn with rocks and other impediments. Our plans must contain a balance of reasonable task durations and reasonable contingency. We must squeeze the fat (or excessive contingency) out of the estimates, yet retain a reasonable cushion for the inevitable effects of Murphy's Law. There are several techniques for dealing with these scheduling issues, including PERT estimates (triple time estimates) and Critical Chain buffers.

But once these plans are drafted, we cannot rely on just a single method of tracking progress. Those of us who were taught to manage via the critical path method soon found that out. If we concentrated entirely on maintaining float (or slack) in the critical path, eventually enough work that was not on the critical path became critical, and the ability to accommodate slippage anywhere in the project had disappeared. If using the CCPM method, a similar danger exists if we put all of our eggs in one basket, by just concentrating on the critical chain.

I prefer to supplement the traditional critical path analysis with something that I call *Accomplishment Value*.

Using Accomplishment Value to Supplement Float Analysis

Accomplishment Value, or Earned Value (a.k.a. Budgeted Cost of Work Performed) pertains to the measurement of accomplishment against the plan, once the work is underway. It is quite easy and practical to employ just part of the earned value protocol, for measuring the *rate of work accomplishment* against the plan. To use the EV approach, identify your tasks, assign a cost (or other weight factor) to each task, and schedule all tasks (either manually or by CPM). The computer will calculate the BCWS or *Planned Accomplishment* for any point of time, by multiplying the planned percent complete of each task by the value (cost) of the task. Now, when it comes time to progress the schedule, just enter the percent complete of any tasks that have started. The system will multiply the percent complete by the budgeted cost, producing the earned value. This gives us a weighted measure of accomplishment, which can be compared to the planned accomplishment. If the earned value (BCWP) is less than the planned accomplishment (BCWS), work is not being accomplished as fast as planned, and you can say that the project is behind schedule.

Interestingly, some of the CCPM advocates knock the EVA methods, claiming that they do not tell an accurate story due to a basis on cost rather than duration. This is not necessarily correct. For a more detailed explanation of Earned Value Analysis, see Section 8.

Parkinson, Murphy, and Shared Contingency

A common thread among all the commentary on shared contingency methods is that we must defend ourselves from Parkinson's Law. It was C. Northcote Parkinson who said "Work expands so as to fill the time available for that work." If we mask the contingency from the real estimate, we tend to realize a self-prophecy that will use the entire duration that was applied to the task (including the contingency). By pulling the contingency out of the task and grouping it with other contingency in the path, we retain the shorter (and achievable) task duration as a target.

Being subject to Murphy's Law as well as Parkinson's Law, we obviously have to allow for tasks to exceed their most likely duration. So the concept of including contingency is entirely defendable. But to counteract Parkinson, that contingency is best left out of the individual tasks and placed in a shared buffer or dummy task.

It has also been my experience that schedule slippage often occurs between tasks rather than within a task. Hence, placing the contingency in a shared buffer allows for this phenomenon.

The other popular theory inherent in the various shared contingency methods is that task durations are more realistic if they allow for 50 percent probability rather than 90 percent probability. The time allowance of the risk that is taken out of the individual tasks goes into the buffers.

Regardless of the disagreement on the various methods, there appears to be consensus on the above issues.

Using Your Options

The bottom line here is to be aware that there are several options available to plan and track project activity. There will be times when applying techniques such as CCPM or PERT for planning projects will provide a better plan. Risk management and contingency planning is always justified (not an option). Tracking options include percent complete, remaining duration, earned value, milestone tracking, critical path tracking, and buffer analysis. I could never say that just one of these is very important and that the others should be subordinated or ignored. Each of these has its purpose.

The concept of shared contingency is one that I can highly support, but there are many ways to do this. The critical chain theory has done much to bring the concept of shared contingency, leaner task durations, and risk awareness to the forefront. We can all learn from it and seek ways to address these issues.

Project success is not as dependent on the planning and control methods and tools as it is on the behavior of managers and other personnel involved with contributing to project performance. It has been well-documented that traditional methods and tools tend to be intimidating to such personnel. Some claim that CCPM lowers this barrier. I'm not sure that this is true. I am certain, however, that improvement in the way that humans operate in the projects environment, and their commitment to good planning and communication, and then execution according to the plan, are the real keys to project success.

CHAPTER 3.3

ESTIMATING TASK DURATIONS

An entire chapter devoted to a discussion on the duration of tasks? He has to be kidding, you say to yourself. But wait! Don't move on to the next chapter just yet. Think a bit about the relative importance of task durations. A project schedule is the result of the aggregation of all the task durations. If the durations lack validity, so does the project schedule. Fidelity in task duration estimating is essential to the development of a wholesome project schedule. And such fidelity can only be achieved via a structured and consistent approach toward establishing task durations.

How Long Does It Take to Catch a Fish?

Here's a good question. How long does it take to catch a fish? Ridiculous, you say. One can't estimate the time to catch a fish. It could be just after you cast a line in the water. It might be never. Or anywhere in between. As ridiculous as this sounds, that is just the feeling that goes through our minds when we are asked to estimate the duration for a task. Our first thought is How the h__ should I know? But we can't get away with this. So we dig in and take a scientific stab at the task duration.

First, we come up with a most likely estimate of the duration. This is the time that we feel it would take about 50 percent of the times that we were to execute the task. But we're not comfortable with a 50 percent confidence factor. So we add some time that we feel we could support about 90 percent of the time.

Next, we think about what we will need to start the task, including what kinds of conditions are required. If we are concerned that we will not have everything that we need to start the task, we add some more time to the task estimate (even though these issues do not impact upon the actual time to execute the task itself).

Then there is the *collection factor*. When a group of tasks come together, we tend to add some more safety margin, to allow for one of the tasks to slip. Similarly, we note that there is a tendency to lose time between tasks. I call this the 5 + 5 = 13 rule. Two tasks, each estimated at 5 days, performed in series, will take 13 days because we lose 3 days between the completion of the first task and the start of the second task.

So what do we do? We compensate for all these factors that are external to the immediate task, by adding time to the task estimate, itself.

Finally, everyone knows that the total duration will not be accepted. They expect to be pushed for a 20 percent reduction, so they add 25 percent to the already inflated estimate.

What Does the Task Duration Really Represent?

If we assign task durations as just described, do we really know what the expected task duration is? Certainly there is justification for all the above mentioned items. However, most of them have nothing to do with the actual time that we need to perform the task.

Furthermore, even the estimate of the actual task duration can take several paths. For instance, here are several approaches to estimating task durations.

Elapsed Time vs. Working Time   We feel that it will take 5 days to actually perform the work. But we know that we will not be working on the task without interruption. So we set the task duration at 10 days, to allow for the elapsed time that we expect to occur.

Task Time vs. Resource Time   We estimate that the task will take 80 hours to perform. Is this 80 hours by 2 people, producing an elapsed time of 5 days? Or is it 80 hours for 1 person, working half time, producing an elapsed time of 20 days? (This issue is addressed in Section 4—on Resource Scheduling.)

Interface Losses and Delays   We noted above that we can expect some loss of time between tasks and when multiple tasks converge. Shall we incorporate these expected losses into the tasks themselves, or set up dummy tasks to allow for these delays?

Tool Tip With any of the CPM tools, it is possible to set a lag between the end of one task and the start of a successor. For instance, to add 3 days between task A and task B, we would define the link between these 2 tasks as FS3. Task B can start 3 days after task A finishes. In reality, the start of task B is not actually delayed. It is just the schedule that will reflect the time allowance that has been inserted.

Theoretical Duration vs. Experience   Here's a situation that always frustrates me. I have a task that I have performed several times. Each time that I estimate how long it should take, I come up with 20 days. I just know that I can do it in 20 days. Yet, each time that I perform the task, it takes about 50 percent longer than the 20 days. Each time there is a different reason for the delay. Nevertheless, I average 30 days to do the job. Now, what do I do? Do I use an estimate of 20 days—the duration that I feel to be most correct? Or do I use an estimate of 30 days—based on past experience? I am justified to use the 20-day estimate. The task should be completed in 20 days and this is what we should use as a target. But if our experience tells us to expect 30 days, aren't we deceiving the team by saying that we expect it to be done in 20 days? And, if we use the 30-day estimate, will we end up taking the 30 days, because that is the time available? Is there a right answer?

Trap Be careful not to improperly use averaging. For instance, we would not want to average performance on parallel paths. Let's say that we have tasks A, B, C, and D, each estimated to take 20 days. A, B, and C actually take 15 days each. Task D actually takes 35 days. While the average still works out to 20 days, the actual duration for the path (for the four parallel tasks) is 35 days.

For another example, we look at two serial tasks, each estimated to take 10 days. Task A gets done in 8 days. Task B takes 12 days. The chain probably took 22 days (rather than 20) because task B didn't start until the eleventh day. (Harvey's Law: A delay in one step is passed on to the next step. An advance made in one step is usually wasted.)

Skill Levels, Learning Curves, and Priorities   How do we handle potential performance modifiers? Do we add time to the duration estimate because we expect that there will be additional time and effort needed to do the task the first time (learning curve)? Should the duration be adjusted based on the skill level of the resources expected to be assigned? Do we actually have an index of skill level? And what if the resources change? Does a higher priority task or project get done faster because of the pressure and attention? These are all things that can impact upon the task duration. But there rarely is a set of guidelines in place to help us with the estimating and to aid in achieving consistency across the project and the team.

PERT Method   This technique provides for a quantitative method of considering uncertainty or risk. It calls for the use of three time estimates for each task. These are called *optimistic*, *most likely*, and *pessimistic*. The most likely is the duration that can be expected 50 percent of the time. The optimistic is the shortest reasonable duration, attainable about 10 percent of the time. The pessimistic is the longest reasonable duration, also with about a 10 percent probability. In the PERT method, a PERT duration is calculated, usually based on the formula: $(a + 4b + c)/6$, where b is the most likely. Using special software, it is then possible to perform a statistical analysis, providing a calculated probability of meeting any project end date. Although it may appear that the PERT method takes a great deal of additional effort, the reverse is really true. In reality, we tend to go through the process of thinking of the possible range of estimates, based on perceived risk and uncertainty. But then, after mentally deriving a single duration, we fail to capture the information that went into the estimate.

Tool Tip Special software is available to support the PERT method of schedule computation. Among the most popular are two products that work with Microsoft Project. These are: Risk + for Project (CS Solutions) and @ Risk for Project (Palisade Corporation).

Welcom Software Technology and Primavera Systems also have offered tools to support the PERT method. These, Opera and Monte Carlo, work with the CPM products sold by these vendors: Open Plan and Primavera Project Planner.

Both Microsoft and Scitor have provisions for using three time estimates, but do not provide full statistical calculation of schedule probabilities. Scitor (PS7 and PS8) allows the user to vary the weighting of the three estimates.

Delphi Method   This decision-aiding technique is rarely employed in determining task durations, but could be applied if desired. It calls for each member of the team to offer their own estimate to the group. Estimates at the extremes (shortest/longest) are defended by the estimator, which often introduces issues that were not considered by the others. Based on the new information, the team votes again (re-estimates). The process is repeated until there is a reasonable consensus and comfort with the task duration.

The Psychology of Task Durations

There is a self-fulfilling prophecy regarding performance of tasks within planned durations. A task is hardly ever completed ahead of schedule. There are several reasons for this. We can demonstrate these using an illustration of a task that has a 50-50 chance of being completed in 5 days, but has been scheduled for 10 days to allow for uncertainty, risk, emergency diversions, and so on.

First, there is Parkinson's Law. Work expands to fill the time available for the work. Work on the task has commenced on schedule and is essentially completed within the first 5 days. But, because 10 days have been allocated for the task, the performer spends the next 5 days fine-tuning the deliverable. This is a natural work ethic of most people. We reach 98 percent completion on our task and, if additional time is available, we attempt to refine it until a delivery deadline is reached.

Second, is procrastination. We are able to start the task as scheduled. But, because there are 10 days allocated, and we know that we need only 5 days, we wait a week to start the task. Now, of course, the contingency has been exhausted before the task has been started, and the potential for a schedule overrun has been increased. But, even if there are no problems, the 5-day task has taken 10 days.

Less obvious are the subtle motivators to avoid early completion of tasks. If we estimated 10 days and complete the task in 5 days, we might be criticized for padding the estimate, even though the extra 5 days was a legitimate allowance for uncertainty. Or we might be under increased pressure to shorten duration estimates in the future. There rarely is a reward for finishing tasks early—only demerits for running over. So where is the motivation to do the task in 5 days?

Trap   The time to complete a task will almost always take a minimum of the allocated time, and probably more. If pressure is to be maintained to minimize the time spent on tasks, it is advantageous to move most contingency out of the individual tasks and allow for the contingency in other ways. See Chapter 6.1, Using and Managing Contingency, and Chapter 3.2, . . . Shared Contingency.

Practical Time Estimating

Recognizing all the possibilities for distorted or padded time estimates, how can we allow for all the perturbations that are likely to impact upon the schedule, without masking the true duration estimate for the task? Certainly, if we do not allow for uncertainty, by adding contingency, we risk a high potential of running late and missing deadlines. However, if we bury the contingency in the individual task estimates, we almost assure that the work will slip to fill the time available.

It is this dilemma that motivated the concepts of shared contingency, discussed in Chapter 3.2. Use of the various shared contingency conventions is one way of addressing many of the issues raised. It is also feasible to deal with some of these issues using traditional CPM methods and tools. Here are a few illustrations.

Example 1   Task should be completed in 20 days, but need to allow 30 days in schedule based on past experience. Enter a duration of 20 days. Create dummy task for contingency, with duration of 10 days.

Example 2   Lump all the contingency for a logical group of tasks in a shared contingency dummy task. Using CCPM philosophy, add up the contingencies and cut in half for the buffer task (shared contingency method).

Example 3   Use finish-to-start (FS) links with a lag duration to incorporate time for delays between tasks.

Example 4   Freely impose Finish-No-Later-Than (FNLT) dates to drive earlier completions. Set FNLT dates equal to the Early Finish dates for tasks that you do not want to let slip.

More important than all the above is the need to develop consistency in estimating task durations. There should be a blanket policy for contingency. At least that way everyone knows the basis for the estimate. Standard guidelines for task duration estimating should be established by the projects function for universal use.

The application of the guidelines should consider the key factors in achieving project success. If getting the job done as fast as possible is a key objective, then contingencies should be minimized and identified. If protecting the firm from delay penalties is a key issue, then contingency allowances play a larger role.

Flexibility, within standardized guidelines, together with notation of and communication of the basis for the estimates, will help reduce the potential for poor estimating and scheduling. But nobody said it was going to be easy.

CHAPTER 3.4

HOW IMPORTANT ARE SCHEDULES AND TIME COMPRESSION?

Have you ever driven along a highway where a construction project seemed to be going on forever? You drive for miles and miles, past thousands of orange barrels and cones, past hundreds of barriers and signs, past dozens of expensive cranes, bulldozers, backhoes and such, and miles of temporary concrete dividers. Yet there are hardly any people in sight. Where are the workers? Why are there 10 miles of detoured traffic and only 10 yards of active work?

Not only that, but you drove by that spot six months ago and hardly anything has changed.

Getting beyond your immediate frustration with the traffic slowdowns, your ever-inquisitive mind drifts to the topic of waste. How much money is tied up in all of this paraphernalia? How much money could be saved by expediting these projects (as well as reducing the inconvenience to the driving public)?

Period Costs and Hammocks

The typical project will contain a combination of labor-based costs, materials costs, and other costs such as equipment rentals and supplies. Consider that many of these are period-based costs. That is, the costs are associated with the duration of the use, rather than the intensity or frequency of the use.

If we look at the highway type projects, such as discussed above, we can list several period-based costs. These would include field trailers, office equipment including computers and phones, earth-moving equipment, and such. What about all of those orange barrels and cones? They must represent a reasonably sized capital investment. What about foremen? The longer the job, the longer the cost.

Good scheduling software will have a hammock function. A *hammock* is a type of task that does not have a fixed time duration. Instead, it automatically calculates its duration from the tasks that it is associated with (or group of tasks that the hammock spans).

You can use the hammock function for all tasks that have resources or costs that are associated with time periods that are dependent on other tasks. For instance, let's say that we rent a backhoe, at $200 per day. We create a hammock task, called *rent backhoe*, and assign a cost of $200 per day. We note a start-to-start relationship with the first task that requires the backhoe, and a finish-to-finish relationship with the last task that requires the backhoe. That's it. If the string of tasks using the backhoe stretches out for 21 days, then the rental cost is automatically calculated as $4,200. If the schedule is compressed to reduce that span to 16 days, then the backhoe cost is automatically recalculated to $3,200.

By setting up these period cost tasks, using hammocks, you can easily see the effect of squeezing time out of the schedule. Often, the additional costs of overtime and/or night work can be offset by the reduction in period costs. Maybe not all the time, but, with this method, you don't have to guess about it. Also, using the hammocks this way, you can also be aware of the true cost of delays.

Tool Tip   The *hammock* feature is not universally available in project management software products. For instance, among the popular CPM packages, hammocks are available in Scitor's PS8, but are not available in Microsoft Project.

Time-to-Market

Here's another thought to ponder. We all read continually about the importance of time-to-market. We hear of constant advances in shortening product development cycles. We know that there are competitive inducements to compressing the time-to-market. And we can postulate that shortening the process might even reduce the cost of development.

But how much has been written that actually quantifies the benefits of shorter development cycles? Well, marketing consultant Geoffrey Moore [*Crossing the Chasm* (HarperBusiness, 1991) and *Inside the Tornado* (HarperBusiness, 1995)] has some interesting figures to offer on this.

He says when a new product is created for a new market, the first one getting to market is most likely to garner at least 50 percent of the total market. The remaining 50 percent is all that will remain for all the other players. No wonder that there is so much pressure on new developments (and, perhaps why some developers are willing to skimp on quality rather than chance delays).

Hey! There's more yet. If the first vendor to the market garners 50 percent of possible sales, while #2 picks up, say, 20 percent, that is not the probable ratio for income. That is because #1 sets the price, which, without competition allows maximizing profits and return on investment. By the time the other vendors join the battle, profit margins will drop (but only after #1 has made its killing). Moore figures that #1 will garner at least 70 percent of the profits pie, in this model.

Now I ask you—is that enough motivation to drive schedule compression and management?

Every day that can be squeezed out of the schedule improves the developer's chances of grabbing the lion's share of the market. The new product developer must not only invest effort in creating fast-track schedules, but must also continually tweak the schedule looking for ways to optimize (shorten) the time cycles. The payoff, for getting there first, is monumental.

Schedule and Cost—Effect on Profit

Here's another bit of data to support our case on the deleterious effect of schedule delays. As project managers and project owners, we tend to worry, equally, about schedule delays and cost overruns. But, according to an oft-quoted study by McKinsey and Company, one of these is more equal than the other.

That study looks at the effect of schedule delays and cost overruns on the expected profit, over a 5-year period. The resultant data indicates that cost overruns in the neighborhood of 50 percent eventually reduced the profit by about 3 to 4 percent. On the other hand, they found that a schedule delay of 6 months often resulted in a loss of a third of the expected profit, over five years.

Certainly, in view of Geoffrey Moore's marketing models, this should not be surprising. Furthermore, the effect of schedule delays on cash flow and return on investment, as noted in the following paragraphs, provides additional support for these findings.

Effect of Project Delays on Return on Investment

I was playing with some numbers recently to explore the effect of extended project completion on cash flow and payback duration. The assumption that I made was that the project was scheduled to be completed in two years, and that I was investing $10,000 per month (at a cost of 8%). The project started on 1/1/2000 and was to be completed on 1/1/2002, at a cost of $260,000. Once completed, the project would return $10,000 per month, and would return my investment on about 3/1/2004, 50 months from the start of the project.

Then, I calculated the effect of a six-month delay, coupled with an increase in monthly expenditure of 15 percent. This schedule and cost overrun is much lower than is typical, according to published studies. When the project was completed, I had put $381,000 into it. With a $10,000 monthly return, starting on 7/1/2002, it will take until about 9/1/2005, or 68 months to get back what I have put into it.

This is just another example of the potential cost of schedule delays and cost overruns. I imagine that if I presented such a project to the sponsors, offering a 68-month payback rather than a 50-month payback, I would have met with considerable resistance. Now, having experienced the extended payback, how well would the project measure up to the project success criteria?

Extended Cash Flow Projections

We typically engage critical path scheduling software to plan and control a project. We normally will define the project as all that takes place from the project authorization or initiation through to the completion of all deliverables. If we use the costing capabilities of the software, it is applied across this time period, generally encompassing all costs incurred to complete the deliverables.

But why stop here? Cash flow can be positive as well as negative. If the project that we are managing is intended to generate a positive cash flow (such as the new product developments discussed above), why not add pseudo tasks that generate income? Now we can model various scenarios and evaluate the best actions for a project. We can go beyond determining the most cost effective plan to complete the project, but rather the best plan to generate the preferred long-term cash flow.

Tool Tip   Hardly any of the commercial project management software products provide direct support for positive cash flow, because they handle only costs, and not income. Super-

Project is an exception, offering this unique capability. However, it should be easily possible to transfer data from your PM database to a spreadsheet and generate the analyses there.

Carrying this process even further, we can evaluate a set of projects and manipulate the mix of projects to optimize support of the full business strategies and plans. We hear a lot lately about Project Portfolio Management. A significant component of this corporate-level strategy is the schedule-based cash flow analysis of multiple projects. (See Section 9, Project Portfolio Management.)

Risk Considerations

Up to now, we have talked about schedules as if they were based on well-defined task durations. But we all know that this is an illusion. Task durations are based on time estimates and effort estimates. These are always based on one or more assumptions, and these assumptions are subject to interpretation. What tends to happen is that all such estimates are developed with some built-in contingency. Yes, we do run into instances where an optimistic individual offers a "best chance" estimate. But most estimates assume that one or more conditions will exist to stretch a task past its achievable duration. So a 10-day task gets 2 days added for possible weather delays, another 2 days for resource conflicts, 1 more day for equipment problems, and perhaps another 3 days just for comfort. Now, with the 10-day task up to 18 days, we add a couple of days because we know that the project manager will ask for a 10 percent improvement, to expedite the schedule.

There are many ways to address this dilemma, such as using multiple estimates (PERT durations) or shared contingency concepts such as Critical Chain and Project Contingency Allowance techniques. (See Chapter 3.2.) However, there is one aspect of this condition of which we all must remain aware. There is a relationship between schedule contingency and schedule risk. The insertion of contingency in schedules is motivated by the urge to reduce risk of failure. Although adding contingency does not necessarily reduce such risk (because we learn to use the contingency to let things slip), it does provide more room for error and corrective action than we would have in a very tight schedule.

If we are to use contingency (which I highly advise) then this must be a managed contingency. By a *managed contingency* I mean:

- We must know the basis for the contingency. That is, if we allow 2 days for weather and 1 day for equipment, this should be noted.
- The contingency should be separated from the real expected duration.

- Pressure should be maintained on achieving the most likely times.
- Time is shifted from the contingency pool to the schedule by the manager, who will maintain an analysis of schedule performance and contingency use.

The tighter the schedule, the less room there is for things to go wrong (there is less time available for corrective action, therefore limiting remedies). This increases the importance of proactive risk management. Management must be fully aware of all areas of risk. These risk areas must be under constant surveillance. The risk averse manager is prepared in advance to take remedial action, by having alternate plans ready for action if needed.

PERT Analysis

As briefly noted in Chapter 3.3, there is a tool available to aid in the analysis of schedules having varying degrees of time contingency. It involves using three time estimates for each task. It is usually called PERT analysis.

The method consists of assigning an optimistic, most likely, and pessimistic estimate to each task. For instance, a task might have a most probable duration of 4 days, with a best-case execution in 3 days. However, it may also be prone to delays, bringing the pessimistic estimate to 10 days. We enter this as 3, 4, 10. The most likely estimate is given a weight of 4 times the others and the sum of the estimates is divided by 6 to obtain a weighted estimate. With Scitor's PS8, we can also set weights to other than the default values. If we want to factor in a bit of extra contingency, we could weight the pessimistic values a bit heavier than the optimistic ones. Calculation of the schedule, based on these weighted estimates, is automatic.

We gain at least 3 advantages from this method. First, by defining 3 estimates, we have a better feel of the true time estimate and the range of risk and contingency for each task. For instance, a task with a 3, 4, 10 estimate would be more risk prone than a task with a 5, 5, 5 estimate.

Second, we can calculate the schedule using various weights. This will let us see projected project completion dates for various degrees of optimism or contingency. It doesn't change how long the project takes. But it does provide insight into the possible outcomes. This is information that management needs to make intelligent decisions.

Third, using special PERT analysis software, we can generate a statistical evaluation of the probability of meeting any of the possible project completion dates. In one of the tests that I conducted on a model project, the project end date that I thought had a 50 percent probability (using just most likely estimates) turned out to have only a 5 percent probability when running the PERT analysis.

The Value of Critical Path Scheduling

CPM has been around for more than 40 years, and has been employed with varying degrees of success. Although subject to criticism at times, for being too difficult to use or understand, it is almost universally employed by serious project managers on serious projects. For most situations, it does the job. It is the basis for the techniques that we have just described: the use of hammocks, project portfolio analysis, and PERT analysis. It is also the basis for other scheduling techniques.

If we operate in a project environment where shortening project duration has a big payoff, these techniques will provide assistance in achieving shorter times and evaluating scheduling options.

CHAPTER 3.5

PRACTICAL SCHEDULING

It is our intention, throughout this book, to provide guidance for the practical application of project management practices and techniques. Within most sections, there is a chapter that aims at fulfilling this objective. In Section 2, we provide guidance for identifying Objectives, Constraints, and Milestones, for developing Outlines and Work Breakdown Structures, and for building a Project Milestone Schedule.

In this chapter, we review the practical application of project scheduling. Later, we look at practical resource scheduling techniques, cost management, scope management, risk management, and communication.

When Will the Work Be Done?

When we talk about scheduling, we are concerned with the timing of the work. We determine when the work will be done. Schedules can be driven by several factors. These may include a combination of any of these:

- *Milestone-driven* The work is scheduled to meet milestones and deadlines that are dictated by the contract or project conditions. These milestones and deadlines are usually captured in the Project Milestone Schedule, which is used to guide the detailed scheduling.

- *Precedence-driven*   The work is scheduled by the computer, based on task durations, constraints, and relationships that have been defined. A pure precedence-driven schedule may not fully support the defined milestones, and assumes that all resources will be available as needed. While this certainly is not realistic, it's a good place to start. Even a schedule that considers the milestones and the resources must also consider precedence relationships if it is to have any validity.

- *Resource-driven*   The work is scheduled when the resources are available to do the work. To do this, we need to start with a preliminary (not resource-constrained) schedule, preferably one that is precedence-driven. Then we define the resources that are to be assigned to the work, and let the computer compute the required resource loads. By also defining the available resources, the computer can compare resource requirements to resource availability. Then by invoking the resource leveling function, the computer can reschedule the work to stay within defined limits. We get into this in detail in Section 4.

A practical final schedule will be one that considers all the above. In doing so, there will be contention for scarce resources, conflicts with established milestones, haggling over priorities, political and territorial squabbles, and consideration of risk. Task durations will be challenged, defined task precedence will be redefined, and even the defined workscope may be modified. Resource availability will also be extremely dynamic, changing almost as fast as it is defined.

Obviously, the computer becomes an essential tool to deal with project scheduling. In this chapter, we provide some tips on how to use these tools to address all of these scheduling dynamics to effectively build a practical project schedule.

Schedule Analysis Using Total and Free Float

The use of float, for schedule decision making, goes back to the original PERT and CPM programs of the late 1950s. It is still a valuable technique, if used properly, and not blindly. *Float* (also called *slack* in Microsoft Project) is calculated by the critical path scheduling function that is the core of virtually all project management software products. Float represents the difference between the earliest time that a task can be performed and the latest allowable time. There are two types of float: *total float* and *free float*. Each type can be used differently.

Total float is the duration that a task can slip without extending the end date of the project. The more total float, the more time contingency there is in the project. We can use this information for two key purposes. The first is to determine which of the tasks are more critical. That is, which task has less time contingency (float or slack) and must be watched more closely. When key dates and milestones are in danger of being missed, total float helps us to determine which tasks need to be expedited.

A further use of total float is to analyze schedule risk and trends. The more tasks there are with low float, the higher the risk of missing target dates. We can compare total float values from the previous schedule update to gauge how much a project is slipping. Even though the most limiting tasks might be running on time, the reduction of float on lesser tasks could be an indication of impending trouble.

It is important to remember that total float should not be used as an invitation to arbitrarily allow work to slide. It should be treated as contingency, to be doled out when appropriate, under management control. We need to also remember that total float is calculated across a chain of tasks. If someone uses the total float for a task that is early in a sequence (by letting the task slip), it reduces the total float for all subsequent tasks that lie within that chain.

Free float addresses this chaining issue. Free float is the measure of how much a task can slip without affecting the earliest start of any other task. Let's look at some roofing work, as an example. Placing the roof shingles has two predecessors: Get Shingles, and Place Underlayment. If the scheduled finish of the underlayment is June 22, and the earliest delivery of the shingles is June 8, we can say that there are 2 weeks of free float on the procurement task. Slipping the delivery of the shingles, by up to 2 weeks, will not delay any other tasks (and might even be preferred for cost or space purposes).

Regarding these two types of float, we can keep in mind that free float can usually be used freely by the responsible task manager, but total float should be managed at a higher level, so as not to affect the work of others.

Working with Dependency and Due Dates

We introduced you to *Date Constraints* in Chapter 3.1. We noted that we could impose dates on tasks and alter the schedule calculations. And we discussed the most popular of these imposed date functions: the Start No Earlier Than (SNET) and Finish No Later Than (FNLT).

Remember to use the SNET dates to delay the start of a task beyond its earliest possible start, as determined by simple task precedence. For example, you're upgrading the guardrails on the expressway that carries traffic to a popular summer resort area. Although your materials will be on site by 8/22, and other preparations can be completed by that date, you don't want to block off the right lane until after Labor Day. So you impose a SNET date of 9/4/01 (the day after Labor

Day) on the tasks associated with the lane closure. If any of the predecessor tasks slip out beyond the 9/4 date, the precedence will override the SNET date.

Use these SNET dates freely, where they are needed to express planned start delays. But avoid using them as an excuse to evade the need to define legitimate task precedence. Also, note that the SNET constraint only affects the forward pass—that which calculates the early dates.

The Finish No Later Than (FNLT) constraint works in just the opposite manner from the SNET constraint. The FNLT date, when imposed, affects the calculation of the late dates. Taking the same highway construction project as above, we provide another example. This time, the work is scheduled in June, and much of the project work will have to continue into the summer. Again, there is pressure to minimize the impact on resort-bound traffic, which picks up around the Memorial Day holiday. So we go to the task that represents the completion of the work that requires the lane closure, and impose a FNLT date of May 24.

By imposing a FNLT date of 5/24 on these tasks, we then drive all other late dates to support that imposed constraint. The FNTL date does not have any effect on the early dates, which are computed during the forward pass. Also, if the defined precedence is more constraining than the imposed dates, the FNLT date will be overridden.

Tip   You can use the FNLT function to incorporate milestones from the Project Milestone Schedule into the detailed CPM. In fact, one can actually start with the PMS, setting the milestones as FNLT dates and then building up the details using the PMS as a schedule framework.

Just-in-time Scheduling

The default CPM scheduling mode is ASAP (as soon as possible). In the example above (SNET) we demonstrated one of the ways to override the ASAP calculations, on an exception basis. But, what if there are parts of your project that you would prefer to occur closer to the required time (closer to the latest dates)?

In most programs, you have the option of selecting the ALAP (as late as possible) mode. In the ALAP mode, the backward pass becomes the schedule driver, and the task dates are set so as to have zero float. This can be done on a project-wide basis or on a task-by-task basis.

But, even with the just-in-time (JIT) mode, I would advise against developing a schedule that reduces everything to zero float. We can allow for some margin or safety by using the *lag* function of the software, or by inserting dummy tasks. For example, we have several items that are needed to support the guardrail work on our expressway project. These may include the new guardrails, fasteners, hole diggers, traffic diversion cones, and lane closure signs. We don't want to purchase or accumulate these items too early, so we designate them as ALAP tasks. But we would like to have them scheduled five days ahead of the planned start of the guardrail work. We can do this in two ways.

One way is to input a finish-to-start lag of 5 days (FS5) between each of these tasks and the start of the guardrail milestone. The alternate is to insert a dummy task, called Accumulate Items for Guardrail Work, and assign a five-day duration.

Trap   Building a schedule with too much float is as bad as not having enough float. It will appear to be unrealistic, and will tend to be ignored. The use of the JIT options allows the development of a more practical and believable schedule.

Building In Schedule Contingency

We discuss schedule contingency at length in Chapter 3.2, including the introduction of an entirely different way of dealing with schedule contingency, using the critical chain method. We attempted to make a case for building contingency into the schedule, and for using shared contingency concepts, where practical.

For the moment, let's assume that you are working with traditional CPM tools. How can we deal with contingency? One option is to use the PERT analysis function, if it is available in the tool that you are using. You'll find a discussion of PERT in Chapter 3.3. Briefly, using the three-duration capability of the PERT mode, and changing the weighting in favor of the pessimistic value (as can be done with Scitor's PS8), will allow you to place some contingency into the schedule.

Another way of inserting contingency into the schedule is to account for the situations that most often result in schedule delays. These situations include:

- Points where a large quantity of predecessors feed into a task. Time is often lost in communication and confirming that the feeder tasks have been completed and that the next task can begin.
- Points where there is a change in the location of the next task or in the parties responsible for the next task. As in relay racing, there is often a problem getting a clean handoff of the baton.
- Points where there is a known or anticipated shortage of resources.

- Your project has a low priority, or weak support from the sponsors.
- Key decision points. These would include design reviews, funding reviews, permitting reviews, or anything that can bring the project to a temporary halt while waiting for authorization to proceed.

Experience has shown that there is a high potential for delays in these situations. Yet we would not want to allow for such delays by adding time to the associated task durations. We lose identification of why the task duration was increased and by how much. Instead, it looks like we are allowing the extra time to do the work, and (due to Parkinson's Law) we end up taking the allotted time, rather than leaving it for the purpose for which we added the contingency in the first place.

The better idea is to add a dummy task at each of these potential delay points. The task should describe the purpose of the delay allowance and be set at a duration that recognizes the potential situation, without adding a ridiculous amount of slop to the schedule. An alternate method is to add a finish-to-start lag.

Then there is the issue of shared contingency buffers. I really like the idea of shared contingency, whether using CCPM or traditional tools. There is nothing to stop you from taking a string of tasks, squeezing the contingency out of the individual task estimates, and creating a dummy task at the end of the string to hold the sum of the contingencies. Using Goldratt's approach, I would reduce the sum of the individual contingencies by 50 percent.

For example, our expressway project has the following series of tasks associated with erection of the guardrail: Lay out and mark the location, Make holes for the support posts, Place the posts, Attach and fasten the guardrails, Paint them, Complete the landscaping. Each of these tasks has a most likely duration of 4 days, but the schedule shows them as 6-day tasks (with 50% contingency allowed for each task). As an option, consider reducing the duration on each task to 4 days, and placing a dummy contingency task at the end, with a duration of 6 days. The overall duration of the string of tasks is reduced from 36 days to 30 days (24 days for the 6 tasks plus 6 days for contingency). Psychologically, we needed the 2-day adder to feel comfortable with any single task, but the 6 days for the series of tasks is within a reasonable comfort range.

With the task durations set at 4 days, we keep the pressure on to perform to the most likely duration. The buffer task (contingency) causes the task to be scheduled early enough to allow for reasonable slippage (even if using the ALAP mode). If any of the tasks do slip, the amount of the slippage is removed from the buffer. This retains the overall timing for the chain (until all contingency is exhausted). By reviewing and managing the buffers, we can keep an eye on the contingency situation. Admittedly, these concepts of buffer management come from

Goldratt's critical chain dissertations. However, practical application of some of these concepts is possible using traditional CPM tools.

Tip When adding dummy tasks for contingency, be sure to mark each of these with a code that can be used to identify such tasks and to select such tasks for contingency monitoring reports. By recording the baseline duration of these tasks (part of the normal *set baseline* function), you can produce a variance report, noting all reductions of durations for contingency tasks. You can even create an exception report, selecting only contingency tasks that have reduced durations.

Regarding schedule contingency, there are three things that you can be certain of.

1. If there is no schedule contingency, the project end date will be missed.
2. If schedule contingency is not managed, the schedule will slip and the project will be completed even later than if there were no contingency.
3. Murphy is working on your project.

A fuller discussion of the entire subject of project risks and contingencies is presented in Section 6.

The Magic of Hammocks

We introduced the hammock function in Chapter 3.4. This capability, which, incidentally, is not found in many CPM packages, has several handy uses. A *hammock* is a type of task that does not have a fixed time duration. Instead, it automatically calculates its duration from the tasks that it is associated with (or group of tasks that the hammock spans). To illustrate, let's go back to that expressway project. There are a number of tasks that are associated with the erection of the new guardrails. We lay out and mark the location. We make holes for the support posts. We place the posts. We attach and fasten the guardrails. We may paint them. Finally, we complete the landscaping. All during this period, we have to close the right lane and operate a flashing sign warning of the lane closure.

How long do we need the sign and traffic cones? This is a piece of data that is required to be entered when we add these activities. The answer is the duration is equal to the length of time that it will take to perform the series of tasks that we outline above. With hammocks, we don't have to calculate this duration. We create a task Set Traffic Diversion Signs and Cones. We establish a start-to-start relationship with the first guardrail task, and a finish-to-finish relationship with the last guardrail task. The computer sets the task duration as equal to the duration of the series of tasks that it spans.

If the work is scheduled to start on 6/1, and run until 6/22, then a duration of three weeks is applied to the hammock task. If the duration of any of the tasks within the chain changes, during either planning or execution, the hammock task will automatically reflect these changes.

If there are daily costs associated with the hammock task, these are also automatically calculated. So, if the signs and cones are costed at $2,000 per week, the budget is set at $6,000. If the chain of tasks is stretched to four weeks, the budget will change to $8,000. The same approach applies to resources that are assigned to hammocks.

Hammocks can be stretched between any two points in the project network. It doesn't have to be a contiguous series of tasks, or be under the purview of a single responsible party. Hammocks can also be used as auxiliary summary tasks, to show the span of time between the two anchor points.

Practical Uses of the Baseline

Most CPM products have a Set Baseline function. A *baseline* is a snapshot of the project schedule at a specific point in time. The early and late dates are saved, as baseline or *target dates*, for later comparison to *current dates*, after the schedule is updated. There should always be an Original Baseline. This is a set of project target dates at the time that the official project schedule is accepted. As the schedule is updated, a variance report can be produced to display the changes from the original plan. The report can be set up to select only variances that exceed a certain threshold, and sorting can be set to order the tasks by amount of variance (largest first).

If your product supports multiple baselines, you will want to consider these additional baseline options. Create a new baseline (while retaining the original) every time that there is an approved major change to the plan. I also like to create a *rolling baseline*. This is a snapshot of each update as it is closed out. When the next schedule update is performed, I compare the new dates and float to the last set (the rolling baseline) to note variances during this last update. Once the update is completed and reviewed, I replace the previous rolling baseline with a snapshot of the current update, ready to use for the next round.

Practical Options to Shorten Schedules

So you've done all the things that we've suggested here. You have developed a list of all the tasks. You have estimated task durations, defined task relationships, imposed date constraints where appropriate, and allowed for contingency. You have a reasonable schedule. Except for one little problem. The resultant project end date is not acceptable.

Is there anything that you can do to shorten the schedule? Our objective is to retain a reasonable schedule. It should still represent something that can reasonably be accomplished, rather than something that we wish would happen. It doesn't take long for the team to see through a window dressing schedule. Here are a few options that you can consider.

Shorter Durations   Are the task estimates really based on the most likely times, or do they have a bit of slop built in? Some contingency is important, but check to see if it hasn't been overdone. Do you want 90 percent confidence? 80 percent? 50 percent? Keep it reasonable and consistent. Check the critical path first, that is, the task chains having the least amount of float. It won't do you any good to reduce the times on the noncritical paths.

Overlapping   Again, look at the critical paths first to see if some of the series tasks can be overlapped. Does task B really have to wait until task A is complete? Or can it start when task A is about 50 percent complete? Selective overlapping of critical tasks is a good way to shorten the schedule. But remember, it has to reflect real conditions, and should not be forced just to make the schedule fit.

Reduce Scope   Schedule too long (or over budget)? Perhaps an option is to reduce scope. It's done all the time, but usually after some of the work has been promised and executed. Why not address this issue early? If the entire workscope cannot be fit into the time available, negotiate reducing some scope or transferring it to a later phase.

Alter Strategies   The schedule will be based on the identified work and the strategies that have been selected to accomplish that work. If the schedule is not acceptable, it may be appropriate to review the strategic alternatives. There may be other ways to accomplish the goal that result in shorter schedules. For instance, re-using older code rather than starting from scratch. Or buying an off-the-shelf component rather than getting a custom part. The initial strategies may have been selected without consideration of the impact on schedule. Now that there is a known problem, you will want to reevaluate the decisions. Again, concentrate on the critical paths first.

Rant and Rave   Well, this won't help the schedule. But sometimes you just have to blow off some steam.

The Useful Schedule

In my travels, I have seen more bad schedules than I would like to admit. I have seen schedules, produced by computers, which bore no resemblance to reality. Sometimes this occurred because the developers of the schedules didn't understand what the computer did with the information that they supplied. In other instances, the schedule was so badly manipulated as to make it impossible to support and most difficult to update. In either case, the result of the scheduling effort is completely useless and makes people resort to alternate means and documents to work with a more usable schedule. In the first case, training (see Chapters 1.4 and 13.1) will help. In the latter case, the scheduler must avoid the temptation to take shortcuts, by forcing dates, rather than defining realistic task duration and precedence. Only after doing so can the override functions, such as date constraints, ALAP modes, and dummy tasks, be used to modify and improve on the schedule. A schedule, thus developed, is the only one that will contribute to project success.

SECTION 4

RESOURCE AND WORKFORCE MANAGEMENT

Resource scheduling is a strange fish. We all know that efficient workforce planning and the scheduling of resources is critical to project success. Millions of dollars are spent on tools to aid in this function, and untold hours are devoted to developing pragmatic resource plans.

The embarrassing truth is that much of this effort is wasted. First of all, when I survey project managers about their use of resource scheduling systems, I get almost a zero reply. That is, hardly anyone is using these capabilities, even when they have them. When I ask why, one answer is that it takes too much effort to learn the system and to describe the assignment details to the computer. But even more frequent is the complaint that these systems don't deliver a usable solution. Personally, I have conducted considerable testing of resource scheduling systems over the past 40 years, and my findings are in agreement with theirs. However, I do think that there is enough to be gained from using resource scheduling systems even if they fall short of perfection.

So we proceed to describe the basic elements of such resource scheduling systems and to discuss the issues involved with getting some benefit from their use. In Chapter 4.1, we present An Overview of the Different Elements of Resource Management. Here we describe the various components of a resource scheduling system and how they work. We cover both traditional and some experimental approaches and comment on their effectiveness.

Resource management (RM) means different things to different people in the organization. So, in Chapter 4.2, we take a role-based look at managing resources in a project-driven organization. We look at resource management from the needs of managers, participants, and other stakeholders.

During the first four decades of what we have come to call Modern Project

Management (MPM), the traditional view of resource management was that it was *schedule-driven*. That is, we defined the work first, then we scheduled the work, and then we adjusted the schedule to consider resource limitations. This was fine for typical project-driven conditions, where resources existed primarily to execute projects. More recently, a new model has emerged, where greater emphasis is placed on the management of resources (than on the management of project schedules). This is not to say that the latter is given short shrift. But rather the primary focus is on workforce management.

There is a subtle, but very significant difference between project resource management and workforce management. This difference stems from the type of organization that is involved and its primary focus. When we talk about project resource management, we are usually focusing on an organization whose business strategy is built upon executing projects. The profit focus (if a for-profit organization) is on completing successful projects, on time, and within budget, thereby preserving the planned margin. When we talk about workforce management, we are usually focusing on a service operation. The firm consists of skilled individuals, who will be applied to work, at billing rates that provide for margin over their actual costs. These service organizations will focus on maximizing the applied time of these skilled individuals, as well as seeking the most productive opportunities for each person—that which will generate the maximum margin.

In each case, we are dealing with the assignment of resources to work. But in the first case, project resource management, we tend to focus on the work, and meeting project objectives. In the other case, workforce management, we tend to focus more on the resources, improving productivity. Nevertheless, the approach that we take to schedule and monitor resources on tasks is not all that different, and we can address the practices and issues in a common section of this book.

As noted above, the algorithms that are built into most of the traditional CPM programs usually fail to deliver the optimal resource loading solution. Recently, this has been improving somewhat. In Chapter 4.3, Resource Leveling and Games of Chance, we present the results of some testing that was conducted a few years ago, and comment on these results. In this chapter, we find fault with how many of these products deal with resource scheduling. But, we also advise ways to make the processes useful.

Ever mindful of our objective to provide guidance for the practical application of project management, our final chapter in this section offers advice for resource scheduling and management. Recognizing some of the limitations in the full value of traditional resource scheduling, we still feel that it is a worthwhile and important part of project planning and project management. In Chapter 4.4, we extract all the usable aspects of these tools, to provide some guidance for practical resource scheduling.

CHAPTER 4.1

AN OVERVIEW OF THE DIFFERENT ELEMENTS OF RESOURCE MANAGEMENT

If you were to ask 10 people to define resource management, you would likely get at least a dozen different responses. Resource management (RM) would be viewed differently when it operates as part of a project management system than as part of a resource management system, an enterprise-wide management system, a human resources system, or a project accounting system. It would, likewise, be viewed differently according to role in the organization, and certainly according to differing sets of needs. Nevertheless, any of these concepts for resource management would likely consist of variations of the basic RM components that have appeared in traditional commercial Critical Path Method (CPM) products.

In the traditional system, it is assumed that the resource scheduling is performed on top of a critical path schedule of the tasks. In other words, the work is identified and scheduled as if there were unlimited resources (see Chapter 3.1). Then, by defining the available resource pool, and by assigning resources to the tasks, the computer can determine a resource loading plan, and can manipulate this plan to meet defined resource and/or time limits.

What follows is a description of the different elements of resource management software systems.

Resource Database

This consists of knowing what your resources are. The data elements associated with this list of resources will vary, and may include:

119

- Resource name—Can be individual resource or class of resource.
- Hierarchical structure (parent/subordinate)—A resource breakdown structure (RBS).
- Information about the resource (some of this can come from or be linked to an HR database).
- Resource's skills.
- Productivity by skill (rare—with good reason—see below).
- Charging and billing rates.
- Availability schedule.

Assignment Database

This consists of knowing what the resources are working on. Again there can be several levels of detail, such as:

- What projects are they assigned to?
- What work within the projects (tasks) are they assigned to?
- What level of effort is planned?
- When is that effort planned?

Time Capture

This consists of capturing the actual time spent on project (and nonproject) work.

- In its simplest form, time charged to projects.
- In more detail, time charged to work items.
- Allocating charges to cost accounts (chargeback).

Performance Measurement

This consists of comparing actual charges to planned charges. To be effective, there must also be a measurement of the actual work accomplished. We often call this Earned Value analysis.

Resource Assignment and Scheduling Protocols

We expect our computer software to provide certain assistance in allocating and scheduling resources. However, to date, most of these systems have been less than satisfactory and are rarely used in practice. Here are some of the options:

- *Assignment Assistance:* We don't see too much of this, although it could be most useful. This requires the use of a skills database. The idea is to define the resource need by skill and to have the system suggest resources on the basis of skill and availability.
- *Top-down Assignment Planning:* This is also a skills-based system. The idea is to associate skills with the work when the work is first defined (may be a planning template rather than an actual, approved project). Work may also be defined at a high level (not detailed). When it is time to actually schedule the work, the skills are replaced by actual named resources. This capability is important to a project portfolio management system, so that prospective and actual project demands can be analyzed. For such a system to work, resource demands must be able to be summarized by skill.
- *Resource Leveling:* Around for decades, this capability is deemed to be essential during the software selection process, and then is totally ignored. Reasons include reluctance to put the effort into defining assignments, and unusable results due to weak resource leveling algorithms.
- A few alternate *resource smoothing algorithms* have been introduced. But these, too, have failed to be accepted thus far. Several of these include some type of "best-fit" approach (see Chapter 4.3).

Resource Analysis

Some of this topic has already been covered. It consists of being able to query the various resource data to analyze resource loadings and demand, resource performance, and so on. It requires access to the data from varied (including remote) locations, with security to control who accesses the data and what data is accessed. It requires that voluminous data be sliced and diced, suggesting that an on-line analytical processing (OLAP) type of capability would be useful. Resource and skills coding is needed to provide a hierarchical roll-up and drill-down capability.

The Requestor/Allocator Approach

Occasionally, a vendor takes a different approach toward assigning resources to work. For instance, ResourceView, developed by Artemis as part of their ArtemisViews suite, has two components. In the Requestor module, anyone can identify work to be done (projects or separate tasks), and add them to a list that goes to owners of the resources. In the allocation module, the resource managers assign resources to the tasks. Resources may also be requested by adding a project from either ProjectView or Microsoft Project. Microsoft took a similar approach in Team Manager. ABT developed a similar Resource Manager component. Although the concept appears to be sound, on the surface, something is not working. Both the Artemis and Microsoft tools have failed to gain acceptance, and ABT has been acquired by Niku, I guess primarily to put a scheduling engine into the Niku PSA (Professional Services Automation) package. The Artemis product has been taken off the market. And the Microsoft and ABT capabilities are not being promoted.

I guess that a contributing factor in this failure is the lack of centralized control. Resource management requires some kind of structuring, mentoring, direction, and coordination—such as we get from a central project office. These requestor/allocator concepts suggest that the system can operate successfully outside a CPO. This failure also suggests that marketing research can sometimes deliver false results.

CHAPTER 4.2

ROLE-BASED NEEDS FOR MANAGING RESOURCES IN A PROJECT-DRIVEN ORGANIZATION

Let's shift gears a bit. In the previous chapter, we look at the mechanics of a resource scheduling system. It was deliberately a narrow look. Our key concern was the tying of resource assignments to defined tasks and creating resource-loaded schedules. But there is so much more to the subject on managing resources on projects. So we need to look at the topic through the eyes of the various resource groups and examine their needs.

In this chapter we explore the objectives, goals, and needs of various disciplines within the enterprise, associated with the management of project portfolios and the resources utilized to support these projects. We then go on to discuss issues and solutions that are associated with these needs.

Each discussion is aimed at a specific segment of the enterprise, such as Operations, Strategic Planning, Projects, and Functional Management. We cover a wide range of stakeholders, both at varying levels of management and contribution, and external as well as internal stakeholders.

A common thread is the strong need for fresh, quality information, accessible by a large community, in forms that support free and clear communication and promote good decisions and selection of alternatives.

Introduction

Today's typical organization is considerably more complex than in the 1960s (when organizational structure and boundaries were fairly well-defined) or in the

1980s (when matrix concepts allowed for greater flexibility in the deployment of human resources across the enterprise, while maintaining defined lines of communication and responsibility). Today, we add to that complexity by using people in various team configurations, for temporary assignments, for differing time periods. We also attempt to deploy people more effectively by recognizing multiple skills and allocating these people to the work on the basis of skills rather than departmental structure. Add to that the use of external supplements to the workforce and we begin to create an environment where loss of control is all too frequent and communication is a screaming, garbled mess.

Now, complicate that with poorly defined objectives, at both the mission and project level, plus a weaker definition of just who the customer or sponsor is and what they want, and we come close to total chaos. Oh! And one other, most important thing. In most of today's businesses, the selection and execution of projects is not just a matter of bringing them in on time and on budget so that they are profitable. Rather the success of projects is essential to survival of the business and/or positioning the business for the next big technological and economic breakthrough.

And so it is that the management of such businesses involves an extensive universe of people, who contribute to, benefit from, or are otherwise affected and impacted by the project-oriented activities of the enterprise. These personnel span a wide spectrum of positions in the organization and may very well extend to positions outside the organization. They will involve multiple disciplines, each with a different set of needs and objectives, and each with a different definition of project success. The group is likely to cross numerous traditional boundaries: physical, such as location; cultural, such as language; economic, such as cost or profit motive; and technical, such as methods and hardware.

Each member of this vast, involved information universe has a specific, different role in supporting the system, as well as a different, specific set of needs from the system. Only in clearly identifying these roles and needs can we expect to be able to implement a set of practices, with supporting tools, to further the objectives of the enterprise in this regard.

This set of practices and tools must facilitate the creation of the needed information, with quality and timeliness, and make it easily available to all involved parties, on a need-to-know basis. They must facilitate open communication, based on current, shared knowledge that will allow the parties to react to changing situations and allow management, on various levels and disciplines, to make effective decisions, while recognizing the impact on all stakeholders and goals. That's a tall order. But the technology is available to support that need, and the failure to put such practices and tools in place will allow the chaos and lack of communication to impact unfavorably on the future of the business.

Acknowledging this, let's proceed to explore the objectives, goals, and needs of various disciplines within the enterprise, with attention to the issues associated with the management of project portfolios and the resources utilized to support these projects.

Stakeholders

If we're going to talk about roles, then we have to talk about stakeholders. First, why are stakeholders so important? It is because the community that is interested in your project, or contributes to your project, or can make or break your project, is larger than you think. Who are these stakeholders? They are people who will have an impact on project success. They are project champions, sponsors, and owners. They are the miscellaneous senior managers, whose measurements (and stock bonuses) are dependent on project success. They are the project participants, including suppliers and clients. They are ancillary groups such as end users, regulatory agencies, and the public. And, of course, they include all the people directly involved in defining, planning, and executing the project.

If we were to look at the traditional view of project success, we might say that it was to accomplish all schedule, budget, and technical objectives, as planned. An alternate view of project success, however, is accomplishing the goals of *everyone* who has a stake in the project.

From a strategic point of view, we have to consider who they are; what they want; how they can impact success; and how they can be satisfied. That is because whether your project has been successful will depend, at least in part, on the perceptions of the stakeholders of what was actually accomplished.

Each stakeholder has a specific role in one or more aspects of the enterprise. These might include: the individual project, the portfolio of projects, the human resources supporting the projects, the capital assets involved in the portfolio, the technical results, the long-term growth or survival of the enterprise, for a few examples. Because these roles differ (as well as the definition of success), the way that these stakeholders interact with the project management system will likewise differ. What stakeholders put into the system and what they need and expect out of the system is unique to their role. For the project management system to work requires that each role be addressed and supported.

Classifications of Role-based Groups

For the purpose of this chapter on Role-based Needs for Managing Resources in a Project-driven Organization, we'll create a group of role sets, based on the general nature of needs and participation in the project management system. There is no standard classification, so we will set a few up.

The Management Groups   Within the general classification of Management, we have several subgroups. We have general senior management, including any senior managers charged with the overall execution of the business. I would include in this group, executives charged with the responsibility for strategic planning, Senior VPs of major corporate divisions, and other Operations-oriented functions. There are the managers of operating functions. There are the managers of the project function and the project managers. Finally, there are the managers of staff functions.

The Participant Groups   Another classification is comprised of the groups that directly participate in the projects. These are people who would likely be charging time to the projects (if time keeping is in effect). These are people directly involved in planning the work and in providing status.

Other Stakeholders   As noted earlier, the universe of people who care about or impact projects is quite large. Often, their role is as important to success as those listed above. One such group is the Owner of the project. This might be an external client, or an internal sponsor. It is the person who represents the organization that is directly or indirectly paying for the work and has (most likely) the greatest stake in its successful completion. Other internal operations that might have more than a passing interest in the ongoing projects would include the Human Resources function, Accounting, and Information Systems. And many organizations depend on external functions as well.

The Roles

It should be easy to see, as we look at all the possible classifications, above, that each group would have a decidedly different need and involvement with the projects information system. We continue, now, by exploring each of these roles and discussing needs, issues, and suggested solutions regarding use of and support of the projects process.

Processes, Not Job Titles, Define Roles

In their 1993 book *Reengineering the Corporation* (HarperBusiness) Hammer and Champy offer the revolutionary concept that we treat the enterprise as *process* rather than *function*. In her 1983 book *The Change Masters* (Simon &

Schuster) Rosabeth Moss Kanter identifies *segmentalism* as a key obstacle to change and innovation.

What do these well-documented observations, of the way things are changing in how we operate businesses, affect how we manage projects? What it tells us, first of all, is that it is not necessarily the position or job title that determines one's role in projects. It is the role in the *process* that is key. Second, projects are more than an independent function. Their effect straddles all segments of the enterprise, and involves a wide range of so-called functions and roles. Furthermore, as traditional segmentalism is pushed aside, improved communication between the segments becomes essential.

All of this points to the necessity to identify all the roles associated with the projects environment, and to define how these roles impact upon the design and use of the projects processes and information system.

The Management Groups

First, within the general classification of Management, we have perhaps four definable subgroups. We have *general senior management*. This would include The CEO and COO, or Chairman or President, and any other senior managers charged with the overall execution of the business. I would include in this group executives charged with the responsibility for strategic planning, Senior VPs of major corporate divisions, and other Operations-oriented functions. Then there is the *direct functional management*. This would include managers of operating functions, such as Engineering, Marketing, Manufacturing, Software Development, and Information Technology.

The third management classification would be *project management*. In a formal projects environment, this would be the Chief Project Officer, or Manager of the Central Project Office. In addition, it would include any managers of individual projects. The final group is managers of *staff functions*, such as the Chief Financial Officer, Chief Information Officer, and Chief Risk Officer.

Remember; we are not so much concerned with identifying job titles as we are interested in identifying roles involved in managing the enterprise. We have established these groups solely for the purpose of providing a basis to discuss the needs of management-level people in respect to the project and resource management process.

Common Needs

What do these groups have in common? First of all, they would be interested mostly in the large picture. While each group might need to have a different perspective of the project portfolio, these views would entail a high-level survey of the data, generally across programs, projects, functions, cost accounts, locations, and so on. Another common condition is that these groups are, for the most part, viewers of the information, rather than suppliers of data.

There is no need for these people to interface directly with the planning and scheduling tool. In fact, if the only way that they could get at the information was to work directly with critical path scheduling software, they are likely to be deterred from such activity. This is because the complex nature of these formats tends to be intimidating to the casual user. What these users need, rather, is access to the projects information, in formats that are not intimidating and do not require the learning of new computer protocols.

The natural solution, considering today's technology, involves designing the management-level subsystem around a webpage format. When properly designed, these formats have the opposite effect—drawing the managers to the information, rather than frightening them away. The solution, however, is more involved than just printing data output in a webpage format. This requires the publisher to predetermine, for each user, exactly what they want to see. This will not support the needs of these users. Their needs are dynamic, and so access to the information must support this need. The web browser must be a doorway into the vast system of project data, rather than a fixed snapshot. While each of the users should be able to have a doorway that is designed for their specific perspective, once they have passed through the doorway they should be able to choose among several rooms of information, and should be able to drill-down, filter, and rearrange the data to respond to their specific need-to-know.

Specific Needs

The formats described above will provide a simple, yet effective means of getting at the essential data of the project portfolio. However, it does not assure us that the desired information will be available, and in a way so as to provide the stories required to support the day-to-day decisions of these executives. There is a world of difference between *data* and *information*. If the data cannot be arranged in ways to provide insight into the projects situations, then it is essentially useless. For instance, the CFO needs to view the data arranged by various budget categories and cost accounts. The strategic planning executive needs to have the data segmented by program initiatives. This cross section would also be of interest to several other senior managers.

The functional managers are most interested in viewing data by skill and resource classification. We could go on and on describing how the data could be sliced and diced to meet the needs of the various executives. The list is only limited by one's imagination. The key to having support for all of this is whether the projects database has been designed for the entering of all the needed data classifications and whether the webpage-based output systems have been designed to take full advantage of such data coding.

Here, then, is a partial listing of the types of information that management-level personnel might be looking for from the project management information system.

General Senior Management CEO, COO, Chairman, President, Strategic Planning executive, Senior VPs of major corporate divisions, other Operations-oriented functions.

- Project information arranged by program initiatives.
- Project information arranged by organization, location, sponsor, client.
- Analysis of project performance, based on variance from time and cost targets.
- Summary, action, and alarm reports.
- Analysis of overall performance against key enterprise objectives.

Direct Functional Management Managers of operating functions, such as Engineering, Marketing, Manufacturing, Software Development, and Information Technology.

- Deployment of resources by skill, department, craft, location.
- Analysis of overloads and underutilization.
- Analysis of outsourced resources.
- Analysis of performance by various resource classifications.
- Commitment of resources, by project and program.
- Overview of time charged vs. plan/budget/commitment.

Project Management Chief Project Officer, Project Manager.

- Analysis of project performance, based on variance from time and cost targets.
- Analysis of achievements vs. objectives.
- Deployment of project planning and control resources.
- Analysis of overloads and underutilization.
- Audit of project management implementation (actual vs. goal).

Staff Functions   Chief Financial Officer, Chief Information Officer, Chief Risk Officer.

- Analysis of cost vs. budgets, arranged by all budget/cost account designations of the enterprise.
- Advance notice of impending major cost commitments and proceed/stop decision points.
- Advance notice of decision points associated with risk mitigation plans.
- A repository for or link to project risk planning and mitigation documentation.
- Analysis of key impact on IT/IS resources and technology.

Implications for Tool Selection

There is no reason why all the above needs cannot be satisfied by a single, highly usable software system. There is also no reason why such a system cannot be applied in such a way as to provide customized, nonintimidating access to these data.

A key aspect to keep in mind, however, is that the project information system cannot be an isolated, desktop solution. Furthermore, you cannot expect the people involved in the above roles to work directly with traditional critical path scheduling formats. Rather, a less arcane model, such as today's popular webpage metaphors, would support both the format and access needs of these groups.

Making It Work

Finding adequate software products to support these defined management roles is not difficult, nor is it the only key to success. While it is important to select tools that will support the defined needs, it is equally important to use these tools to build a bridge between the various management groups (many of which act more to defend territories than to seek the synergy of collective management). With differing needs, goals, and measurements, we often find operations management, financial management, functional management, and project management working at cross purposes, each supported by a separate information system, none of which communicate with each other.

By considering the roles of each group, and designing/selecting a projects information system that respects and supports these roles, we can bridge this deleterious gap. Such a solution will facilitate broad and effective communication using up-to-date data that is consistent between groups and can be trusted and shared by all.

The Changing Environment

The world of project management has been changing. While this should come as no surprise, what is startling is the rate of change and the dramatic effect that it is having on all aspects of this special discipline. It is affecting how we organize for projects, and how we communicate project information. It is especially affecting the roles that people play in projects. Because of these changes and equally because of the latest developments in computer technology, it is also affecting the design and use of the tools that support project and workforce management.

If we follow the stream of names that have been given to these project management tools, we can get an idea of the ever-changing model of the project management world. For the longest time we just called all the tools *project management software*. Whether designed to run on mainframes, mini's, or personal computers, they focused on the *project* as the center of the universe, and addressed each project individually. Resources were either dedicated to the project or on loan to the project.

During the past decade, we moved through several changes in this model, as the relative importance of projects to the typical firm's bottom line and future was realized. The first sign of growth was the ability to address multiple projects (although one of the most popular PM tools remained notably weak in this area). Next, we started to reach out beyond the project-centric view and latched on to Enterprise Project Management. A few years ago, the reach was extended to include accounting and human resources elements, as we integrated project management capabilities with Enterprise Resource Planning (ERP). We address this area in Section 10.

With the realization that projects were becoming an essential element of the firm's success, we acknowledged a need to bridge the traditional gap that existed between the projects side and the operations side of the enterprise. Soon, Project Portfolio Management became the fashion of the year.

In the past few years, yet another model was born: Professional Services Automation (PSA). The significance of this latest craze is its concentration on human resources. In each of the earlier modes of project management, there was a growth in attention to the resource side of projects. However, with PSA, and its companion title, Workforce Management, we see an increased focus on what is being called Human Capital. In many ways, the PM/PSA solution addresses the needs of service-oriented industries as the PM/ERP solutions did for the product-oriented sector. We take a look at PSA in Section 11.

While all of this was happening, the environment of the workforce, itself, was changing. One very significant element of change was the growing scarcity of workers. Another was the greater specialization of workers. Both of these often meant that a firm had to go outside the immediate organization to obtain resources with the proper skills to perform committed work. Furthermore, these temporary workers and many of the regular staff might be located off-site, or at least remotely from their managers. Communication, always a critical factor for project success, became more difficult.

Impact of the Changing Environment

Now, let's look at what may be a typical scenario for today's participants in projects. They are temporarily assigned to one or more projects. They may not work directly for the performing organization. They are located remotely from senior management, taking direction from a team leader. They are independently minded, knowing that their skills are in demand and that they have a choice of where to work.

Even in a more structured environment, there has been resistance to supporting traditional project control activities, such as statusing and time reporting. How then, in this more informal environment, do we get today's individual contributors to support traditional project and resource management activities? Certainly, as we pay greater attention to the human resources involved in projects, we must recognize that there are many diverse roles and that our tools must address the needs of each. Also, we must make the process as simple and nonlaborious as possible. And one more thing: I have found that people are much more willing to provide information to a system when that system can also provide information to them that allows them to be informed contributors.

The Participant Groups

In our introduction we chose to define three classifications of roles associated with project management. These are: the Management groups; the Participant groups; and other Stakeholders. We looked at the roles of the Management groups. Now, we look at the next classification, the Participant groups.

Here we are talking about the people who are directly involved in the projects. These are people who would likely be charging time to the projects (if time keeping is in effect). These are people directly involved in planning the work and in providing status. We can split these into subgroups, based on the degree of involvement with the project information system. The key project team members or leaders of the primary supporting functions would require greater access to the system than those primarily providing status and time-spent data.

Tool Tip   PlanView (PlanView, Inc.) is a project management tool that deliberately approaches system use on a role-based design. In its default roles, PlanView recognizes these two levels of participants, calling them Deluxe Contributor and Contributor. A simple Contributor would be expected to feed periodic time and expense data into the system, and possibly work status data. A Deluxe Contributor, or team leader would also need to be able to add or modify work items.

Both levels of contributor would need ready access to the data, via a process that we call Reports. Of course, the concept of reports has changed considerably since the early days of 11″ × 14″ green-bar computer sheets. Today, reports are likely to be screen views, giving the user almost immediate access to any of the data. However, the big gain from today's reporting technology is not speed—it's customization. When we printed voluminous reports, we tended to create one-size-fits-all outputs. Everyone, regardless of role or need, received the same pack of reports. As such, they received much more than they could use, generally in a format that required them to search through the reports to get the information that was specifically useful to them.

This is self-defeating. There is no reason, today, to create general use reports, with excess data. Reports can be, and should be, designed for each user. To do this, we would first identify the roles that would be receiving the data and design a set of model reports for each defined role. Then we can go further. Each individual can have his or her own set of reports, using a personal selection criterion.

Tool Tip   The capability, in PlanView, of having a HomeView for each individual epitomizes this concept. This not only provides access to the specific information needed by each contributor, but also limits access to the data that the individual needs.

Access should not be overly restrictive. The information available to the contributors should be enriched enough to inform them of the larger picture as well as their particulars. It should also provide warnings of current and pending critical items, missing items, and news of general interest. Here again, we would expect that the Deluxe Contributors would have a wider span of interest and responsibility than the simple Contributors would. Access and level of information may be different for internal workers, external workers, contractors, and clients.

Remember that the well-informed contributor is likely to feel more a part of the enterprise, and therefore participate with more enthusiasm. On the other hand, we should avoid information overload, lest we confuse and discourage such participation. We need to seek a reasonable balance.

Of course, getting data out of the system assumes that data has been put into the system. Therefore, it is essential that we promote the inputting of good and timely data. This, too, is a product of the design of appropriate and personal data input screens. The principle at work here is the same as for reports. We develop models for each role for each type of required data. Then we individualize them further by customizing them for each contributor. This generally entails using selection criteria that will create a timesheet (or expense sheet or status update sheet) that already lists the items that the contributor is expected to report against. There is no reason to require the contributor to input work item descriptions or task codes. The predefined list should include nonproject items as well.

Team leaders will need more than just input screens. Depending on the extent of their roles, they will need access to the work planning and resource assignment screens, to allow the addition or modification of these data. The ability to analyze performance, explore alternatives, and communicate progress, problems, and issues should be supported.

Summary Comments—Participant Groups

A key to contributor involvement (and project success) is a project management information system that is conducive to frequent and accurate data inputs and one that provides tailored information to the participants. Such a system is role-oriented, personal, and easy-to-use. It is accessible from offsite locations, but secure from accidental inputs and unauthorized eyes. It supports the needs and involvement of the full span of interested parties, while providing customized access for the wide span of roles.

Other Roles

We have been exploring the expanding roles of participants in projects, as we enter the twenty-first century. We have taken note of the shift from a project-centric focus to a resource-centric focus, and the emergence of modern workforce management. We have taken note of a revolution in the concepts and technology of communication, especially as it applies to project and workforce management. And we have taken note of the expansion of the concept of stakeholders, recognizing that whether your project has been successful will depend, at least in part, on the perceptions of the stakeholders of what was actually accomplished.

Thus far, we have discussed the role-based needs of two segments of the stakeholder community: the management groups and the participant groups. We conclude this chapter with the needs of the remaining stakeholders.

Other Stakeholders

As noted earlier, the universe of people who care about or impact projects is quite large. This extends well beyond the involved management groups and the directly involved participants. More important, these other stakeholders can be as important to success as the management and participant groups. One such group is the Owner of the project. This might be an external client, or an internal sponsor. It is the person who represents the organization that is directly or indirectly paying for the work and has (most likely) the greatest stake in its successful completion. Other internal operations that might have more than a passing interest in the ongoing projects would include the Human Resources function, Accounting, and Information Systems. And many organizations depend on external functions as well, such as Professional Services Organizations, Outsourcing groups, and Business-to-Business alliances.

Communicating with Stakeholders

One of the biggest causes of project failure, especially in Information Technology projects, is the lack of continued participation and communication by this more remote segment of the project community. Actually, it seems ludicrous to refer to the owner or sponsor as remote. Yet, in practice, these people are often out of the loop. We accept the project and then limit communication to brief, disconnected, periodic reports.

One thing that managers and clients despise is surprises. But we tend to go merrily along our way, reporting that all is well, until we can't hide the slippages, overruns, and technical problems. Then we suddenly break the news that the client will not get what was expected. In most projects, problems such as these can be expected. If frequent communication and disclosure is maintained, these problems become part of a natural, shared resolution process. But the sudden shift from a state of "not to worry" to a state of "all hell has broken loose" leads to a breakdown of trust.

This regretful state can be avoided. A key to doing this is communication. Such communication should be frequent, concise, and consistent. It should facilitate bi-directional discussion and exchange of information.

In the past, our culture seemed to support the hiding of information. We often felt that we should tell people as little as possible. But this protectionist attitude often backfired. Today, we tend to be more open and to share information with others. This has led to improved participation and trust. Let's examine this new communication environment as we look at the role-based needs of clients, sponsors, and peripheral stakeholders.

Fidelity in Communications

As I look back at four decades of participation in the management of projects, I recall far too many instances of breakdowns in communication and trust. The first (breakdown in communication) leads to the second (deterioration of trust). We all know the story about the project that quickly reaches 90 percent complete, then stays there forever. Obviously, the earlier 90 percent figures were more wishful thinking than fact. In another common scenario the sponsor inquires (on a regular basis) as to the project status and is told that things are moving along just fine. Then, when the fantasy can no longer be sustained, the project suddenly jumps to negative variances that obviously didn't just happen. And just as bad is the situation where multiple sets of data just don't match. There is a lack of fidelity in the information and, with such, a complete breakdown of trust.

The Need to Communicate

There is much to be gained from regular and trustworthy communication with all parties to project success. This is what the stakeholders need. And this is what we can give them, using today's improved communication technology. I know that I'm repeating myself, here, but for such communication to work, it must be regular and consistent (to maintain believability). It must also be consistent with any other data about the project. The data itself should be supported by narrative discussions of the impact of the data. Such discussions should advise the recipients of things that require their action or response, as well as provide early warnings of potential action items. Remember; a primary object is to avoid surprises. (Another is to facilitate broad participation in problem resolution.)

Perhaps *data* is not the proper word to use. I remember seeing a cartoon many years ago that depicted a man up to his ears in computer-generated characters, exclaiming, "Drowning in data while starving for information!" This is a great message. The data that we provide must have meaning. They must be related to areas of interest of the receiver. For the owner, this means tying the data to the owner's objectives. The client or sponsor wants to know how we are doing against these objectives. It is not enough to say The project will be completed on 9/1/01, or We've spent $120,000. Is this good or bad? If it is the latter, are actions being taken to reverse the situation? Is there some action required of the owner?

Likewise, reporting that a technical objective is in jeopardy is not full communication. Again, the owner should be informed as to the prognosis and possible remedies, as well as the diagnosis. And, again, the owner should be invited to participate in the solution. There are at least two advantages to this philosophy. First, the client/sponsor may actually be able to contribute to the remedy. Second, the client/sponsor is less likely to dump the entire blame for the failures when he/she is invited to participate (and when mutual trust is maintained).

All too often, the project team will wrestle with a problem, such as attempting to achieve a requested technical objective. Finally, after exhausting large amounts of effort and funds, the team communicates the problem to the sponsor, who responds, "That objective wasn't really that important." Think of what could have been saved if the sponsor had known of the situation earlier.

Other Internal Operations

Most projects will require the support of several internal support functions. It may be the Human Resources Department, or Training, Financial, Information Systems, Graphics and Printing support, or any of the traditional internal support groups. Here, too, there is a tendency to keep these groups in the dark, until we need their services. Then, we hit them with a request for immediate support and cry that they are not responsive when they won't drop everything for your project. The lack of advance communication on your part should not be justification for bringing the internal graphics group in on a weekend to meet your needs.

If you are maintaining a project plan, there is no reason not to include these internal support groups in the distribution of selected information. The objective is to identify parts of the project that will have an impact on these groups and to maintain periodic communication of the status of these items.

Other External Operations

In some firms, some support functions may be external or outsourced. That should not make a big difference. Similar communication is in order. A supplier may require two weeks advance notice of the start of a contracted effort. Why not provide an early estimate and update it regularly? The contractor will appreciate it and provide better service. Again, a key is to design a customized view of the appropriate data, for each stakeholder.

Software Systems Considerations

A key factor of system design for this other stakeholders group is whether communication is uni-directional or bi-directional. For the Participants groups, we obviously need bi-directional capabilities. This may not be necessary for other stakeholders. If this is the case, an effective method of communication is *web publishing*. This would allow the target receivers of the information to access the data via a web browser. The web pages would be designed specifically for each target, and there are no security problems. When reverse communication is warranted, the web pages can have e-mail links to the people most likely to be contacted.

A disadvantage to web publishing is that the publisher determines what the viewer sees and when it is refreshed. But this can also be viewed as an advantage, as the publisher has a chance to review and validate the data before broadcasting them. Another advantage of web publishing is that the format is preset and the reader needs to know no more than how to access the web pages.

Of course, all stakeholders can be included in the full, bi-directional system. Security can be set to allow queries, but disallow data entry. This gives full (or limited) access to the data, on demand, without exposing the database to unauthorized inputs. For the broadest access, from remote locations, a web-based system will usually serve these users better than a client/server system. With the former system, the users do not require any PM system software on their computers.

Role-based Needs

This concludes the chapter on role-based needs for managing resources in a project-driven organization. We have tried to show that there is a vast community of stakeholders who support or impact projects—each with information needs and many with information contributions. The effective system designer will consider the specific needs of each stakeholder and accommodate those needs. The design will consider both the type of information required and the best format to facilitate delivery and receipt of such information.

There is no excuse for a one-size-fits-all approach. Ignoring individual roles and their need for tailored project communication vehicles will further the probability of project failure. This need not happen.

CHAPTER 4.3

RESOURCE LEVELING AND GAMES OF CHANCE

In Chapter 3.1, we alert you to possible deficiencies in traditional resource scheduling software. That function is most commonly called *resource leveling*. In this chapter we dig deeper into this situation, disclosing results from tests conducted on several products and looking at remedies for such deficiencies. The actual testing was conducted several years ago, so we won't reveal the actual products (these versions are no longer available). However, the test results still serve to illustrate the problem and provide a basis for discussion on techniques that work. The benefit to you, from this discussion, will be increased knowledge of what is involved in resource leveling, increased awareness of the critical issues in software selection and use, and practical approaches toward achieving reasonable resource-loaded schedules.

Is It Blackjack?

We start this chapter off with a trick question. Let's say that you play a game 30 times. Thirteen times, you come up with 17. Nine times you come up with 16. Six times you come up with 18. Once you get a 20, and once you get a 15. What game are you playing?

Sounds a bit like blackjack, doesn't it? But it's not! How about roulette? Wrong again! I know—*it's the resource leveling game.* Right on! It's the actual results that I obtained from a resource leveling test.

In life, they say that two things are certain: death and taxes. When it comes to computer-based resource leveling there are also a couple of things that you can bet on. First, don't expect to obtain an optimum solution. Second, you will rarely obtain the same solution, even within the same program. And, we might add, there are no assurances that the higher-priced or more functionally endowed products will provide shorter or more consistent results.

That is not to assume that the software designers are either lax or inept regarding the resource leveling function. On the contrary, a lot of effort has gone into most of these products to support effective resource scheduling, and excellent resource leveling capabilities have been available for more than 20 years. The problem is primarily one of tradeoffs, and of real world considerations.

It may very well be possible to generate an optimized solution. However, you may not wish to pay the price for executing such routines. First, it would tend to require extensive computer resources. Second, it would require so many iterations to slow down the process to an unacceptable level. However, even more important, it would require the user to make critical and unnecessary decisions long before they are needed, and then to relinquish control of this complex process to the computer. And because conditions change as the project is being scheduled and executed, the decisions made at the beginning may no longer be appropriate down the line. User intervention may be required to produce the right resource schedule.

The issue here is that there are usually sensitive criteria that must be considered when deciding which task should get the limited resources. In the first place, it would be tedious to define all of these decision factors to the computer (after all we are already protesting the amount of detail that must be entered to produce a decent project model). But, more to the point, it would be even more difficult, and unrealistic, to make these determinations very far in advance of the period of work execution.

There are definite benefits to be gained from employing computerized resource leveling routines, especially to get the big picture. But, if we want to be realistic, relative to detailed resource scheduling, we will need to take a short-term prospective, and fully interact with the computer.

Tool Tip   Responding to my philosophy that resource leveling to the end of a two-year-long project may be unrealistic, Scitor added a Level until xx/xx/xx Date option in PS7 and PS8. Look for this option in other products, as well.

I have been researching this subject for quite some time, and the more involved in it I get the more I find it Byzantine and intriguing. It is a fairly complex topic. There is probably more information here than you need to know. We start by looking at some of the issues and problems involving resource leveling. Then, we study the resource leveling process, itself, and examine the results of 13 products on some test projects. Next, we look at the resource scheduling attributes and calculations of these products. We also look at some alternate software for resource management. Finally, in Chapter 4.4, we explore the Practical Uses of Resource Scheduling.

Wheel of Misfortune: The Resource Leveling Process

Resource leveling is certainly not new, and neither are the issues pertaining to the best and practical methods to be used. I was recently browsing through a 1981 P/2 manual (PROJECT/2 from Project Software & Development, Inc.). P/2, then running on IBM mainframes and the DEC VAX, offered powerful resource scheduling options. The user had the choice of four leveling methods, two parallel and two serial modes.

The *parallel mode*, which is seldom used today, will usually (but not always) produce a shorter-duration, resource-constrained schedule. The parallel method looks at the project by time periods. For each time period, it looks at all the tasks that are scheduled to be worked and assigns resources according to the user preferred ranking criteria. Activities that cannot be scheduled in that time period, due to insufficient resources, are postponed until a later time period. Then the system moves to the next time period and reconsiders the next set of tasks that are ready to be worked.

The *serial mode* considers the project on an activity by activity basis, and generally takes less time to process. For any particular time period, it starts out as above. However, when it cannot schedule an activity on its earliest start period, it looks for the first available period (resource availability) and immediately schedules that activity at that future time. It is possible, therefore, that when the system gets to a later time period, one or more tasks may already be scheduled, before checking for the best choice or closest support of the ranking criteria. We will find that the serial method of resource leveling is almost universally employed in today's popular products.

With either method, the user is often allowed to identify a set of *ranking factors* (sometimes called ordering, prioritization, or heuristics). These are conditions that will influence the selection of tasks where some tasks must be delayed. Common factors are date values (ES, EF, LS, LF), float values, task duration, assigned priorities, task IDs, and user sort sequences. During resource leveling, the system first looks at the precedence and imposed date results (the CPM schedule) and then the ranking factors. There is no sure way of telling (in advance) which ranking criteria will produce the shorter or smoother schedule. (Those 30 seemingly random numbers mentioned earlier came from running the same test project on 13 programs. Those programs that allowed the setting of preferred ranking criteria gave several different answers, depending on that setting.) Experimentation, with varied ranking factors, is necessary in order to get close to the best solution. In addition, in the serial method, the ranking criteria are used only when a task is first considered for resource scheduling. The tasks are not reordered during the process.

Even with the multiple options for advanced resource leveling, available in P/2, PSDI, in that 1981 document, advised that the system is not designed to achieve the optimal results. In addition to the demand on computer resources, they suggested that the process needs to be timely and dynamic. Today, two decades later, that reasoning is still valid, and, with the universal use of the serial method, optimization cannot be expected.

We cannot, within this book, hope to resolve all the issues of efficient and effective resource leveling. We will endeavor, however, to make you more aware of the realities of resource leveling, and of the capabilities and limitations of the popular project management software products, with regard to resource leveling. Perhaps as a byproduct, we will keep the heat on ourselves and the software developers to make resource leveling a more useful function than it is today.

Place Your Bets: A Review of Resource Leveling Results

Looking at the results of resource leveling tests performed on 13 project management software products, it is startling to realize the range of answers obtained, and the effect on project duration and resource utilization. Here is an overview.

Test model A (producing the results that were mentioned earlier) consists of 14 resource-loaded tasks, requiring either 1 or 2 units of a single resource. There is a total of 30 MDs of effort. The unleveled CPM is 11 days. Leveling, with 2 units of the resource available, should be able to produce a 15-day schedule. Yet, in 30 trials (without invoking splitting options, where available), only 1 iteration produced the 15-day result. Others ranged from 16 to 20 days. (Splitting options, available on 6 of the programs, produced schedules of 15 and 16 days. However, activity splitting was not necessary to obtain a 15-day result via manual leveling.)

Let's say that you are the project or resource manager on this job. Would you be willing to pay for 40 days of effort (20 days for 2 people) when you could get the job done with 30 days of effort?

Test model B consists of 7 tasks and 2 resources. Unleveled, the CPM duration is 4 weeks, but there is a resource overload in week 1. After resource leveling, the result should still be 4 weeks, as there is room to move 1 task, within the available float. Yet several products delayed more than 1 task, underutilizing available resources in week 1, and adding 1 week to the project duration.

In both test cases, it was possible to obtain the optimal solution manually, following a set of pre-defined ordering rules. Yet the process of serial leveling (routines to immediately place tasks that are ready to be worked), often resulted in periods of resource underutilization that were unnecessary.

Test model C is the most revealing. It consists of only 3 tasks and 1 resource. Only 2 of the tasks require the resource. Depending on the ranking factors used, resource leveling can add either 1 day or 5 months to the schedule. For those programs that offer a choice of ranking factors, it is up to the user to determine which method of prioritization will produce the better result.

And don't look for help from the user manuals and other documentation on resource leveling ranking factors. I read, in one manual, that Late Start (LS) will usually produce the shortest resource-constrained schedule. Another source suggested that least Total Float (TF) should be your first try. Yet, in my experiments, the best results in test model A were obtained using Early Start (ES) and test model C worked best with Late Finish (LF) or least (shortest) duration.

Better Odds at Blackjack?

What I learned, from my research and testing, is that the chances of getting 21 were far greater than the chances of obtaining optimal leveled schedules from project management software. Oh! If only we could employ *elastic* resources, I thought, wishfully. But resource pools that grow as needed are even rarer than the successful cloning of project managers.

No, the only immediate, practical solution (outside of software improvements) is to recognize the limitations of today's project scheduling systems, and to work within these limits. This will require interaction between the person doing the resource management and the project management software system.

Tool Tip   Good news! Although the serial leveling algorithm continues to dominate the traditional CPM tools, the results delivered by the latest releases are more likely to provide a better solution than the products that I reviewed for my series of tests. While still benefiting from user interaction, the computed results from these latest releases are much more dependable than they were a few years ago.

Options That Affect Resource Leveling

Before we get into practical techniques for resource management, let's consider the various differences in the resource scheduling and leveling capabilities in project management software products. In addition to the basic leveling methods that we discussed earlier, we can identify several dozen design attributes that can affect the ability to define a project's resource parameters and influence the resource leveling outcome. The variations are extensive. Figure 4.3a presents most of the attributes that directly affect the resource leveling function.

Practical Uses of Resource Scheduling

In Chapter 4.4, we look at *practical uses of resource scheduling*. Here is a preview of some things that you should find interesting.

Long Term/Short Term   Practical resource scheduling is best achieved via a balance of long-term resource aggregation (analysis of predicted resource loads) and short-term resource leveling (possibly with user intervention). We outline a recommendation that should suit most applications.

Use of Total and Free Float   Have you been taught that we use CPM scheduling so that we can obtain a measure of float? And that we use these float values to help us make decisions on priorities, and to analyze project schedule risk? Get ready to learn all over again. When we use resource leveling, we can forget about using the resultant float values as a time management tool. I explain why, in Chapter 4.4.

Use of Accomplishment Value in Place of Float   There are other techniques available to help analyze project progress. Accomplishment value (based on popular earned value protocols) can be used, even without using the cost management features of your project management software.

A Design for Optimized Resource Scheduling   Is there a better way of doing resource scheduling using project management software? We share some ideas on this subject.

Trends in Resource Management

Resource management may well be the real oldest profession. Certainly it is not a new function. I'll bet that even when the pyramids were built, there were fairly well-structured practices in place for managing the projects and the resources. Frederick Taylor, at the turn of the twentieth century, published new

Figure 4.3a Options That Affect Resource Leveling

Here is a list of resource scheduling attributes that may be found in traditional CPM products. The range of attributes is quite wide. Some of these are unique to a single product. Most items on the list are available in many products, but in less than half of them. So, in selecting project management software, you cannot assume that even the most popular and rudimentary capabilities are supported by any product. Price, by the way, is not directly related to the number of supported resource scheduling functions.

- User choices for ranking.
- Multiple iterations or ranking calculations.
- Effect of imposed dates (Note: Some products use fixed dates that interfere with resource leveling).
- Trial and Error—Perform what-if, but do not replace until accepted by user (or perform *undo*).
- Manual (interactive) adjustment (most Windows products).
- Activity splitting.
  Entire project only (this is useless—must be able to select by task).
  By task.
  By task with definable conditions.
  Automatic contouring (system varies loading by time period to adjust for resource availability).
  Discrete loading via spreadsheet.
- Overtime.
- Activity Stretching (called *Stretching* or *Re-profiling* in some products or *Flex* in another). Reduces loading per time period and increases time periods (I wonder if we want to let the computer make this decision without human interaction).
- Min-Max or Threshold Options. Defines preferred limits and maximum.
- Limit for resource.
- Resource substitution (rare).
- Leveling audit or results report.
- Depletable resources.
- Producer resources (unique to SuperProject).
- Span dates for resource leveling (if we can choose to limit our resource leveling to a reasonably short time frame, then we can afford to implement more exacting leveling algorithms).
- Minimum crew size (available in a few packages).

concepts for utilizing resources more efficiently. When the first CPM systems emerged, in the late 1950s, it didn't take long for tool developers to add resource scheduling functionality.

A most interesting trend can be observed at the current time. It relates to new practitioners of project management and new users of project management software. Businesses are realizing that the work that they are doing is centered around *projects*. For those of us who have been immersed in the project management scene for a while, this is no major revelation. But what is happening is that a project orientation is more of a normal modus operandi, today, rather than a special situation. Hence, there has been a growth in interest in project management and in computer-based systems to help them plan and schedule this work.

That they are looking to project management software for this purpose is essentially good! But wait! There's more (why keep it simple?). These businesses are also realizing that a key item to be planned and managed is the *assignment and use of resources* on these projects. Again, businesses are looking to project management software, as well they should. There can be no doubt that traditional project management software packages can be excellent tools to support this important function.

In our model project environment, we need to do critical path scheduling, and adjust the schedules for resource limitations. We need software that will allow us to:

- Identify the project workscope.
- Organize the identified work (outlines and work breakdown structures).
- Schedule the work.
- Identify available resources.
- Assign resources to the work.
- Evaluate and adjust the schedule and resource assignments.
- Analyze and report schedule and resource information, oriented by project and by resource structures.

These are all functions that are fully supported by project management software, and I would recommend the use of such software for most applications. However, traditional project management software may not be the ideal solution for every application. There are certain plusses and minuses that must be considered, especially when alternative software choices exist.

The strong point of project management software is its ability to do critical path scheduling. These tools are optimized to produce and display schedules of the work, based on defined task durations, dependencies, and date constraints (and, optionally, resource constraints). They are designed to analyze and display resource schedules and loads (as well as costs). They would appear to be complete systems for planning and control.

The issue is that these project management software systems are rarely connected to the corporate accounting systems. Yet the latter are usually the only complete and dependable repositories for resource charges (time sheets) and cost data. Also, many of these project management software systems are optimized to present a project-centric view of the work, often leaving functional and resource managers with less information and control than would be desired.

So our discussion of computer support for resource management functions would not be complete without mentioning some of the non-CPM tools that are available for this purpose. Here are some options for software that can be used in place of or to supplement our traditional project management software products.

Alternative Algorithms

A few alternative resource smoothing algorithms have been introduced during the past decade. But these, too, have failed to be accepted thus far. Many of these include some type of best-fit approach. One appeared in Best Schedule (Parsifal Systems), but is no longer on the market. Another was built into Team Manager (Microsoft). This product also failed to achieve significant position in the marketplace. Yet another best-fit concept was introduced in Project Toolbox (adRem Technologies). This product is no longer available, but the technology was acquired by jeTech Data, for inclusion with their Project Enterprise product. Project Enterprise has since been acquired by Microsoft.

It is strange that despite the potential for these tools to provide improved resource scheduling results, interest in such solutions remains very low.

Non-CPM Resource Planning and Analysis Tools

Representative of tools that have been specifically designed to address these deeper resource issues is *Allegro, The Resource Management System,* from Deltek Systems, Inc.

Allegro *is not a critical path scheduling tool.* It is a resource planning and analysis tool, employing a spreadsheet metaphor as a convenient mechanism to input to and analyze a comprehensive project and resource database.

Each Allegro installation is custom designed to interface with the company accounting system. Most of the project and resource information can be brought over to Allegro from the accounting system, and regular upload/download between these two systems (and to other data systems) is supported.

There are hierarchical structures for both projects and resources. The Project WBS is three levels (default is Department/Phase/Task). Also each project can belong to a specified group of projects (accumulators) for further summarized analysis.

Each individual resource can belong to a group or class of resources. Resource assignments can be made at the group or individual level. This supports a real world environment, where we often wish to evaluate the impact of pending and future work, without assigning that work to specific individuals. An especially helpful feature of Allegro is the ability to reassign work from a resource class to individuals, either manually or automatically. In the automatic method, Allegro considers the workloads for resources assigned to the project when it makes these assignments. Allegro can do this because it maintains a record of resource availability.

The master calendar, in Allegro, can be set to define up to 54 custom, variable periods. Normally, you would set up a few historical periods, followed by weekly periods for a few months, and then go to coarser periods, such as months and quarters. A period can be any number of days. Each period becomes a column in the spreadsheet.

Data can be analyzed by project, resources, timeslice, and so on at any level of detail. All analysis views are in the spreadsheet format, with a freeze column at the right and a freeze row at the bottom (user selectable). Data can be viewed in Hours, Revenue, Labor (costs), or Percentage of Available Time. All views can be printed. In addition, there is a report writer for graphs and customized reports.

All of this goes just a bit beyond the typical capabilities of traditional project management software. But Allegro users must forgo critical path scheduling, or use a CPM program to generate the schedule. In Allegro, each work item (project/dept/phase/task) is assigned a start and end date, which is used for assigning resources. Resource assignment can be uniform, or can be discrete (by loading each time period), or automatic (considering availability). Additional features include: user specified billing and costing attributes, an award probability (percentage) multiplier, project and contract accounting fields, and several project and resource classification fields.

Time Keeping Software   Traditional project management software assumes that task progress will be entered into the system, as start and completion dates and percent complete. It also assumes that actual resource usage will be entered directly into the resource assignment records, on a task-by-task basis. But this is not normally the best way to enter resource time data.

Most traditional project management software tools now provide a *timesheet* view, which facilitates the entering of time spent on tasks, as well as supporting manager review and approval of such entries. These features will optimize and satisfy the needs for time keeping, from the project point of view. However, they tend not to be robust enough to meet the resource accounting requirements of most firms. If you are to avoid the redundancy of operating two timekeeping systems (project and accounting), you will need to consider specialized project timekeeping software. Such tools are designed to interface directly with many of the popular project management software packages, while being robust enough to provide management-level features and a tie-in to corporate accounting systems.

Tool Tip It is important for these software packages to allow the user to design a time capture input form or view that will allow time sheet data to be entered on a resource by resource basis, across multiple projects.

A key difference between a full-featured time keeping program and just a time input form is the level of administrative control provided. We can see this by looking at the attributes of one of the special timekeeping programs that have been developed for use with project management software. This product is representative of a myriad of excellent add-on products for timekeeping.

Time$heet Professional, from TIMESLIPS Corporation, has been around for several years. It has features and capabilities suitable for large resource groups. A data exchange utility is included with the product, supporting data transfer to and from many CPM products.

Time$heet Professional is a corporate time and project tracking software using a timesheet metaphor. While it can be used as a stand-alone program, it works very well as an adjunct program with traditional project management software. It tracks time and expense data for projects, clients, employees, and tasks.

Custom reports support multiproject consolidation, with several analysis options. A Stopwatch Timer automatically records time spent on tasks. Many of the terms can be customized to match the corporate jargon. Tasks can belong to billing groups or cost centers. Using the data exchange utility, projects and tasks, with their assignments, can be downloaded to Time$heet Professional, and the entered timesheet data can then be brought back over to the project management software.

Similar capabilities are available in products such as Time Control (HMS) and Time Wizard (AC Software). And don't forget that many of these features are available in modules that are packaged with traditional CPM systems.

Whoops! Gotta run. They're opening up a new blackjack table.

CHAPTER 4.4

PRACTICAL RESOURCE SCHEDULING

Practical resource scheduling is best achieved via a balance of long-term resource aggregation (analysis of predicted resource loads) and short-term resource leveling (possibly with user intervention). *Resource aggregation* is the tally of effort for each resource for each time period. These results can be viewed in *resource histograms* or *resource tables* (spreadsheets). Resource leveling is not required.

For a *long-term* evaluation, use resource aggregation to observe the potential impact on resources. Generally, a coarse view (weekly for a project over six months) will be sufficient. Identify periods of potential overloads. Identify strategic alternatives (shifting priorities, delaying lower priority projects, outsourcing, extra hires, overtime, reducing scope, reducing quality, panic, burying head in sand).

Tip There is no justification for producing a resource schedule, to four decimal places, way out into the future, when we can usually be assured that significant changes to the task schedule, to the available resources, and even to the workscope will nullify the results of that effort.

For the *short term*, look at unleveled and leveled solutions. If the leveled solution has a good utilization factor (not too many peaks and valleys), you may wish to use the computer-produced schedule, as-is. If not, use the computer data to determine a reasonable resource pool (if adjustable) or a reasonable task load (if resources are fixed), and determine an optimum short-term schedule (i.e., next two weeks), using the computer to display the results of the various what-ifs.

Tool Tip   Software that allows you to preview a result before accepting, or that has an undo feature, can be helpful in this optimization exercise.

Warning: Use of Total and Free Float Disallowed   We use *total float* as an indicator of the time that a task may slip without delaying the shortest completion of the project. We use *free float* as an indicator of the time that a task may slip without affecting the start of any other task in the project. When we use resource leveling, we can forget about using the resultant float values as a time management tool.

The system may use float in determining the priorities for scarce resources. So it is important to develop a sound schedule, which contains valid float values. But, once we execute the leveling process, we can no longer assume that sliding out the work while staying within the float is not going to hurt the ability to get the work done on time, because we need to consider the effect on resource availability. This being the case, it should serve to further justify a short-term philosophy.

Trap   Once you have adopted a resource-leveled schedule, the indicated schedule floats are no longer useful as a measure of allowed schedule slippage. Any deviation to the planned performance of a task, even those having float or even those not requiring resources (except non-resource tasks having free float), will cause a change in the resource loads.

A Review of Basic Resource Scheduling Practices

Project Model   The first step of the resource scheduling process is to build a sound model of the project work that is to be performed. We highly recommend the use of critical path based software to aid in this task. This initial plan should support the key dates as outlined in the Project Milestone Schedule. Also, through the use of Work Breakdown Structures and Organizational Breakdown Structures, the defined work should be organized and coded in ways to assist later in assigning resources. The why and how of this type of scheduling is discussed in Section 3.

Resource Database   You will need to build a Resource Database (sometimes called the resource dictionary or resource library). This consists of knowing what your resources are and certain information about skills and availability. The data elements associated with this list of resources will vary, and may include any of the following:

- Resource name—Can be individual resource or class of resource.
- Hierarchical structure (parent/subordinate)—A Resource Breakdown Structure (RBS).
- Information about the resource (some of this can come from or be linked to an HR database).
- Resource's skills.
- Productivity by skill (rare—with good reason—see Trap).
- Charging and billing rates.
- Availability schedule.

Trap   Caution is advised when you are working with the productivity of skills. This is usually very sensitive information, which should not be available to the general public. Before attempting to add these data, the situation should be reviewed with the human resources and legal departments and approved at a high level of management. At the least, such data should be restricted to need-to-know personnel. In practice, most users do not use a productivity feature and many products do not support such a function.

Assign Resources   Next, from this resource database, you will select which resources are to be assigned to which tasks. This assignment can be by individual, that is, Jack and Betty. Or it may be by class or skill, that is, Plumber or System Analyst.

The assignments will need to be quantified. Jack is assigned full time to the task but Betty is assigned only at half time. Also, Betty cannot start work on the task until 1 week after Jack starts. Or, perhaps on this 3-week task, Jack is assigned for 120 hours, and Betty for 40 hours (half time for the last 2 weeks). Most systems will allow the user to input this level of detail.

For class or skill assignments, you might simply assign 2 plumbers to the task. But you can also specify that a third plumber plus a pipefitter will join the resource team for the second week of the task. The idea is to define the intended work assignments so as to facilitate the computation of a resource-loading profile.

Evaluate Resource Demands   At this point, I like to review the scheduled demand on resources, without invoking any of the resource-leveling functions. The CPM systems should be able to calculate the demand on each resource, for each time period, and display this data in both graphic and spreadsheet formats. This is sometimes called *resource aggregation.* In the graphic view, the defined availability is usually shown as a horizontal line, with the demand shown as vertical bars or columns. It is easy to see where the bars rise above the availability lines, indicating a resource overload. An advantage to the spreadsheet view is that you may view several resources at once. The actual demand (loading) values will change from black to red (in the typical system) when that value exceeds the defined availability.

Trap   If the resource aggregation data show that there are extended periods of time when one or more resources are in a high overload condition, it would be a waste of time to continue with the resource leveling utility. Resource leveling cannot manufacture resources for you. If the indicated overload is small or sporadic, it should be possible to eliminate the overloads by such actions as shifting dates within float (done by the computer) or allowing some overtime (defined in the resource database). But forecasts of extended periods of significant overloads will require other action.

Remedial Options   What can you do if such a high impact overload exists? This will depend on the particular situation and set of conditions. If time is of the essence, something will have to be done about either the work or the assignment. It is perfectly valid to re-examine the workscope and strategy in the areas where resource support is hurting.

The first line of action might be to seek alternative resources. If there is a pool of resources available, in which some resources are underutilized, can any of these substitute for the primary choice? If so, does the effort level need to be changed to reflect possible productivity differences? We do this all the time (independent of computer-driven scheduling). Tom is our go-to guy for a particular type of task, but is up to his ears in alligators. This isn't exactly Fred's bag, but he can handle it in a pinch. So we have Fred pinch-hit for Tom, but perhaps throw a few hours in for Tom at the start of the task, to provide guidance, and again at the end of the task to review the results.

Another early consideration, in the case of significant shortages, is to consider farming out some of the work, or bringing in temporary resources. If the entire workscope is essential, and time is limited, this may be your only viable recourse.

Can any of the scope be shifted to a different phase of the project, where resources are less stressed? Can you use a prior design or lines of code rather than starting from scratch? There's no law that states that you can't reduce quality or increase risk (understanding the possible consequences and doing it within reason). Can resources be shifted from a lower priority project?

Trap When managing multiple projects with shared resources, it is normal to re-evaluate project priorities to choose which project gets first pick of the limited resources. Such action will not resolve your severe shortages, but will only shift which project ends up with the short stick.

If the indicated overload is way out in the distance (i.e., six months or more) you might want to look at the resource aggregation data as a warning of potential resource problems rather than trying to fix things immediately. There is too much chance that the work will change, that the work timing will change, and that even the workforce availability will change. To be aware of a potential problem is the first step in mitigating the problem.

Resource Leveling. Are you ready to let the machine help with smoothing the resource loading? There are several choices on how to go about this. You may choose to emphasize time limits or resource limits (or, with some products, both). Here are a few examples (depending on your software's feature set).

Time-Constrained Resource Scheduling. The situation: The CPM calculated end date is 3/1/02. The resource aggregation shows that there are several, sporadic overloads, for some of the resources. The contract (or sponsor) allows completion by 4/15/02. The action: Perform a time-constrained resource scheduling (leveling) with the end date set at 4/15/02. See if that will alleviate the resource overload. If not, re-evaluate the peaks and look again at the earlier options (resource substitution, outsourcing, scope change).

Resource-Constrained Resource Scheduling. The situation: The CPM calculated date is 3/1/02. The resource aggregation shows that there are several, sporadic overloads, for some of the resources. The resource availability is frozen. The action: Set the resource leveling function so that resource limits cannot be exceeded and let the computer calculate a new end date.

Tip It is possible for there to be situations where the computer cannot find enough resources, at any time, to satisfy the defined demand. In such instances, the system will usually ignore the defined limits and leave the overload. It might send a warning notification.

Combined Resource Scheduling. The situation: As above. The action: Define the normal and maximum resource availability. For instance, Jane's normal availability is 8 hours per day. Knowing that October is going to be a tough workload month, she has agreed to work up to 2 extra hours per day during that month. Set the maximum hours to 10 per day, for October. Or, for class-type resources: The normal availability of technical writers is 4. A retired tech writer is available on call. Set the normal limit for tech writers at 4 and the maximum at 5.

Set the required end date for 4/15/02 (if that is still a good date). The system will attempt to level the resources, staying within the normal limits. If that computation pushes the project completion beyond 4/15/02, the system will re-evaluate the resource availability, up to the defined maximum limits. If it cannot achieve a leveled schedule within the maximum limits, it will slip the schedule out beyond the 4/15/02 date.

Tool Tip The Combined Resource Scheduling capability is not available in most programs. This function can be accomplished by manually adjusting the availability of the critical resources and running the Resource-Constrained mode. This can be repeated until a satisfactory result is obtained.

Manual Intervention. As noted several times, it is unlikely that an optimized, resource-constrained schedule will be obtained without coaching the computer to adjust the loading and schedule. Optimal scheduling is a reiterative process and will usually require user intervention. This is one of the advantages to using the computer for this function. You can test a scenario—say, what-if—and try various combinations until you accept a solution.

When testing various scenarios, you can also try different combinations of ranking criteria, activity splitting, re-profiling, and so on, depending on what features are supported by your software.

Tip If the resource leveled schedule is satisfactory through the first six months of the project, but indicates problems further out into the future, you may as well accept the result and move on. The future is likely to be too dynamic to try to lock-in a resource loading plan that far in advance. If your tool supports it, you can instruct the system to level the resources only out until a specified date, rather than until the end of the project.

A Design for Optimized Resource Scheduling

What if you really want the computer to assist you in developing an optimized, resource limited schedule? What should we be looking for, in the way of a practical and efficient method? It seems to me that all we would need is a combination of functions that are already available in various project management software packages. If we buy the premise that realistic resource leveling should be short term and interactive, why couldn't we have the following set of functions in our resource scheduling system?

- Use the Parallel method algorithm (or one of the best-fit processes).
- Specify the limited time span to apply the algorithm.
- Specify the preferred ranking criteria.
- Allow activity splitting as a task-level option (and overtime).
- Allow activity stretching or reprofiling, or contouring (selective).
- Employ an interactive window for user override.
- Provide a resource table or spreadsheet view (to view several resources at once).
- Provide an undo function, to facilitate what-if experiments.
- In a multi-project environment, it would be useful to be able to designate resources as assigned or available to specified projects, at specified proportions.

In operation, the interactive window would pop up whenever a decision is required, showing the computer's default recommendation and other options. An interactive window of this nature was available in Time Line for Windows, as the Co-Pilot feature. In addition to allowing the choice of the task to get the limited resource, it would also suggest when activity splitting, stretching, or overtime could be used, and allow the user to define the split or overtime parameters at that time. Splitting or overtime could be set to automatic or discretionary, for any task. However, this product is no longer available.

Trap No combination of resource scheduling optimization capabilities can be assured of delivering the best results for any situation. There are subtle conditions that cannot be considered by any software, especially far in advance of the assignment time. The various smoothing capabilities will usually deliver better utilization of resources (on paper). But the computerized solution might not actually represent the best use of the resources. For instance, splitting assignments on tasks could result in fragmentation of the effort, with loss of efficiency or quality. Splitting and profiling functions, if available, must be applied on a case-by-case basis, with expressed parameters.

If enough resource information is available on the screen (perhaps in an optional window) we might even offer the user the ability to substitute for a scarce resource, on the fly.

Isn't this essentially what resource managers do on a project (or projects)? They look at the planned schedule for the immediate future, and at the available resources. They try to figure out the best way to get the necessary scheduled work done, when required, within resource limits. When they find a situation that does not support these criteria, they look at slipping tasks, using overtime, or reassigning work to less loaded resources. Why shouldn't we be able to provide them with support for that process, within the software that they are using to develop the project plans?

Personally, I am a strong supporter of the use of computers for project planning and control. On the other hand, you just can't beat the old weekly planning meeting concept. When we had an important project, the project team met early each Monday morning to firm up a plan for that week's activities. We started with an updated plan based on status as of the end of the previous week (usually computer generated). Then, armed with data about what work needed to be performed and who was available to do that work, the team confirmed the plan for the current week.

The computer was a significant part of the process. But we just couldn't let the computer make the final decisions, which were better left in the hands of the project team. While it is in the realm of possibility to describe all the factors needed to make an electronic decision, it would not be practical to do this. Thus, a computer-assisted decision process, fine-tuned by the project team, on a short time frame basis, would appear to be the way to go.

SECTION 5

BUDGETING AND COST CONTROL

Cost Management: The Weakest Link

A generic definition of *project management* would undoubtedly talk of planning, controlling, and balancing the scope, schedule, resource, and cost aspects of the project. Yet, when we read about project management, discussion of the latter item, *cost*, tends to get the least attention. This is often carried over to the design of software for project management. Many of the heavy-duty products, at least back before the PC era, addressed scope, schedule, and resource management and ignored cost management entirely. They left the design of the cost component of the software up to the user. And with good reason.

If you were to ask a dozen project management experts to list the primary functions and protocols of scope, schedule, and resource management, they would speak with almost a single voice. Although there might be variations in emphasis and style, the fundamentals would follow a similar philosophy and purpose. But not so for cost management.

Ask those same dozen project management experts about cost and you might get 15 opinions. First of all, many project management applications mainly ignore cost. And those that do consider cost have varied motives and objectives. Second, cost is usually the domain of the firm's financial staff, rather than that of the project managers. Frankly, financial managers and project managers are from two different worlds. Without favoring either group, I can say that generally they have a different view of what has to be managed, how to manage it, and how structured they are in performing their duties. Furthermore, if we also define project management as attempting to satisfy the wishes of all the stakeholders, we will find that the accountant stakeholders have a different definition of success from the other stakeholders.

In my experience, there are two important aspects of cost management that separate it from the other project management functions. The first is that each firm has a very specific way that they do it and a very specific set of terms that they apply. It would be difficult to apply a pre-defined practice and a canned program, out of the box, that would satisfy the firm's accounting requirements. We need only look at the Enterprise Resource Planning (ERP) applications to see the effect of this situation. Firms such as Oracle, PeopleSoft, Baan, SAP, and J.D. Edwards sell project financial management systems for several hundred thousand dollars (or more) and then charge that much again to tweak the system to the client's specific needs. There is no such thing as out-of-the-box finance systems, unless you are willing to abandon any in-house practices and accept the system that has been built into the software as a default.

The second is that the accountants (financial analysts, bean counters, finance managers, whatever you want to call them) would never pass control or even share control of the cost management function with PM people. Let's face it. If the accounting protocol is to process time cards and costs every two weeks, it will happen. Nothing can get in its way. On the other hand, if the scheduling protocol is to update the plan every other week, this will happen only if one of the daily crises doesn't get in the way. Traditional companies rely on cost data to satisfy their basic operational measurements. These costs are processed by the financial group, to a very structured set of practices, following generally accepted accounting protocols. When projects are involved, we often have had to duplicate the cost processing so that the costs are related to the project work.

Some progress has been made in integrating the accountant-managed cost data with the project-associated data by linking PM systems with Enterprise Resource Planning (ERP) systems. See Section 10 for a discussion of PM and ERP.

An Overview of Budgeting and Cost Control

Without getting into the details of any costing application, we can still discuss the general requirements and issues of project budgeting and cost control. We do this in Chapter 5.1.

Software Support for Cost Management

Regardless of your methods for cost management, it will not be done on the back of an envelope. The question is whether you will use special cost management tools, basic CPM tools, or integrated systems. We discuss the options and make some generalized recommendations in Chapter 5.2.

There are additional topics that impact on this subject of budgeting and cost control. Change control and managing costs associated with scope changes are discussed in Chapter 7.1. The area of performance management, including using cost variance measurements for measuring performance, is covered in Section 8. Project portfolio management is discussed in Section 9. The integration of project management and ERP tools is covered in Section 10.

CHAPTER 5.1

CONCEPTS AND ISSUES OF PROJECT BUDGETING AND COST CONTROL

Who Needs Cost Management?

In every firm, cost management will exist in some form, usually under the control of the finance function. Our problem as project managers is that often that form is not consistent with the project management function, and that the cost data cannot be integrated with the other project data. As a result, many of the critical management questions concerning cost go unanswered.

For instance, if the monthly accounting report notes that Omega Project has accumulated costs of $123,999, is this good or bad? Without integrating the accounting data with the other project data, much of the data is worthless.

How do we go about answering such common questions as:

- How much are you going to spend?
- How much did you spend? Is this good or bad?
- How much will you have spent when the project is over? Is this good or bad?
- If I'm in trouble on costs, what can I do to turn things around?
- How shall the costs be distributed?
- How can I control my resource costs?

Effective cost management must address such questions. This requires an integrated schedule and budget plan. It also requires integrated participation by leaders of the projects, resources, and financial disciplines.

Trap I have often run into situations where the schedule is being processed using a CPM tool, while the cost plan is processed in a spreadsheet. This continually leads to a mismatch of data. For instance, I have seen instances where the schedule was deliberately slipped by two months, but the cost spreadsheet did not change. Of course, the costs are driven by the schedule. So the spreadsheet-based budget was now totally out of synch. But nobody seemed to know or care. This is not an acceptable practice. The schedule and cost plan must be integrated.

Phases of Cost Management and Sources of Data

There are several phases of cost management. These may include:

- Proposal or preplanning phase.
- Spending authorization.
- Project cost plan (or budget).
- Collection of actual cost data.
- Billing and chargebacks.
- Cost performance analysis.
- Remedial actions.
- Replanning.
- End of project analysis and recommendations.

Several different disciplines within the organization have defined roles in support of these cost management phases. The baton is often passed between participants, and many phases require inputs and actions from multiple parties. From the list above, you can see that cost management is much more than just setting a budget and collecting actuals. In this chapter we discuss practical practices for each phase of the process.

Trap A common error in cost management is to exclude some sources of cost from the project cost database. If the project charter initiates the authorization to charge costs to the project, what happens to the costs that were associated with developing the project opportunity? Costs that are associated with preparing proposals or developing offerings should be accumulated and inserted into the project cost database. Likewise, there are often costs associated with project closeout that are not accounted for. The budget should allow for project closeout costs, including punch list items and disposition of resources and assets.

Functions and Subsystems Associated with Cost Management

There are several functions and subsystems that are often associated with cost management. Some are erroneously believed to be the equivalent of cost management, but fall short of satisfying the full requirements. Rather, they are only elements of a full-fledged cost management system.

Project accounting is not cost management. Most often, a project accounting system is no more than assigning an ID number to each authorized project so that costs can be allocated to projects. There is no budgeting within the project and there is no facility to evaluate performance or to know whether anything is wrong.

Activity-based costing (ABC) is a process wherein the budgeting and cost collection are associated with the defined workscope. It provides for much more detail than project accounting, facilitating greater control and performance. ABC is heavily promoted by Dekker, Ltd. Dekker TRAKKER is a product that integrates many project management and project accounting elements, and facilitates integration of project management with Generally Accepted Accounting Practices (GAAP). ABC is very useful when you need to perform detailed costing and profit analyses, down to a deep level of the various breakdown structures.

Work Breakdown Structures (WBS) is a protocol that facilitates the building of a hierarchical structure of the work. The project is broken down into several levels, as in an organization chart. This allows data analysis and reporting at any level of detail. WBS is an essential component of an Earned Value analysis system.

Earned Value analysis (EVA) is the term used to describe project performance analysis. In using the EVA protocol, the *Cost Variance (CV)* can be determined for any segment of the project. The CV is based on "what did it cost to do the work that was accomplished." In the absence of EVA, accountants often produce a CV that expresses actual costs vs. planned cost. This means nothing, as the planned cost may not be anywhere equal to what has been accomplished to date. Also, EVA data can be used effectively for progress billing. Performance measurement, measuring the value of work accomplishment, and EVA are covered in detail in Section 8.

Costing Areas

Something that I used to hear about a lot (but less so, recently) is *cost engineering*. There are a lot of practices that are associated with cost engineering that are not within the purview of this text. Still, there is an abundance of things that can impact upon the cost of doing the defined work. Part of the function of cost management is to identify and evaluate all the options that can bring costs down or (the downside) blow up your budget. Here are just a few.

- Risk and cost—We try to get off to a fast start. Sometimes it's too fast. The design criteria are not set. Or the sponsor isn't sure what he wanted. Or work on the task did not wait for the predecessor information. We may have to start over. Time is important, but it's not everything. These items could hurt in the pocketbook.
  Costs of doing it over.
  Costs of changing design in midstream.
  Trickle down effect on other parts of the job.
- Time and cost—Faster is sometimes cheaper. In Chapter 3.4, we discussed how period costs could be reduced by expediting the project. Later in this chapter, we discuss the potential cost efficiency of overtime.
  Reduce period-based costs by shortening duration (includes: cranes, safety barriers, foremen).
  Overtime hours may cost less than standard time (burden costs are already factored into base rates).
- Reuse and cost—What is the value of *invention* as compared to *efficiency*? Left in the hands of a designer, the objective is likely to be a new, fresh product that raises the bar in technology or service. Left in the hands of the cost manager, the focus might be on reusing as much "old stuff" as possible. This reduces time, cost, and risk, but might not deliver the best solution. These options need to be explored and evaluated and a balance made that comes closest to satisfying all stakeholders and objectives.
  Reuse code or boilerplate.
  Reduced risk.
  Reduced learning curve.
  On the other hand, older may be less efficient.

- Resource selection—When we estimate the costs for a task, we generally make an assumption of the resources that will work on the task. The budget is set based on that assumption and estimate. However, there may be several resource assignment options available to the team. Here's one example of how such options can impact upon the cost to perform the task.

    The Task: Commercial Communications Division—User's Guide for Advanced Messaging System.

    The Plan: 100 hrs over a 5-week period.

    The Budget: $2,500, based on $25/hr.

  - Option 1: Tom, on loan from Military Communications Systems.

      Uses extra time to learn CCD methods and style.

      Runs up 120 hrs.

      Cost is $3,000.

  - Option 2: Lou, operating under Parkinson's Law (Work expands so as to use all the time available for the work).

      Charges 180 hrs (5 wks @ 40 hrs, less 20 hrs on unapplied charges).

      Cost is $4,500.

  - Option 3: Jim, a new technical writer, requiring review of his work by a senior writer.

      Charges 100 hrs plus 10 hrs @ $35/hr for senior writer.

      Cost is $2,850

  - Option 4: Alice, "been there, done that."

      Is best for the task, but is overloaded.

      Gets assigned to task with approval to work overtime.

      Gets job done in 80 hrs, including 40 hrs OT @ $28.50.

      Cost is $1,000 (RT) + $1,140 (OT) = $2,140.

From the resource manager's view, nothing was actually saved because sooner or later, someone will have to pay the penalties for Tom, Lou, and Jim. But from the project manager's view, getting the overworked Alice assigned to the project saved the project money.

Trap We can see from this example that the cost objectives and the definition of cost success can be very different for project managers and functional managers. The project manager is interested in getting the resource on the job that can perform the work (up to standards) at the lowest cost. The functional managers' emphasis is on getting the maximum applied hours for their staff.

Tip There is a general misconception that overtime work costs more than regular time work. This is not necessarily accurate. For instance, if a person's regular billing rate were based on a wage cost of $15/hr plus overhead of $15/hr plus $3/hr profit, we would bill $33/hr for normal time. If that individual was paid a 50 percent premium for overtime, the billing rate would be $24.75/hr ($22.50/hr plus $2.25 profit). There is no need to include a charge for the overhead, which is covered by the charges for the first 40 hours per week.

In this example, OT for Alice was billed at a 10 percent premium. Although Alice gets a 25 percent premium in pay for OT, the overhead costs for OT are lower because most OH charges are already factored into the base (40 hr) rate. In a high OH environment, OT hours can actually cost less than regular hours.

A Detailed Look at the Phases of Cost Management

Earlier, we outlined the phases of cost management. Let's take a closer look at each of these.

Proposal or Pre-planning Phase   There are too many variations on how organizations go about dealing with proposals and opportunity management to be able to cover in this book. Much of this is dependent upon what kind of business you are in, whether your projects are internal or external, for profit or expense recovery, and so on. Yet this phase is perhaps the most important. It is very difficult to achieve widespread stakeholder satisfaction (project success) if the project proposal or preplan is flawed.

A proposal should not be a dream of what you would like to see happen. Projects that must take three years to complete can't be delivered in two years, just because the customer asked for it and the salesperson agreed to it. Projects that must cost $2 million can't be executed at a cost of $1 million, just because that was as high as the client would go. Yes, these reductions in time or cost can sometimes be made by reducing scope, increasing risk, reducing quality, or any combination of these. If such project restructuring is invoked, then it is important that these alterations be fully documented and the expected effect on time and cost be passed on to the project planning and budgeting phase.

Trap   Try this one on for size. The development team develops a proposal with an expected cost of $2,000,000. With profit, the project should be priced at $2,300,000. However, the sales group sells a project at a reduced price of $1,900,000. Senior management now expects the project team to hold costs to $1,650,000 (to retain the expected 15% margin). The project team prepares a plan, with a budget of $1,950,000 (already attempting to squeeze a few bucks out of the budget—recognizing that the job was sold at too low a price). With a high awareness of the pressures on costs, the project team delivers at a total cost of $1,875,000. This is 6¼ percent below the original estimate and almost 4 percent below the already reduced budget. Yet, it is 13½ percent above the management target (based on the sales price). Should the project team be commended for their excellent cost performance (I think so) or should they be criticized for missing the (artificial) target? If you want to have a valid budget for performance analysis, that budget should be tied to the full identified workscope, rather than an artificial, sales price basis.

Spending Authorization   Time or expenses should not be charged to a project until such charges are authorized. A good vehicle for this authorization is the *project charter*. The authorization document should specify who can charge and to what accounts the charges can go. Spending authorizations may be granted by phases. The project team should establish *phase gates*, which are used to evaluate project progress before proceeding to the next major phase.

The Project Cost Plan (or Budget)   We allocate project costs to elements of the plan. If we can, we allocate costs taken from the estimate data. All too often, however, the cost estimate structure and the plan structure do not match, making it difficult or even impossible to use the estimate data. An alternate method is to build a new cost estimate using the CPM plan and letting the system calculate the budget based on resources and other expenses that have been assigned to the tasks. If this method is used, it is a good idea to then reconcile the CPM-generated budgets with the original estimates.

Tip It is a good idea to try to use a common WBS for estimating and developing the schedule. However, this is not always practical, because estimating is often based on common quantities, involving several individual tasks. Try to compromise by having at least one or two common levels in the WBS and the estimating structure, before branching out as needed to facilitate each function.

Once the CPM budget has been developed and approved, it should be set as a baseline. The *baseline* is a snapshot of the approved budget before changes and actuals are processed. The baseline is used for measuring status and performance.

Collection of Actual Cost Data Actual cost data may come from multiple sources. Labor-based costs are usually derived from time sheet inputs and the library of billing rates. Other expenses will come from invoices. There are several issues that need to be addressed when one is setting up the cost collection system. These include:

- Who has authorization to process charges against the project?
- Have you set up all the cost buckets (accounting-based charge numbers)?
- Have you synchronized the timing of the cost status with the timing of the task status? This is needed to have a valid analysis of costs vs. accomplishment (see EVA in Section 8).
- Is there a procedure to review and accept charges?

Trap Invoices rarely have information on them that detail which tasks to apply the costs. For purchasing and CPM integration, the buyer should note the reference task IDs on the purchase order. POs are often issued for items that involve more than one task. In such cases, the buyer must allocate the costs to the tasks (by percentage or actual values).

Billing and Chargebacks If you have set up a robust system for the collection of actual costs, as described above, you will have the capability to create automated billing and chargeback documentation. You will have an audit trail of the charges and costs that are being passed on to the client.

Tip If your contract calls for progress payments, you should tie the billing into the measured accomplishments, rather than the actual costs. See EVA in Section 8.

Cost Performance Analysis   This is the place to employ EVA and ABC capabilities. In order to do this, you must have set up a structured set of cost buckets (to hold the appropriate costs) and have established a budget (so that there is something to which to compare actuals). The budgets will be maintained in the baseline plan. Forecasting also takes place at this time. Based on the performance analysis, there should be forecasts of when the project will be completed and how much it will cost to complete.

Remedial Actions   Most projects are very dynamic in nature. The workscope changes. The plans change. Things go wrong. Priorities change. Forecasting will precipitate remedial action. The project team will continually be making changes, many of which will impact upon the project costs. Without a structured set of practices for the management of change, things can get out of hand in a hurry, destroying the ability to monitor progress meaningfully, to bill accurately, and to measure performance. We discuss change control and scope management in Chapter 7.1.

Replanning   When changes are made and the project plan is adjusted for such changes, it may be advisable to create a revised baseline (snapshot of the new budgets). Whether or not to do this is a factor of whether the replanning is part of a negotiated restructuring of the project or just the result of poor progress on the original plan. If the latter is the case, the baseline should be left unchanged.

End of Project Analysis and Recommendations   What is that well-known saying "Those that fail to learn from their mistakes will have to re-live them"? This is what we do time and time again when we fail to carry out the cost management to the logical end of the project. Cost management does not end with the collection of data. It needs to be continued through a final analysis of the costs and through to a set of recommendations. The analysis will document what went wrong (or right) and why. The recommendations will be your legacy to the following generations of project managers—so that they can learn from your mistakes.

Trap   There is a consensus that about half of the value of planning and control comes from developing the plan. The remaining half is divided between maintaining/progressing the plan and the final analysis and recommendations. When we terminate the cost management process at the end of the project (or a bit before the end) and we do not prepare a final analysis and recommendations, we are throwing away at least a quarter of the total value of the planning and control efforts.

CHAPTER 5.2

SOFTWARE SUPPORT FOR COST MANAGEMENT

We noted in the introduction to this section that software support for project budgeting and cost control is usually weaker than support for the other project management functions. This is deliberate. One reason is that each firm has its own, very specific, way of handling things that fall under the domain of Finance. Another reason is that this domain of Finance is usually somewhat isolated from the other functions. While I understand the reasoning behind this thinking, I feel that it doesn't have to be that way.

Here's just one example of the problems with isolating the cost elements of the projects from the other parts. This is a true story. A major power systems manufacturer was involved in several large turnkey projects. On the 4th floor of an administration building, a team of 40 people was involved in implementing project control, using a respected CPM product, in a minicomputer environment. They were issuing monthly reports on a project, noting that the progress was not keeping up with the plan.

On the 6th floor, the Finance Group was accumulating costs on the project. These costs were compared to the budget and cash flow plan. About halfway through this project, they noted that, financially, things were in good shape. Their data indicated that the cash flow plan called for the project to be about 50 percent expended, and that they had charged only 45 percent of the costs, thus far.

Boy, were they ever wrong! If the financial data had been coordinated with the progress data, it would have been noted that only 40 percent of the planned work had been accomplished. Not only was the project behind schedule (40% vs. 50%) but they had spent 45 percent of the budget to accomplish only 40 percent of the work. The finance report, of good cost results on this project, was misleading and wrong.

This example is used later in the book (see Section 8) to build a case for using earned value analysis techniques. But it's also important to note it here, in defense of integrating the cost function with the other project management elements. There is no justification for isolating the financial data. It is okay to utilize different tools to support these functions, and it is even okay to have different parts of the organization responsible for each part. But they have to be connected.

Options for Cost/Schedule Integration

It is debatable whether it is better to have all of the costing and scheduling functions supported by a single program, or located in two or more specialized tools. There are advantages and disadvantages to both and there is no clear winner.

The case for the single, integrated solution is headed by the ability to have just one set of data, in one location. Anytime that you have multiple programs with multiple databases, you are prone to several problems. One is that the data in the two locations may have differences. We have better things to do than to spend our time explaining to senior management, or the client, why a screen that they are looking at says that $100,000 has been spent, and our screen shows $94,000.

Another problem is the timing of the data. It could well be that the database with the $100,000 expense has a data date of 5/1 while the lower cost was as of 4/15. As soon as you have more than one database, you always have to wonder which one is the latest and most valid. Furthermore, the 5/1 database may very well be entirely valid, but the 4/15 database is the one that is synchronized with the scheduling data. Such synchronization is essential for performance measurement operations, such as earned value analysis.

Also, in favor of the single product approach is the ability to enter data just once. With two separate systems, the possibility of data errors is doubled. And one more thing: With a single system, you are always certain of a data match between the cost data and the schedule data. There will be a one-to-one relationship of all elements.

So it would appear that the single product approach is the way to go. But let's hear the arguments for the other options, first. The biggest argument is that any costing functions that are built into a traditional CPM program are likely to be weaker than those in a specialized financial management program. The latter is likely to have support for all types of overtime and overhead (burdens). It will allow for multiple billing and cost rates. It may support multiple currencies. It will have extensive capacity for various code of accounts structures.

Then there is the ownership of the systems and data. The two systems will be owned and maintained by two different groups, with the probability of two different sets of standards, practices, and cultures. Just recently the projects organizations and the operations organizations are learning to work together. Finance operations have traditionally been isolated from the rest of the firm. This has been by design, to prevent contamination from the other disciplines. Now, we are trying to reverse this age-old tradition by getting the finance people and the projects people on the same playing field.

There is a third option. This is a full integration of two systems, which share a common set of data. One system is optimized for project planning and control—usually a traditional CPM system. The second system is optimized for financial management. A bridging program facilitates the collection of data for both systems and the transfer of information between the three modules.

Such solutions became available in the late 1990s, as the popular ERP vendors, such as Oracle, PeopleSoft, SAP, Baan, and J.D. Edwards created Projects modules, designed to integrate their financial management modules with many CPM programs. The potential for these to be an ideal solution has been there, but the jury is still out on how successful the early implementations have been. The upside is that these systems should be able to support all the specialized needs of the financial and operations community, as well as the projects community, while avoiding duplicity of data. The downside is complexity, cost, and the time to implement such solutions. We discuss this area of PM/ERP integration in Section 10.

Recommendations

Your choice of the available options should be based on what your needs are. The simplest solution is a robust CPM program with strong costing capabilities. This option will work only if you do not have specialized financial management needs that are integrated with projects, or if the financial management systems do not have to address projects data.

If you need exceptionally strong costing functions, but still would prefer to work with a single program, look into one of the CPM-type products that emphasize cost management.

If total integration of schedule and cost functions is needed, and the cost side of the integrated system must be a full-featured cost management system, then you will need to look into the PM/ERP type solution with a projects module to facilitate the integration. Again, be aware that this is a very big commitment, of both cost and effort.

I can't recommend that two separate (nonintegrated) tools (CPM and financial) be employed to deal with project costs. This is asking for trouble.

SECTION 6

RISK MANAGEMENT AND CONTINGENCY

Did I just say that Cost was the weakest link (Section 5)? I take that back. It is *Risk Management* that seems to get the least attention. Why is risk management virtually ignored as an integral part of the project selection and management process? We all recognize that risk is an important part of all projects. If we thought about it, we would all acknowledge that the management of risk could be the most critical factor in project success. Yet as I look at the practices that have been put in place in most firms, and at the tools that are being used to support these practices, risk analysis and management are most often missing.

"Risk Is a Four-letter Word (But Denial Is Our Biggest Enemy)"

This was the name of an article that I wrote in 1999. I was shocked by how often otherwise intelligent professionals could ignore the potential downside of a proposed project or business venture. This was usually because they didn't want to admit that a potential downside existed or they were afraid that, if they acknowledged the potential risk, the proposed project would not be granted approval. You cannot make risk go away just because you don't like bad news. Risk must be evaluated, and, where the risks can significantly damage the project, there should be risk mitigation plans in place.

The Many Colors of Risk

There are many sources of risk and they can take many shapes. We just need to look at some of the more well-known catastrophes to see the breadth of this thing that we collectively call *risk*.

- **The *Titanic*—**There was such a low chance of risk, from sinking, that the possibility was entirely discounted and ignored—with a devastating outcome. Lesson: Even a very low risk can produce gross consequences.
- **Denver International Airport—**Did anyone think about the effect on time and cost from the failure of the automated baggage handling system? Is it possible that the team just assumed that this entirely new technology would be absent of risk just because the small-scale mockup worked? Lesson: Don't put all of your eggs in one basket. There should have been a backup strategy.
- **The Standish Chaos Report—**This 1998 study of information technology projects indicated that these projects averaged a 50 percent schedule delay and a 186 percent cost overrun. Imagine the effect of this on cash flow and profitability. And what about the effect on the time to recoup the investment (see Chapter 9.3)? Can there be project success with this kind of performance? Lesson: A successful project requires realistic estimates, time and cost contingency, effective management, and comprehensive risk analysis and mitigation.
- **Where's Murphy?—**Why do so many people feel that they are exempt from Murphy's Law? Murphy visits every project. Lesson: It is folly to think that "what can go wrong will go wrong" does not apply to your project.
- **Elastic task durations—**We first raised this risk issue in Chapter 3.3. Sometimes, we are overly optimistic and fail to allow enough time margin for things to not go perfectly on each task. At the other extreme, we add time contingency for every imaginable delay, and then add a cushion to boot. The first action produces an impossible-to-meet schedule. The second action produces an overly long schedule and causes the schedule itself to produce project delays. Lesson: Schedules should be realistic. In many instances, using three time estimates, as in the PERT method, will produce more reasonable schedules plus an analysis of schedule risk.

Recognizing that risk, on projects, can take many shapes, here are just a few of the recognized approaches to dealing with project risk.

PERT Estimating Models

There is an ability to model risk with PERT estimates. This is the method where we use three time estimates for each task and employ Monte Carlo simulation to generate a statistical analysis of the probability to meet any project completion date. Despite my personal aversion to anything that has a sigma in it, there is significant value in using the PERT estimating protocol. But, there is also a serious limitation to this method. It only addresses uncertainty in *time*.

Risk Identification, Quantification, and Mitigation

Certainly, risk in projects goes well beyond time issues. There is the potential for technical risk and cost risk, as well. In addition to several software packages that support the PERT method for risk, there is also software to address all risk issues. This class of tools is used to identify risk areas, to quantify these risks (probability of occurrence and impact of occurrence), and to record risk mitigation plans. In my opinion, no project should move forward without applying this risk analysis method.

Contingency

We cannot talk about risk without talking about contingency. Contingency is one of the ways that we deal with risk. Contingency also can take many shapes. We can consider contingency for time, cost, resources, and workscope.

Contingency for time (schedule contingency) has gained increased attention from the Theory of Constraints concept that was advanced by Dr. Eliyahu Goldratt, in his book *Critical Chain*. We discuss this concept and the entire topic of shared contingency in Chapter 3.2.

Because contingency is an issue for schedules, resources, costs, and workscope, we have discussed this subject a bit in the sections devoted to those topics. However, if contingency is a way that we deal with risk, then we need to cover it here as well. In Chapter 6.1, we bring everything about contingency together and devote an entire chapter to the full span of project contingency concerns.

In addition to the formal methods for risk analysis and management, there are several things that we can do to address risk issues that are just based on common sense, and do not require any special tools (besides traditional CPM software). We cover this in Chapter 6.2, Risk Management for the Sigmaphobic, as part of our commitment to presenting practical project management.

But then, there are also some good special tools for risk analysis and management that deserve our attention. We discuss these analytical concepts and the supporting software in Chapter 6.3.

Risk is also an essential part of project portfolio management. So we'll save a little part of our attention to risk for a chapter on project selection and risk, in Section 9. If you are concerned with risk (which you should be) please don't miss this chapter in the Project Portfolio Management section.

CHAPTER 6.1

Using and Managing Contingency

Part 1—Schedule Contingency

A major aspect of managing projects is the balancing of objectives and constraints involving project time, resources, costs, and workscope. These are four key dimensions of any project and for each of these elements there is always the risk of missing defined targets.

More often than not, there are penalties involved in missing such targets. Some penalties may actually be spelled out in the contract. Others may be more subtle and ambiguous. Some targets may be imposed as a condition of the contract. Others may be implied by a sponsor as a set of objectives. In either case, there is a price to pay when the targets are missed. It may be an inexplicit penalty, such as a dissatisfied client. Or it may involve a significant fee reduction.

A missed schedule target could leave a client without key services, or lead you to miss a window of opportunity. The unavailability of key resources when needed could throw a schedule out of joint. Cost overruns or adverse cash flow can turn an otherwise successful project into a financial loss. Any of these could affect the workscope, resulting in a reduction in deliverables, or a reduction in quality.

A well-planned project addresses these issues. A well-planned and managed project will identify potential schedule, resource, cost, and workscope problems and will provide defined contingencies for each risk element.

Quantifying Contingency

As part of the risk analysis process, we identify risks, the probability of the risk, and the impact of the risk. As part of the risk mitigation plan, we identify actions that can be taken to avoid or minimize risks (or the deleterious effects of risks). We also identify alternatives and decision points (when to consider implementing the alternatives).

In many cases, rather than allowing for each individual risk, we gather risks into natural groups, for which we then provide for a collective contingency. These contingencies may involve time, resources, money, and even the scope of work. The amount of contingency will depend on the degree of risk and the penalties for missing targets.

Here are a few examples.

Building In a Reasonable Time Contingency

Those of us who use critical path scheduling to calculate a project end date may be lulled into thinking that the date that was generated by the computer is a valid project end date. But you must realize that a CPM schedule would normally represent the *most likely* duration of the project. That means, in essence, that the calculated end date is at the mid-point of the range of dates that could be realized. In this case, zero float (or zero slack) means a 50 percent chance of meeting the schedule. Is that good enough? Well, that depends on a couple of things.

The first one is: What is the penalty for missing that date? I can relate this to my philosophy for driving my car to various appointments. For a person who preaches the use of contingency, I am notorious for not allowing any contingency in my planning to get places. My subconscious reasoning, I guess, is that there usually are no deleterious consequences from my being a few minutes late to a doctor's appointment or a dinner engagement. In other words, there is an acceptable risk. On the other hand, if I am driving to the train station or airport, I do inject some contingency into my driving schedule. It is worth the time contingency to avoid the risk of missing a flight.

The message, therefore, is to evaluate the potential consequences of a schedule delay, and to factor in a contingency that is consistent with the degree of risk. Certainly, we would take greater schedule precautions in the case of a $10,000 per day penalty contract than we would in a contract without a delay clause.

But getting back to the 50 percent issue. The project completion date, that is supposedly a most likely calculation, is based on the workscope that has been defined to the system. If our model has not recognized several activities that might pop up later (a normal situation), doesn't the project completion date have even less than a 50 percent chance? How much time contingency should we allow for unidentified work?

The point is that we must allow a time cushion. How much of a cushion will depend on:

- The degree of acceptable risk or penalty for delays.
- How complete the definition of the workscope is.
- How well the work will be managed (if pressure is not kept on the schedule, slips of up to 50% can be expected).
- How active Murphy is on your job.

The easiest and safest way to build in a time contingency is to extend the project end date to a point where there is a comfortable amount of positive float. But this may not be practical for several reasons. It may not be cost effective. It may not be acceptable to your client. It may not fit with other programs associated with your project. However, it is not prudent to proceed with a zero float plan if meeting the end date is important. Therefore, if the end date can't be moved, then the work must be replanned to create a schedule with reasonable positive float (time contingency). Replanning, to gain schedule float, can involve one or more of the following:

- Selective overlapping of tasks.
- Increased resources or use of overtime.
- Reducing scope.
- Outsourcing.
- Alternative strategies.

As the available time cushion is reduced, the alternatives are to take preemptive actions to prevent high-risk incidents from occurring, and to increase efforts to identify all the work as early as possible.

Tip When the schedule contingency is too small to allow slippage, more effort must be spent on managing task interfaces. My experience has been that as much time can be lost between tasks as in the execution of the tasks themselves.

Advanced Time Contingency Methods

Most project managers seem to agree that the most common weakness of project schedules is the *task estimates*. We have trouble estimating the *duration* of tasks, as well as the *effort* required to execute the tasks. There are volumes of writings on the problems of task estimating, and there would be considerably more published on the subject, if anyone had any really good solutions for the problem of estimating.

There are two well-accepted (but competing) structured methods for dealing with the fallacy of task estimating and the tendency to inject schedule contingency into the task estimates. The older, well-established method is often called the PERT method. A newer approach is called the critical chain method. Both have a strong following and are effective ways of quantifying schedule contingency within a structured planning environment.

In both cases, we avoid fuzzy, undocumented schedule contingency and create a measurable and manageable basis for improved time estimating.

The PERT Method

This concept relies on three time estimates per task, rather than a single estimate. You won't find the three time estimate approach to be in great demand. After all, if we have such a terrible time arriving at a reasonable single time estimate, won't the PERT approach just give us a very precise error? This is certainly possible, and we have to evaluate the justification for this estimating mode on a case basis. On the other hand, it is often easier to provide three estimates for which the basis of the estimate is clear, than one estimate that considers multiple scenarios and blurs the basis for the calculation.

Given the softness in our base estimates, what do we gain from the triple estimate approach? First, we are more likely to gain precision in the time estimates. When we ask a performer to estimate the duration of the task, we often get a biased estimate. The performer may be overly optimistic, assuming that everything will go well (Murphy is on someone else's job). Or the performer may be afraid to make a commitment based on a best guess so he adds a little time as a safety factor. So just what does 10 days mean? Is it 10 days if everything goes well, but more likely to be 13 days? Or is it most likely to be 8 days, but we'll add a couple of days as a cushion?

With the PERT approach, we can ask for three distinct time estimates. An *optimistic* estimate is usually a duration that would be achievable about 10 percent of the time. Likewise the *pessimistic* estimate is usually a duration that would occur about 10 percent of the time. The third estimate is the *most likely*, which we are now able to obtain without deliberate bias. The traditional PERT formula, for calculating task durations, is A + 4B + C over 6, where A is the pessimistic, B is the most likely, and C is the optimistic.

Other advantages are: (1) we gain a range of task and project durations, (2) we can adjust weight factors (in some programs) to generate schedules with higher or lower confidence factors, and (3) we can evaluate the potential for achieving any selected project end date. We also expand the capability for performing what-if analyses. We can use this increased information about durations in our analyses of the schedule, whether performed by simple observation or via computerized probability analysis.

There is computer software available that supports the PERT approach. Many of these execute a statistical analysis of the resulting schedules, which will provide a confidence factor calculation for any projected end date. In my experience with such programs, I have frequently found that the original calculated end date had less than a 50 percent probability.

I don't necessarily recommend these programs for everyone, or every project. But when the basis for estimating task durations is weak, or meeting a schedule date is important, and especially when there are dire consequences from missing schedule deadlines, these programs will generate better estimates and an understanding of the potential (or improved confidence) for achieving the end dates.

The Critical Chain Method

This is a concept, documented by Eliyahu Goldratt, in his book *Critical Chain*. In it, he codifies the concept of shared contingency and extends the approach well beyond the simplified shared contingency that I (and others) had written about several years earlier.

Goldratt has popularized this approach and has also developed a loyal group of disciples, who extol the virtues of *critical chain*, shoot down any of its critics, and champion the cause of this new scheduling elixir. The concepts of critical chain deserve our attention. It makes absolute sense to move the inferred (but undefined) contingency out of individual tasks and to grouped, calculated contingency in a shared buffer.

In brief, Goldratt builds on the premise that project schedules are always too long, due to the safety factors that are added to the task estimates. He claims that estimates are usually based on a 90 percent confidence factor (rather than 50%). In addition task durations are also padded unless the performer is assured that everything needed to do the task will be ready at the start of the task (which is usually not the case). To this, we generally add a collection factor whenever a group of tasks come together, providing some margin in case one of the tasks slips. Similarly, a safety allowance is added by each level of management. Finally, on top of this, everyone knows that the total duration will not be accepted. They expect to be pushed for a 20 percent reduction, so they add 25 percent to the already inflated estimate.

The Shared Contingency Idea

Essentially, Goldratt's solution might be called *shared contingency* (my term), and is applied in several stages. First, he locates the critical path and reduces task durations to be consistent with a 50 percent probability rather than 90 percent. Half of the removed duration is added at the end of the path, as a *project buffer*.

Next, the feeder paths are located and treated in a similar manner, and half of the removed duration is added at the end of each feeder path, as a *feeder buffer*. The overall project schedule is reduced. Emphasis is placed on monitoring the project buffer and feeder buffers (for shrinkage), rather than managing the critical path.

The moving of the inflated portion of task estimates to a collective buffer has always been an option in traditional critical path programs, and does not require the abandoning of such programs just to adopt the shared contingency protocol. However, commercial products that support critical chain have extended functionality to address buffer analysis and additional critical chain features.

Trap   If you were to adopt the full critical chain philosophy and support programs, you would also have to adopt the full set of rules and processes associated with critical chain, and abandon many of the important features of traditional CPM, such as earned value and milestones. So be sure that you want to do this before changing over to CCPM.

Managing Schedule Contingency

Now that we have defined several ways to improve task estimating and to create schedule contingency, we have to provide for the management of such contingency. It would be wasteful to just move inflation values to a buffer and then assume that the buffer duration is up for grabs. In fact, that would have a reverse effect. Float, slack, or buffered contingency are not slop time. They must not be treated as extra time available to waste.

Schedule contingency should be reserved for changes to the plan, rather than to account for poor performance. Of course, in reality, there is no way to exclude the latter from eating into the contingency. However, the project team should not make the mistake of thinking that as long as there is contingency then it is okay to let things slip.

Every effort should be made to hold the team to the estimated and planned durations, allowing the contingency to be available for unplanned additions to task list and uncontrollable delays. Buffers and planned contingency tasks should be monitored and the project manager should maintain awareness of shrinking buffers and the cause.

Here are three things that you can be certain of:

1. If there is no schedule contingency, the project end date will be missed.
2. If schedule contingency is not managed, the schedule will slip and the project will be completed even later than if there were no contingency.
3. Murphy is working on your project.

Part 2—Cost Contingency

The use of contingency for schedules is quite common and practical. Similar practices are available for resources, costs, and workscope, but often receive even less attention. The following discussion addresses both cost contingency and scope creep.

The Concept of Management Reserve

There are two primary causes of cost overruns. The obvious one is that more money is spent for the defined work than was budgeted. The second cause is that work is added to the project without additional funding to cover the cost of the additional work. In any discussion of cost contingency, we must address the common incidence of scope creep, which we do below.

As we get into the subject of cost contingency, I introduce the concept of *management reserve*. This is a term that I use for cost contingency, because it better defines the methods that I employ to address the issues of cost and scope management.

Management reserve is a sum of money that is put into the project budget, but is set aside for work that has not been specifically defined and planned. Hold on to this thought for a moment as we explore the conditions that lead to the need to employ management reserve.

Avoiding Scope Creep

The project management literature is overflowing with horror stories on scope creep. In the Information Technology area, especially, we are often hit with a double whammy. The project workscope keeps escalating (often without providing additional funding or time) until the project runs out of time, money, or both—and then gets delivered with even less than the original planned content.

So there are several reasons to control the baseline and the project workscope. We need to have some means of containing the project workscope. This is not to say that additions to the workscope are necessarily bad and must be forbidden (I did have a client who felt that way). But rather, that we must *manage* the additions to scope, in order to control project costs. But, you've all heard this before. We all know that scope creep is something that we wish to avoid. However, our aversion to control seems to take precedence. We avoid the C word, at all costs, but then pay the costs, big time, for the lack of simple, but meaningful controls.

Some Simple Scope Management Methods

Let's look at a few examples for managing the workscope. This first example addresses issues associated with maintaining a valid baseline for Earned Value measurements. But the concepts are useful for managing cost contingency, even if EVA is not employed on your project.

We'll assume that the project has been planned, and that a list of work items has been defined to support the project charter. This workscope matches the contents of an approved contract or an approved work authorization, and spells out the work to be performed to meet the commitment.

In many cases, this list of work items will have time and effort data associated with it, such as schedule dates, effort hours, and costs. Following generally accepted project management practice, we freeze these data as a project baseline. We then proceed to execute the project, and track progress against the plan.

Separating Legitimate Changes from Performance Issues

Here's where the fun begins—and the project baseline gets infected with the black plague of the project world, the uncontrolled-scope virus. It doesn't take long for the plan to change. In the initial weeks upon implementation, we often find that (1) we have left things out of the plan, (2) we have to change the way that we will do the work, (3) some of the estimates for time, effort, and costs have been challenged, and (4) the project sponsor or client has requested additions to the scope.

All the above are typical situations that can affect the defined scope of work and the costs associated with that work. This is all in addition to performance issues, such as that it is taking longer to do the work and the estimated costs for materials did not hold up.

This first group consists of legitimate conditions that will affect the project budget. How do we contend with all of these changes and maintain control of the costs, as well as the workscope?

Managing Scope Creep

Here is a recommended procedure for both maintaining control over the workscope and maintaining a valid baseline for EVA.

1. Establish a standard practice for adding to the project workscope.
2. Provide forms, either printed or electronic, to facilitate the practice.
3. Identify roles, including who may originate a scope change and who may approve a scope change.
4. When a scope change is proposed, the work to be performed is to be fully defined, preferably as a list of work items (task, activities, whatever) with work breakdown structure IDs, schedule, effort, costs, as applicable to the current methods in place.
5. The source of funding is to be identified. Is the project budget being increased? Is it coming out of a contingency fund? Theoretically, work should not be added to the project database without an adjustment for the added costs.
6. Maintain a record of all scope changes.

By the way, scope changes can be negative. That is, they may involve a scope reduction. This is actually a legitimate means of balancing schedule, cost, quality, and scope requirements, wherein the scope is reduced to meet schedule, cost, and quality objectives. In the case of a scope reduction, the same procedure should be followed. The work items slated for removal should be deleted from the project baseline. Such changes should be fully documented and approved.

Note that this procedure may violate what is often presented as a project control axiom. We are often told that we create a project plan and freeze a baseline. Yet, in this proposed practice, we allow continual updating of this baseline. It is my belief that a project baseline is managed, rather than frozen. It should always reflect the plan values for all authorized work. However, the changes to the baseline must adhere to a rigid protocol.

A Simple Change Control Method, Employing Management Reserve

In Figure 6.1a, we illustrate a simple spreadsheet-based method for logging changes to project scope. We use this illustration, both for an example of providing an audit trail of such changes, and for registering any changes to the project baseline for EVA purposes.

In this example of a telephone system installation project, we see that it is a commercial, for-profit contract for an outside client. However, the basic approach can be applied to internally funded projects, with some modification. This example also supports my philosophy that divides the contract into three cost segments. Segment One, the Task Budget, includes all the work that has been specifically identified and planned. This Task Budget is the original Baseline for the EVA. If we were employing a traditional CPM system for planning and control, its content would consist of all the work items included in the Task Budget, including schedule, effort, and cost baselines.

Figure 6.1a   Change Control: Summary and Log

	BASE	Chg #1	Chg #2	Chg #3	Chg #4	Chg #5
Task Budget		$3000	$2000	$4000	$3000	-$2000
	$100000	$103000	$105000	$109000	$112000	$110000
Mgmt Reserve		-$3000	-$2000	$0	-$1500	$0
	$15000	$12000	$10000	$10000	$8500	$8500
Margin		$0	$0	$600	$0	$0
	$15000	$15000	$15000	$15600	$15600	$15600
Contract Total				$4600	$1500	-$2000
	$130000	$130000	$130000	$134600	$136100	$134100
Effect on Schedule	15-Jun-92	15-Jun-92	25-June-92	15-Jul-92	15-Jul-92	15-Jul-92

Explanation of Changes

Change #1   Forgot L.P. Materials – Add $3000 – Take from MR
Change #2   Conduit stuffed – Need extra – Add $2000 – Take from MR
Change #3   Add 20 phones and new IDF – Add to contract: $4000 + 15%
Change #4   Existing trunk line inadequate – Split $3000 cost
Change #5   Delete data lines from bldg A – Deduct $2000 from contract

Wouldn't it be grand if we were so wise as to be able to identify every work item at the onset of the project and even enjoy the benefit of foreseeing the future to pre-identify all potential problems? However, we have learned from experience that such is not the case. We somehow manage to omit some items from the original plan. And, sooner or later, a few unplanned problems will pop up. So we learn to allow a contingency for these situations. Segment Two, therefore, is what I call Management Reserve. It is a contingency amount (in this case 15%) that has been set aside (based on experience) for items that we expect to add to the project workscope, but have not yet been defined (because we don't know what they will be).

It is called Management Reserve because it is a fund that is to be managed, rather than a bucket of dollars available to any passerby. Funds are moved from Management Reserve to Task Budget only when a specific cause is noted and the resulting work is planned. Funds so moved to the Task Budget become part of the revised EVA baseline.

Segment Three is the Project Margin or profit. It is the Contract Price, less the Task Budget and the Management Reserve. At the conclusion of the project, unused Management Reserve, if any, becomes part of the profit. By the same rule, an overrun of either the Task Budget or the Management Reserve will eat into the profit.

Figure 6.1a shows the base dollars and schedule, plus an audit trail of five approved changes. Where the changes were not chargeable to the account of the client (and were not due to performance issues), dollars were moved from the Management Reserve to the Task Budget. In each of these (Changes #1 & #2) additional work was defined and added to the project plan, and to the EVA baseline.

In Change #3, the additions were chargeable to the client, and in Change #4 the extra work was split with the client. The source of funding is immaterial to the Task Budgeting process. In each case, the extra work is defined and added to the baseline.

In Change #5, we have a deletion from the workscope. The effect on the Task Budget is similar. Only this time, we identify work to be removed, and the Task Budget and EVA baseline are reduced.

Controlling Costs Using Management Reserve

Let's examine what we have gained from employing this simple, spreadsheet-based, change control system.

- We have an audit trail of all changes.
- We maintain control over the Management Reserve fund, as well as the makeup of the contract dollars.

- We have a negotiated and accepted change in the project completion date (chg. 2 & 3).
- We have a valid basis for calculating schedule and cost variances for EVA (if employed).

In the example, above, three of the changes involved increased costs to the project, which were not funded by the client. Where did the money come from? It came from the Management Reserve.

Note that the spreadsheet only shows changes to the project budget due to approved changes (both funded and unfunded). It shows that there is now an approved project budget of $110,000. The spreadsheet does not display any of the actual project expenditures.

But when we get down to analyzing the project cost performance, we will have a revised (and proper) budget figure to compare to the actual costs.

Imagine if we did not have such a change control system. What do we use as the project BAC (Budget at Completion)? Is it $100,000 or $115,000? Which is fairer? To answer this, we continue to look at this example, assuming that the project gets completed at an actual cost of $108,000.

If we use the lower budget figure ($100,000), and the project comes in at $108,000, then we are apt to report that the project had overrun the budget. Yet $10,000 of work had been added to the project. Would it be fair to penalize the project team for the overrun, when it really wasn't such?

If we use the higher budget figure, which includes the Management Reserve ($115,000), then we give the team credit for cost performance that was not due to actual project performance but rather to unused contingency.

With our change control log and management system, we know just what the actual cost performance was. The project team spent $108,000 to do $110,000 of work. A valid basis for performance measurements was retained. It can be fairly reported that the team brought the project in under budget—by $2,000.

Managing Cost Contingency

The same concluding comments that I wrote for schedule contingency would apply to cost contingency.

It would be wasteful to build in a cost contingency and then assume that the extra funding is up for grabs. Cost contingency should be reserved for scope changes to the plan, rather than to account for poor performance. It is a reserve for unforeseen extras, which are not funded by the client.

Here, again, are the three things that you can be certain of:

1. If there is no cost contingency, the project budget will be overrun.
2. If cost contingency is not managed, the funds will be used up and the project will cost even more than if there were no cost contingency.
3. Murphy is still working on your project.

Part 3—Resource and Scope Contingency

In the previous parts of this chapter, we devoted most of the discussion to the use and management of schedule contingency and cost contingency. In this concluding segment, we will cover resource and scope contingency.

Resource Contingency

The use of contingency for schedule and cost is essential for establishing attainable and manageable schedule and cost targets. There may be times when contingency should be applied to resources and workscope, as well. However, you will not come across much discussion of these two items. We touch on them briefly here.

As noted previously, it has been my experience that attention to resource contingency is rare. For some reason, project managers, even those who have allowed for contingency in their schedules and budgets, do not see the need for similar practices when it comes to planning and managing resource loads. In fact, we often see the opposite. Resources are assigned to work using an overload model. That is, the resources are assumed to be available at a level that is a bit greater than full time.

I can understand the rationale for such a seemingly irrational approach. First of all, many of the automatic resource leveling processes look for periods of time when the assigned resources can be applied to a task without interruption. Therefore, they tend to leave gaps showing periods of unassigned resources when there is work waiting for those resources.

Perhaps another consideration is that resources are more flexible than time or budgets. The logic is that we can always squeeze a little extra out of a resource if the pressure is on.

Perhaps the real reason is that nobody trusts the schedules. Why plan well out into the future, lining up resources for the scheduled work, if when the time comes, the schedule has changed, or the tasks have changed, or perhaps even the project has been shelved? Of course, better schedules will help. But the nature of most projects is that there is a high level of uncertainty. We must consider schedule flexibility as a matter of course and be prepared to be flexible with resources as well.

So can we apply contingency methods to resources? I think not in the way that we use contingency for schedules and budgets. But here are a few things that we can do.

- Improve effort estimates.
- Apply the PERT concept to effort estimates. That is, use three estimates: optimistic, pessimistic, and most likely. This will provide a range of effort, which will illustrate the risk of exceeding the most likely figures.

> **Trap** Unfortunately, no computer program yet exists that considers three *effort* estimates and provides a statistical analysis of the values.

- Avoid deliberate overloads. Assume that resources will be available less than every hour of the day (which is certainly realistic).
- Plan the immediate future in detail (for resource loading), but use long-range schedules only to get an idea of the resource load factors (rather than being concerned with which resource is working on which task six months into the future).
- For long-range resource planning, concentrate on the class of resource (skills) rather than specific people.
- Where the long-range projection indicates a potential overload situation, make early (flexible) plans for bringing in additional resources. Identify options and sources.
- Where possible, identify alternative resources (skills) that can be used if the preferred resource is in short supply.

In essence, contingency planning is a form of risk management. We identify areas that might impact on our meeting of objectives and take actions to mitigate any deleterious effect.

> **Tip** Whether you need to allow some resource contingency will depend in part on the density of the forecast resource usage. If the resource usage histogram for the accepted baseline plan shows resource loadings at or above the planned resource availability, for most of the schedule periods, then

some resource contingency allowance is in order. However, if the resource usage histogram shows a mix of peaks and valleys, especially well out into the future, it may be okay to wait until you are closer to the period in question before making firm contingency plans.

Workscope Contingency

We note at the start of this chapter on contingency that project management involves the balancing of schedule, resource, cost, and workscope objectives. If this is so, it means that the project workscope may be considered to be negotiable. Usually, at the outset of a project, we assume that the workscope is set in concrete. In order to maintain the contract workscope, we may adjust (usually overrun) schedules, resource effort, and costs. We may, in order to maintain the other objectives, even compromise quality or reliability.

However, in reality, the workscope may not be totally fixed. In fact, studies have shown that most development type projects are delivered with less than the contracted scope. If time or cost ceilings are fairly rigid, then it may have to be the workscope that gives way.

Tip *A Corollary to Parkinson's Law*   C. Northcote Parkinson noted that "work expands so as to fill the time available for that work." In some projects, we can state that in reverse. That is, the workscope is reduced by the limits in time and money available to do that work. In some cases, we reduce the content or functionality of what is delivered. We may even eliminate an item in its entirety.

Perhaps, as part of a full-featured project plan, it is prudent to identify, up front, those parts of the workscope that could be modified, reduced, eliminated, or delayed until a later phase. This would be part of the deliverables risk evaluation. Then, as the project moves along, the project team would periodically evaluate the workscope, along with the schedule and costs. This is part of that balancing of schedule, resources, costs, workscope, and quality—an essential element of the project management process.

Again, this is not contingency management as we described for schedules and cost. But it does influence us to identify the more flexible parts of the contract workscope and to be proactive in evaluating options and alternatives. In this regard, it can be considered to be contingency management.

Tip The life cycle of a project consists of a series of closing doors. Early in the project, there are usually numerous alternatives for satisfying the project objectives. As we move along further in the project, constraints in time, cost, and technology tend to reduce the number of available options. As a basic part of project management, and specifically a component of contingency management, the prudent project manager identifies the critical decision points and notes the deadline for making such decisions. Evaluations of alternatives should be scheduled sometime prior to the closing of critical doors.

Some Closing Thoughts on Contingency

In this chapter, we have discussed the concepts of schedule contingency, cost contingency, resource contingency, and workscope contingency, and have provided some examples of practices that can be applied to these concepts. We justified the need for contingency planning and management based on the following realities of the typical project environment:

1. At the initiation of the project, we often don't know the details of the entire workscope.
2. At the initiation of the project, there is a good chance that we left something out of the defined workscope, by mistake.
3. The initial calculated project end date is usually too optimistic. We tend to bow to sales pressures or promise anything to get the job. Also, the calculated end date often does not consider project risks.
4. The initial project budget may not allow for escalation, accidental scope omissions, repeating failed elements of the job, and project delays.
5. The defined project workscope may have to be modified due to technical problems, schedule deadlines, or budget limitations.
6. Resources may not be available when needed, or in the right mix of skills.

Being flexible is not a sign of weak management. On the contrary, excessive rigidity could more easily be faulted. However, prudent flexibility should be part of a structured, proactive process.

Contingency, for time and cost, should be factored into the project at the start. The contingency values should be based on an evaluation of risks, completeness of the project definition, and other contract factors, such as delay penalties.

Contingency must be managed. Where an allowance has been made for time and budget, there should be an audit trail of the amounts that are moved from the contingency category to the project baseline.

Alternatives for critical content should be identified in advance, and project reviews should be scheduled prior to the deadline for exercising such options.

All of this is part of the risk management aspects of a project, with the immediate objective of balancing schedule, cost, resources, and workscope, and an end objective of maximizing client satisfaction and project success.

Contingency planning and contingency management are essential to project success.

CHAPTER 6.2

RISK MANAGEMENT FOR THE SIGMAPHOBIC
Managing Schedule, Cost, and Technical Risk and Contingency

L ots of things make me nervous, but none like the sight of a sigma, that weird, E-like gizmo that signifies the sum of a series of often obscure values.

I was reminded of this phobia when I browsed through a series of articles on Decision Analysis. I'm wondering if there are other people like myself, who prefer a more visual and pragmatic approach. I'm not knocking Monte Carlo, decision trees, and other probabilistic techniques. It's just that I'm not mathematically oriented, and can't get comfortable with this stuff. I can't even pronounce Taguchi, let alone understand Taguchi methods. Can we take something called Fuzzy Logic seriously?

I wholeheartedly support the premise, presented periodically, that CPM, and its various network modeling techniques, cannot be relied upon as a sole determination of a project schedule, or the basis for schedule-driven resource and cost planning. Certainly, we must recognize that we can rarely capture, in such a CPM model, all the conditions that can affect the project schedule.

Given the above, and the desire (necessity) to manage project risks, are there pragmatic means, other than these structured probabilistic techniques, that we can use to identify, quantify, and minimize risk? The answer, I believe, is a resounding YES! And these pragmatic means are available to anyone using today's typical project management software products.

Pragmatic Methods to Control Risk

Actually, there is not much material in this chapter, or the next, that is not discussed elsewhere in this book. We present concepts such as accomplishment value (a variation on Earned Value analysis), PERT durations, schedule contingency, cost contingency, and (by popular demand) Monte Carlo schedule analysis techniques. We draw these techniques together here to present a set of common sense options for risk avoidance and risk management.

This chapter concentrates on low-tech, common sense methods to address potential risk issues, for time, cost, and technology. We then, in Chapter 6.3, submit to the demand of the more statistically oriented project managers, who argue in favor of proven Monte Carlo risk analysis techniques.

All techniques can be supported by readily available software that is inexpensive to acquire and simple to use.

Risk Avoidance

First, let's agree that it is better to avoid risk (via better planning, not avoidance of opportunity) than it is to manage risk (or problems arising out of insufficient planning and contingency). That is, risk control requires proactive management, rather than reactive management.

Trap Some people define avoidance of risk as avoidance of opportunity. That is, rather than taking calculated risks, they avoid anything that contains any risk. This, of course, reduces the number of options that are available to achieve stated objectives. In development projects, it often means that the product is weakened by excluding the latest technical advances. A safer, risk-free strategy can lead to an unsuccessful project just as much as a project with risk. When we talk about risk avoidance, we are talking about qualifying risk, not avoiding it.

Here are some of the major components of the risk management for sigmaphobics approach.

Employ Strategic Planning Techniques

- Identify objectives and constraints.
- Probe opportunities, threats, and issues.
- Perform stakeholder analysis.
- Gather project team early.
- Gather widespread inputs and gain stakeholder buy-in to strategies.

Remember Murphy's Law—Everything That Can Go Wrong, Will Go Wrong

Consider all undesirable risks—evaluate consequences.

- Identify reasonable defenses.
- How they can be avoided.
- How damage can be minimized.
- Compute allowances (time, resources, costs, quality) for the above.

Build In a Reasonable Time Contingency

Repeating what we say in the previous chapter, remember that a CPM schedule would normally represent the most likely duration of the project. That means, in essence, that the calculated end date is at the mid-point of the range of dates that could be achieved. In this case, zero float means a 50 percent chance of meeting schedule. Is that good enough? We will need to ask "what is the penalty for missing that date?"

The message, therefore, is to evaluate the potential consequences of a schedule delay, and to factor in a contingency that is consistent with the degree of risk. Certainly, we would take greater schedule precautions in the case of a $10,000 per day penalty contract than we would in a contract without a delay clause.

Remember, the project completion date, that is supposedly a most likely calculation, is based on the workscope that has been defined to the system. If our model has not recognized several activities that might pop up later (a normal situation), doesn't the project completion date have even less than a 50 percent chance? How much time contingency should we allow for unidentified work?

The point is that we must allow a time cushion. How much of a cushion will depend on:

- The degree of acceptable risk or penalty for delays.
- How complete the definition of the workscope is.
- How well the work will be managed (if pressure is not kept on the schedule, slips of up to 50% can be expected).
- How active Murphy is on your job.

The easiest and safest way to build in a time contingency is to extend the project end date to a point where there is a comfortable amount of positive float. But this may not be practical for several reasons. It may not be cost effective. It may not be acceptable to your client. It may not fit with other programs associated with your project. However, it cannot be acceptable to proceed with a zero float plan if meeting the end date is important. Therefore, if the end date can't be moved, then the work must be replanned to create a schedule with reasonable positive float (time contingency).

Replanning, to gain schedule float, can involve one or more of these.

- Selective overlapping of tasks.
- Increased resources or use of overtime.
- Reducing scope.
- Outsourcing.
- Alternative strategies.

As the available time cushion is reduced, the alternatives are to take preemptive actions to prevent high-risk incidents from occurring, and to increase efforts to identify all the work as early as possible.

Also, when the schedule contingency is too small to allow slippage, more effort must be spent on managing task interfaces. My experience has been that as much time can be lost between tasks as in the execution of the tasks themselves.

Use Accomplishment Value to Supplement Float Analysis

Accomplishment value, or earned value (a.k.a. Budgeted Cost of Work Performed) pertains to the measurement of accomplishment against the plan, once the work is underway. Normally, when we have a critical path schedule, we rely primarily on total float to see how we're doing. If we maintain the desired float, we assume that the schedule progress is satisfactory. This can be a false security. If you read the manuals on the use of the critical path method, you probably were told that CPM analysis helps you to focus on the work that is most critical. The problem is that we can be watching the critical items while the rest of the project gets less emphasis on maintaining schedule.

Trap Using CPM-based models and relying primarily on total float (slack) to have us focus on the critical work can actually lead to schedule slippage rather than preventing it. This problem occurs when we concentrate so much on the activities that lie on the critical path that much of the other work does not get done when planned. Eventually, all the work loses its float and there is no time margin left to deal with any problems that might crop up.

I monitor this by doing a periodic float analysis, to see if more and more tasks are joining the low-float group. The more tasks there are that have low float, the less room there is to manipulate the work to adjust for problems. This float analysis can be a very important early warning system.

But what if you do not have a critical path schedule, or do not feel comfortable with the float measurements? Are there other ways to measure progress and schedule risk? One alternative is to use Earned Value.

The EV method requires that we assign some kind of weight factor to each task. This can be resource hours, or budgeted cost. Or it can be an arbitrary estimate that allows us to balance the value of each task against the others.

The capability to use earned value measurements is available in most project management software products. But it is rarely utilized, for two primary reasons. First, it asks the user to learn several new terms and acronyms. How about BCWS, BCWP, ACWP, CPI, SPI, CV, SV, BAC, EAC, and other alphabet soup terms? Secondly, the use of this feature is usually associated with *cost* performance analysis, a function that is not universally utilized. But you need not be scared off by either the terminology or the costing aspects. It is quite easy and practical to employ just part of this earned value protocol, for measuring the *rate of work accomplishment* against the plan. Here's how.

Forget about the alphabet soup, except for these two terms: Budgeted Cost of Work Scheduled (BCWS) and Budgeted Cost of Work Performed (BCWP). *BCWS* is really the value of the work that was planned to be accomplished at any point in time, per the target or baseline schedule. *BCWP* is the budget for the work times the percent complete, at any point in time. In fact, why don't we rename these terms *planned accomplishment* and *earned value* (or accomplishment value, if you prefer). You may even find that your software uses these terms, instead of or in addition to the acronyms. You do not have to have a CPM to use this earned value technique. You do have to have a list of all the work to be performed (identified as tasks in your scheduling database), a schedule for the work, and some kind of weight factor for each task. If you are controlling only labor-based tasks, you can use the *planned labor hours* as the weight factor. If you are using mixed resource values, you will find that the *planned task cost* is the lowest common denominator, or weight factor.

To use the EV approach, identify your tasks, assign a cost (or other weight factor) to each task, and schedule all tasks (either manually or by CPM). The computer will calculate the BCWS or planned accomplishment for any point in time, by multiplying the planned percent complete of each task by the value (cost) of the task. If you are using a work breakdown structure (WBS), the computer will roll up the data to any level of detail. By summarizing to the highest level, you can get a weighted planned accomplishment curve for the entire project—essentially a cash flow or *project expenditure graph*.

Now, when it comes time to progress the schedule, just enter the percent complete of any tasks that have started. The system will multiply the percent complete by the budgeted cost, producing the earned value. This gives us a weighted measure of accomplishment, which can be compared to the planned accomplishment. If the earned value (BCWP) is less than the planned accomplishment (BCWS), work is not being accomplished as fast as planned, and you can say that the project is behind schedule.

Monitoring the earned value against the planned accomplishment (the Schedule Performance Index) provides an early trend analysis to guard against poor schedule performance. We can assume that if the overall production rate is below par, then the computed project end date is in jeopardy. This technique also works very well for monitoring the progress of subcontractors. I use a below par SPI to convince subcontractors to put on additional crews to get back on schedule.

Tip Use the Schedule Performance Index (SPI) to plot the rate of work accomplishment. The SPI is the earned value divided by the planned accomplishment (BCWP/BCWS). You are looking for an SPI of 1.0 or better. If you plot the SPI on a periodic basis, you can see if the rate of accomplishment is improving or faltering. A low SPI, which fails to improve with time, is a clear indication that meeting the schedule objective is in danger.

Build In a Managed Cost Contingency

Cost contingency, also called management reserve or *water*, is often frowned upon, because it is incorrectly used as a cushion for poor performance, rather than a managed reserve for unidentified work. A properly priced job (where the market will allow it) will have three cost components. These are (1) the work budget, (2) management reserve, and (3) margin.

The first item is the *budget for the identified work*. It is the sum of all task budgets in your CPM (or other plan). It does not contain any contingency costs.

Management reserve is funding put aside for unidentified work. In most projects, we are not so perfect as to clearly identify every work item to be performed. Just as we can surely expect incidents that add time to our project, we can expect to discover cost items that did not go into the original plan. By excluding this contingency from the task budget, the latter remains pure—for measurement of progress and performance. Only when new work is defined do we move funds from management reserve to the task budget.

A log should be maintained of scope changes, and their effect on the task budget, management reserve, and margin (and schedule). If new work is defined, which will not be paid for by the customer, then the cost of that work is moved from management reserve to the task budget. If new work is added by request of the customer, the tasks and their costs are added to the task budget, without touching the management reserve (I use an Excel spreadsheet to record all changes). Managing the contingency precludes any use of those funds unless the new tasks are defined and added to the CPM baseline.

If we put contingency directly into the task budgets, at the start, we have no way of managing these dollars, and they eventually are considered to be available for spending. If we have no contingency at all, we can almost be assured of overrunning the project budget. The answer is a managed contingency—the management reserve.

Managing Technical Risk

The avoidance and management of technical risk could warrant a whole additional chapter. Let it suffice, here, that technical risk must be addressed at least as much as schedule and cost. Needless to say, here too, we need to take a proactive approach. As we scope out our projects and develop our plans, we need to ask:

- What if it won't work?
- What alternatives and options do we have?
- What is our backup strategy?

I can't help but wonder if this approach was taken on the Denver International Airport project, and whether the problematic baggage handling situation would have caused such a disaster if it had been. Are we prone to believe in our own infallibility (the *Titanic* syndrome)? Whether schedule, cost, or technical design, we usually develop an appraisal that contains a most likely scenario, and a potential upside and a potential downside. Then we say that the downside will never happen. Such thinking is suicidal. Preparing for the downside allows us to manage these risks.

Not Very Scientific—But It Works

Time contingency, float management, earned value analysis, management reserve, and technical risk analysis are all very basic, nonscientific, practical means of managing and avoiding risk. All of these practices can be supported by commonly available tools, such as project management software and spreadsheets.

CHAPTER 6.3

Some Computer-based Approaches to Schedule Risk Analysis

In Chapter 6.2, we illustrate several nonstatistical approaches toward schedule and cost risk avoidance and management. These included practical, nonmathematical, common sense approaches, such as time contingency, earned value analysis, and management reserve (cost contingency). When I have written on this topic before, several of my colleagues, who are defenders of traditional statistical methods, wrote to challenge some of my claims. One distinguished expert in this area noted that my claim of a 50 percent probability for traditional CPM calculations was highly optimistic. This was fully borne out by my experiments with the risk analysis software. In fact, the CPM calculated finish, in one test model, was shown to have less than a 5 percent probability, when run through a popular PERT-based risk program.

Further support for risk management came from a consulting firm specializing in project control and risk management methodologies, for IS and high-tech manufacturing. They report continued success in helping firms to set realistic schedule and cost targets and then to meet those targets, using a homegrown methodology called Risk Averse Project Management Process. The process centers on improving estimates and "having the good common sense to create Managed Contingencies and Risk Reserves." This sounds just like what we talked about in the previous chapter.

There exists a volume of evidence in support of multiestimate, statistical-based computer analysis of risk. Therefore, ignoring my fear of the mighty sigma, we include discussion of these tools so that you will have a complete kit of methods with which to address risk. We continue now with a look at a few simple, computer-based methods of working with schedule risk.

The first three methods are based on what is often called the PERT method. This concept relies on three time estimates per task, rather than a single estimate. The latter two examples (both risk management programs) allow the user to either specify discrete values for each of the three estimates, or to apply a defined formula for the optimistic and pessimistic values. While calling this the PERT approach may not be technically correct, we will yield to this popular label for the various three time estimate methodologies.

The Three Time Estimate (PERT) Approach

You won't find the three time estimate approach to be in great demand. After all, if we have such a terrible time arriving at a reasonable single time estimate, won't the PERT approach just give us a very precise error? This is certainly possible, and we have to evaluate the justification for either estimating mode on a case basis. Let's look at some of the advantages and disadvantages of each mode.

First of all, project managers seem to agree that the most common weakness of project schedules is the *task estimates*. We have trouble estimating the *duration* of tasks, as well as the *effort* required to execute the tasks. There are volumes of writings on the problems of task estimating, and there would be considerably more published on the subject, if anyone had any really good solutions for the problem of estimating. Given the softness in our base estimates, what do we gain from the triple estimate approach?

First, we are more likely to gain precision in the time estimates. When we ask a performer to estimate the duration of the task, we often get a biased estimate. The performer may be overly optimistic, assuming that everything will go well (Murphy is on someone else's job). Or the performer may be afraid to make a commitment based on a best guess, so he adds a little time as a safety factor. So just what does 10 days mean? Is it 10 days if everything goes well, but more likely to be 13 days? Or is it most likely to be 8 days, but we'll add a couple of days as a cushion? With the PERT approach, we can ask for three distinct time estimates. An *optimistic* estimate is usually a duration that would be achievable about 10 percent of the time.° Likewise the *pessimistic* estimate is usually a duration that would occur

°Note: Early PERT practices used 1% and 5% probability for the extremes. Modern practice has left these values up to the user. Other options are to select a standard deviation formula and a distribution curve, rather than three distinct time extimates.

about 10 percent of the time. The third estimate is the *most likely*, which we are now able to obtain without deliberate bias. The traditional PERT formula, for calculating task durations, is $(A + 4B + C) / 6$, where A is the pessimistic, B is the most likely, and C is the optimistic (the most likely is given a weight of four times the optimistic and pessimistic). But there are other options, as we will soon see.

Other advantages are: (1) we gain a range of task and project durations, (2) we can adjust weight factors to generate schedules with higher or lower confidence factors, and (3) we can evaluate the potential for achieving any selected project end date. We also expand the capability for performing what-if analyses. We can use this increased information about durations in our analyses of the schedule, whether performed by simple observation or via computerized probability analysis.

It's time to look at our three computer-based approaches to duration analysis. In Chapter 6.2, we argue that traditional CPM schedules produce a project end date calculation that could have a 50 percent or less possibility of being met. These programs address this issue, in varying degrees of sophistication. They are easy to understand, even if you are sigmaphobic. But ease-of-learning and ease-of-use do increase with the level of sophistication. I don't necessarily recommend them for everyone or every project. But when meeting a schedule date is important, and especially when there are dire consequences for missing schedule deadlines, these three programs will generate better estimates and an understanding of the potential (or improved confidence) for achieving the end dates.

Using Project Scheduler 8

Example one features a general purpose CPM program that also offers support for the three time estimate (PERT) approach. Several products have a PERT capability, but we will look at Project Scheduler 8, from Scitor, because of some of its special PERT features.

In PS8, we can activate the PERT mode and add a PERT DUR column to the task table. We can enter the three time estimates, and (in a special PS8 feature) adjust the weighting factors. In Figure 6.3a, we can see that (using the traditional 1/4/1 weighting) the calculated project duration is 21.33 days (vs. the 20 days using the single estimates).

By adjusting the weight factors, we can calculate various degrees of optimism or confidence. Using a 1/0/0 weighting, we calculate the project using only the optimistic durations. In this case we can say that the best possible project end date is 10/16 or 16 days. By changing to a 0/0/1 weighting (all pessimistic) we can project a worst case of 11/1 or 32 days.

Another option is to deliberately add time contingency, by giving more weight to the pessimistic dates. In the model above, setting the weight factors to 1/4/5

Figure 6.3a   PERT Mode in Project Scheduler 8 (Scitor)

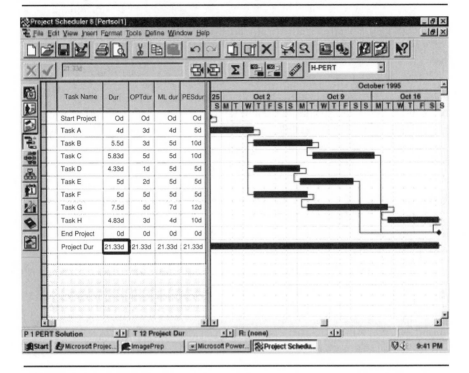

will generate a 25.6 day schedule. While PS8 has this unusual capability to select the weighting factors, it does not provide support for statistical analysis and probability of various end dates (normally expected in a PERT-type program). Our next two examples do.

Using Risk+ for Microsoft Project

When the PERT approach was first developed, in the late 1950s, it was customary to perform a statistical analysis (whoops, here come the sigmas) to calculate the confidence factor for each potential project completion date. Today, there are several add-on programs that work with popular PC-based CPM programs. We look at two of them here, starting with Risk+ for Project, from C/S Solutions Inc. Most of what Risk+ does is virtually transparent to the user, and no expertise in statistics is needed to operate the program or to understand the results.

Risk+ attaches itself to Microsoft Project, when installed. Then, when you boot up MS Project, the Risk+ functions are directly available from the Project Toolbar. A Risk Gantt View is automatically added to the View Menu. Users can enter their own (triple) estimates, or can have the system spread the optimistic and pessimistic values based on a set of user-defined preferences. Where Risk+ departs from the capabilities of PS8 is in the ability to compute the probability of meeting any schedule date. This program and Monte Carlo, our next example, do not try to average the three time estimates (as in the prior example) but rather make several passes through the network, using random selection of the (defined) possible task durations.

When we run the Risk Analysis routine in Risk+ (selecting 1,000 iterations), the results are similar to (actually slightly more conservative than) those with PS8, except that, with just a single analysis run, we obtain a complete set of dates and probabilities. In Figure 6.3b, we can see that there is less than a 10 percent chance to achieve the CPM completion date of 10/20. We have calculated a 50 percent probability of meeting 10/23, and a 90 percent probability of meeting 10/26. If we really wanted to play it safe (100% probability) we would not want to commit to anything earlier than 10/30.

A second capability, not handled by simple PERT solutions, is the problem of *merge bias*. It may not be readily apparent that the probability of a schedule being

Figure 6.3b   Risk Analysis Using Risk+ for Project

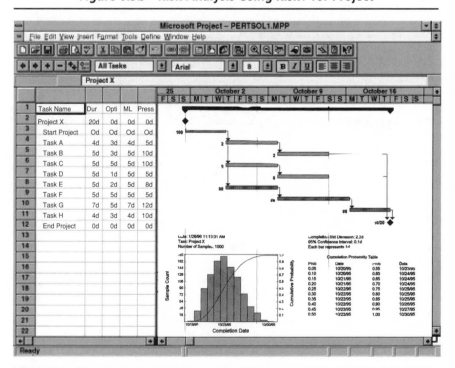

met will be adversely affected by the number of paths that converge at a single point. At least, this phenomenon is not taken into consideration in traditional CPM calculations. But merge bias will have considerable impact on project end date confidence.

For instance, in the example (Figure 6.3c), we extend the durations of tasks 5 and 7 so that there are three equal paths. Each of the tasks might have a 50 percent probability, and each path might have a 50 percent probability. But it just takes a delay in any of the tasks, in any of the paths, to delay the project end date. When we run the risk analysis on the model with the three equal paths, we find that the 50 percent probability date has moved out to 10/25, and the 100 percent date to 11/4. In fact, the risk analysis says that we have less than a 5 percent chance of meeting a 10/22 date, which is 2 days later than the simple CPM project calculation. Would you want to bet the store on 10/20?

Note, also, that our bar chart displays the degree of criticality of each path. A simple bar chart would indicate that all three paths are equally critical (because they all have zero float). The risk analysis bar chart indicates that the upper path

Figure 6.3c   Risk Analysis Showing Merge Bias

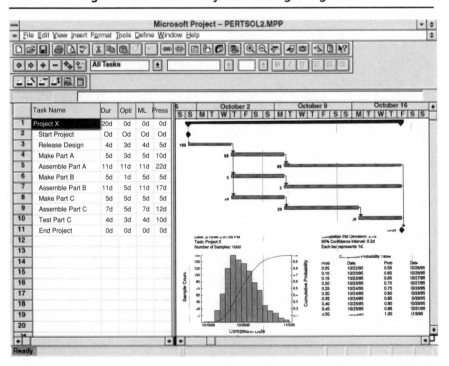

was critical for 68 percent of the iterations, and the lower path for 30 percent. (In our earlier illustration, Figure 6.3b, the lower path was shown to be critical 98 percent of the time. Yet, we didn't change the duration of that path or the project.) With risk analysis, we gain both greater sensitivity to the effect of converging paths, and additional information to direct our attention to the tasks that are at the greatest risk to extend the project.

Risk+ can also perform risk analysis for costs, as well as time. The discussion here is deliberately limited to schedule analysis.

Using Monte Carlo

Our second risk management software example is Monte Carlo, from Primavera Systems, Inc. Monte Carlo sits on top of Primavera Project Planner (P3). When Monte Carlo is loaded, it can be accessed from the P3 menu. You can use Monte Carlo on any project file that has been saved in the P3 format (from P3 for Windows, SureTrak for Windows, or P3 for DOS). As with Risk+, Monte Carlo can analyze both schedule and cost risk, and generate date and cost probability graphs. Where Monte Carlo goes beyond Risk+ is in its ability to handle probabilistic and conditional branching, and several other statistical functions. You can skip that part, if you're sigmaphobic. I had to read the manual several times before the process sank in. The basics are not really that complex. But many of the advanced features can be a challenge to the statistically disadvantaged.

Basic Risk Analysis in Monte Carlo

Basic schedule and cost risk analysis, in Monte Carlo, is similar to that in Risk+. Click on Monte Carlo and you get a chance to specify risk parameters and number of iterations. Initial results are shown in Primavera Look (an output reader). Monte Carlo employs ReportSmith (bundled with P3) for detailed reporting. Several predesigned reports are furnished.

Advanced Analysis in Monte Carlo

Up to now, we have looked at routines for analyzing schedules based on a fixed work flow. We defined potential variables for the time of each task. However, all tasks were assumed to be performed, and in the defined sequence.

A frequent planning concern is the scheduling of alternative strategies. Monte Carlo deals with this in two ways. The first is *probabilistic branching*. You would use probabilistic branching when you want to define the percentage likelihood that a specific activity will occur after another activity.

Conditional branching goes one step further, adding a condition that will determine which branch should be taken. You would use conditional branching when the choice of the successor task is tied to the status of a defined condition task.

Another feature of Monte Carlo, applicable to all modes, is the ability to define *probabilistic calendars*. Here, you can select dates that might not be available for work, and specify the probability of that unavailability. Monte Carlo also has a provision for defining three resource usage values (Opti/ML/Pess), extending the risk analysis into the resource usage and cost area.

While Monte Carlo offers several capabilities for advanced risk analysis, it raises the learning curve both for understanding the technology and for following a set of involved routines.

Working with probabilistic and conditional relationships might not be for everyone or every project. Yet, when there is significant sensitivity to missing dates and budgets (high risk), it's nice to know that there are simple, PC-based software products available to facilitate the analysis of such risks.

Other Products and Resources

The three products used here to describe three software-based methods of schedule risk analysis are not the only ones available to perform such tasks. Readers seeking information on such products might also consider *MS Project* (Microsoft), which can operate on PERT calculations, using macros and/or Excel. *SuperProject* (Computer Associates) provides actual probability analysis, based on three time estimates and standard deviation.

Palisade Corporation's @ *Risk for Project* supports probabilistic and conditional branching. Distribution functions can be applied to any numeric field.

Welcom Software Technology developed a risk analysis capability, first published as a program called *OPERA*. Now, the features of OPERA have been incorporated into Welcom's Open Plan Professional CPM software.

Risk Tracking Databases

There is yet another class of software that has been developed to aid in identifying and tracking project risk. These programs provide structured formats to facilitate the identification of risk items, and the quantification of these items. The quantification is based on defining the probability of the risk item and the impact of the potential risk. The key use of these programs is in making it easier to address risk issues, to record mitigation plans, to track the status of risk items, and to communicate all risk data to all team and management personnel.

As with the software previously discussed, some products in this category are standalone risk software and some are traditional CPM products that have incorporated risk support within the single product. Examples of the latter are two products from Primavera Systems, Inc., Team Play and P3e. PlanView just added risk and change management to their PM product. Risk Services & Technology offers a standalone product, called RiskTrak.

Wrap-up

Risk management requires a proactive culture. You cannot afford to wait until something bad happens, to first consider a response. It's usually too late to prevent serious damage by then. You must evaluate and anticipate possible failure and plan for alternatives in advance. You must evaluate the "windows of opportunity" for alternatives and check for satisfactory performance while there is still time to act (or while shifting strategies is still economically viable and within an acceptable time frame).

Earlier in this section, we discussed several nonstatistical approaches toward schedule and cost risk avoidance and management. Those, and the simple, program-based statistical methods, that we just discussed, will arm the project manager with important information needed to support this proactive activity. Obviously, it is not practical to consider every possible problem that could adversely affect your project. Risk analysis helps you to focus on those areas that have the highest sensitivity to things not going as planned. The prudent project manager will take advantage of methods and tools such as these, when schedule and cost risk is an issue.

Tip Risk mitigation is usually easier when the risk opportunities occur early in the project. As you move further into the project, there are fewer options, there is less time, and there is greater cost for alternative or corrective action. Risk avoidance and mitigation plans should attempt to trigger early detection of risk incidents and early corrective action.

SECTION 7

MAINTAINING THE PLAN

I have to start this section with a few stories. As odd as they may sound, these were actual experiences. As they say, truth can be stranger than fiction.

In the first instance, I was conducting a project management seminar for the engineering department of a major U.S. city. On day three, I was about to open my discussion on Change Control and Scope Management, when the city engineer stopped me and said, "You can skip this session, Harvey. We don't allow changes."

The second incident was reported in my local newspaper, just the other day. The executive director for the Center for Environmental Sciences and Technology, at Albany University, had just announced a major addition to the facility. Responding to speculation that the project was behind schedule and over budget, the director stated that these claims were unfounded, because these two items had not been established. "We never announced a date to start or a specified cost for the project," he said during an interview with reporters.

I suppose that a project manager's life would be much simpler if there were never any changes to the workscope, and if the schedule and cost never had to be cast in concrete. But, for most of us, that's not the way it works. The typical project has a defined workscope, and a target schedule and budget. Therefore, a basic component of managing the project consists of maintaining the plan, and managing changes to the plan.

Of all the areas of discussion on project management, it is Maintaining the Plan that allows for the most diversity, both in philosophy and in effort. If we were to poll the users, we might get responses such as these:

- We're too busy doing the work to bother maintaining the plan.
- The plan keeps changing. It is too difficult to maintain.
- In planning, we get 70 percent of the benefit from 30 percent of the effort.

In maintaining the plan, the reverse is true. We get 30 percent of the benefit from 70 percent of the effort.

- Plan maintenance is not necessary. We don't allow changes.

There are some legitimate issues here. Most managers agree that the greatest benefit to effort ratio is obtained in the planning stage. Frankly, if I had to choose between limiting the effort to just planning, or not being able to do it at all, I would certainly go with the limited planning. Otherwise, we may find ourselves moving swiftly ahead, but on the wrong path.

The first two items also reflect the typical project environment. We do experience conflict between addressing the project problems and incorporating changes and status into the plan. And plans do change and workscopes change. It is a natural part of projects, regardless of the few Neanderthals who refuse to see this. Dealing with scope and plan changes need not be that difficult or time consuming. See Chapter 7.1 for a practical approach to this function.

Trap Failure to maintain the plan or to incorporate changes and scope modifications will quickly negate the value of the plan. Perhaps we can think of the plan as a garden. Much effort goes into planning and planting the shrubs and flowers. But the failure to perform periodic treatment and trimming will quickly turn the garden into something even more unattractive than the original void.

Furthermore, as we discuss in Section 8, the failure to maintain the plan and a valid baseline makes it difficult to measure and manage project performance.

Maintaining status and incorporating changes is mostly very easy. The easiest part is statusing. On a periodic basis, we need only to note when tasks have started and when they were completed. For tasks in progress, it is customary to note the percent complete. There are several acceptable methods of doing this. A detailed discussion of accepted practices for expressing percent complete is presented in the next section, in Chapter 8.1.

The tricky part is making changes that affect the work flow, such as changing predecessors and successors. This often occurs when work is performed out of sequence. Making such changes is best left to the people who developed the original work flow and defined it to the CPM system. But you need to communicate these changes to them. Remember, there is no law that says that you cannot do work out of sequence just because the plan showed it that way. The plan is a statement of the team's intentions. In most cases, it reflects the preferred way to do the work, rather than the only way to do the work. In developing the CPM, the planner must choose a single alternative, although several options may exist.

Obviously, it is a good idea to communicate with the project manager or team leader when you are deviating from the published plan. But it is not practical to assume that the plan is cast in concrete.

There are two misconceptions regarding updating the plan that need to be exposed and critiqued. The first one is the implied advantages of real-time statusing. This popular capability, achievable today due to recent advances in real-time access to project databases, can actually be a disadvantage, especially when implemented without management oversight. We discuss these issues in Chapter 7.2.

The other misconception is something called *automatic updating*. Any thought of maintaining the plan by assuming that everything is occurring as planned, or that status changes do not need to be evaluated and managed, should be promptly challenged. We discuss why in Chapter 7.3.

Traps Caution is advised when you are using today's instant updating and access capabilities. Data needs to be evaluated and tested for validity before broadcasting it to the project universe.

Caution is also advised when you are using the automatic updating capabilities of today's tools. Allowing the program to assume that work was done as planned, without human involvement in the statusing, does not constitute plan management.

CHAPTER 7.1

CHANGE CONTROL AND SCOPE MANAGEMENT

Part 1—About EVA and Baselines

This chapter consists of a four-part series on practical applications of the earned value analysis (EVA) concept. EVA is a valuable, simple, and practical concept for use in maintaining a valid plan and measuring performance. We will focus on two of the most important functions associated with project performance management. These are Managing the Baseline and Controlling Scope Creep. You'll find that it is easier than it looks.

Introduction

Long before the structured, computer-based project planning systems (PERT and CPM) came on the scene in the late 1950s, project mangers struggled with the task of measuring work accomplishment. This measurement was needed for several reasons. One reason was the need to measure performance, which required a comparison of accomplishment against a plan. Another was to provide a basis for progress payments.

The performance data was needed so we could avoid surprises and make decisions. Without performance measurements (which depend on measuring accomplishment) we cannot determine how well a project is proceeding or forecast the end conditions. Therefore, a common occurrence would be to believe that a project was on time and within budget until the schedule and budget were exceeded. And even then, no one knew how extensive the overruns might be until the project was completed.

Where contracts involved progress payments, a similar situation existed. A plan of effort over time would be produced, which was used as a basis for periodic payments to the contractor. Without the measurement of what was actually accomplished, periodic payments were made to the contractor according to the planned effort. However, most projects run into some kind of problems that delay the work. Whether these be technical problems, weather delays, labor strikes, contract disputes, or design changes, the work is often accomplished at a lesser pace than in the plan. But if there is no formal measurement of the work accomplished, the contractor ends up getting paid according to the original plan (an overpayment) or gets into a dispute with the client.

Therefore, the need for formal methods of measuring work accomplishment was soundly established many decades ago, and such methods have helped to address these problems.

Earned Value Analysis and Performance Measurement Systems

With the advent of computer-based project management systems, the industry, spurred by such U.S. government agencies as the Department of Energy and Department of Defense, developed a formal approach toward the analysis of schedule and cost variance, which we commonly refer to as *Earned Value analysis*. This would include DOE's *Performance Measurement System* and DOD's *Cost/Schedule Control Systems Criteria*.

Many people, erroneously, assume that EVA systems are only for major government-type contracts, such as Aerospace and Defense. I strongly disagree. A key element of any EVA system is a method of measuring the work accomplishment. Such EV measurements are useful (I might rather say essential) for any kind of project, if the project manager is to maintain control of the project, make practical decisions based on knowing what is going on, and avoid surprises when the project is late and overexpended. This would apply to any size project as well as any type of project in any industry. It would also apply to internal projects as well as projects being performed for an external client.

Baselines and Scope Creep

One of the more challenging aspects of performance measurement systems (we'll use EVA for short) is maintaining a valid baseline. All EVA systems assume that there is a baseline plan (schedule and usually cost and effort), which is used to calculate variances. In theory, we talk about *freezing* the baseline, early in the project. But we all know that a *frozen baseline* is like the abominable snowman. It is a myth, and it melts under pressure.

So the issue becomes: What are valid changes to the baseline and how do we incorporate such changes into the database? There are some reasonable and practical approaches, which we share with you, here. There is also an auxiliary benefit from addressing baseline management. It also provides a basis for controlling the demon of all projects: *scope creep*.

A Basic EVA Concept

When we develop a project plan, we identify the work to be performed (activities and tasks), which we then schedule and budget. Once we have negotiated a feasible plan, one that balances the work objectives with schedule, resource, and cost considerations, we establish that plan as the *baseline*.

A basic premise of the earned value analysis protocol is that we establish such a project baseline and then evaluate progress against that target. The traditional EVA nomenclature uses this target, the Budget at Completion (BAC), as an essential component of the base formula. The planned effort to date, which we call the Budgeted Cost of Work Scheduled (BCWS), is calculated by multiplying the BAC by the planned percent complete.

Sounds complicated? It's really not. If you have identified a task and a cost (budget) for that task, then you have the BAC. If you have scheduled that task, then the system knows the planned percent complete at any point in time. When the system multiplies the budget by the planned %C, it has calculated the BCWS, which is the planned accomplishment at a specific point in time. Your software will do all of this for you. All that you have to do is read the results of the calculations.

Later, when you have entered the task progress, the system will use the actual %C to calculate the Budgeted Cost of Work Performed (BCWP). Schedule variances are then determined by comparing the work accomplished (BCWP) to the plan (BCWS).

Tip Got a language problem? Let's substitute some everyday terms for the EVA jargon:

BAC (Budget at Completion).   The budget.
BCWS (Budgeted Cost of   Planned accomplishment (at
   Work Scheduled).   any point in time).

BCWP (Budgeted Cost of Work Performed).	Earned value or accomplishment value (at any point in time).
ACWP (Actual Cost of Work Performed).	Actual cost to date.
SV (Schedule Variance).	Difference between planned accomplishment and EV.
CV (Cost Variance).	Difference between actual cost and EV.

So it is essential that a baseline be established and controlled. For the most part, this is a simple and straightforward process. However, there is the potential for complicating circumstances. For instance:

- What if the project workscope changes? Does it invalidate the EVA? What constitutes a legitimate baseline change?
- How do we manage the baseline for phased projects, wherein each phase defines the successor phases?

In this chapter, we discuss how to build a project baseline, followed by illustrations of pragmatic practices for managing the baseline and avoiding scope creep. We also address the challenges noted above.

Building the Project Baseline

Let's make this really simple. The project baseline is essentially a project plan. Even if you were not planning on measuring performance, you would still want to develop a basic plan for the project. Figure 1.1a (pg. 7) illustrates the basic activities and products associated with developing a project plan. These include:

- Identification of the work.
- Scheduling of the work.
- Assigning resources.
- Budgeting.

As we develop the plan, we balance objectives and constraints associated with the defined workscope, and schedule, resource, and cost issues. The result, a list of scheduled tasks, with resource assignments and cost estimates, becomes the project baseline plan.

The process is made much easier if we develop structures for the workscope and the schedule at the start. We use a Work Breakdown Structure (WBS) to organize the workscope. This is essential if we are going to use the baseline plan for EVA. For scheduling, it helps to develop a Project Milestone Schedule to identify time objectives and constraints and to guide the process.

It is possible to conduct performance measurement operations without having a project budget, but we assume that there is one for these illustrations.

Now, let's look further into managing the project baseline and avoiding scope creep.

Part 2—Managing the Baseline

(Note: Much of the material presented in Parts 2 and 3 of this chapter is also included in Part 2 of Chapter 6.1, where it is discussed as a solution for managing cost contingency. It is repeated here to maintain continuity and flow, during this discussion on change control and scope management. Contingency management and baseline management involve many of the same concerns and practices.)

Avoiding Scope Creep

It is difficult to read stories about projects without coming across references to scope creep. In the Information Technology area, especially, the stories tell of a double loss. The project workscope keeps escalating (often without providing additional funding or time) until the project runs out of time, money, or both—and then gets delivered with even less than the original planned content.

So there are several reasons to control the baseline and the project workscope. Even if we are not doing Earned Value analysis (EVA), we need to have some means of containing the project workscope. This is not to say that additions to the workscope are necessarily bad and must be forbidden. Rather, we must *manage* the additions to scope, both for controlling project costs and to maintain a valid baseline for earned value analysis. We all know that scope creep is something that we wish to avoid. Here are some easy ways to deal with the problem.

Some Simple Scope Management Methods

Let's look at a few examples for managing the workscope. This first example addresses issues associated with maintaining a valid baseline for EV measurements.

We assume that the project has been planned, and that a list of work items has been defined to support the project charter. This workscope matches the contents of an approved contract or an approved work authorization, and spells out the work to be performed to meet the commitment.

In many cases, this list of work items will have time and effort data associated with it, such as schedule dates, effort hours, and costs. Following generally accepted project management practice, we freeze these data as a project baseline. We then proceed to execute the project, and track progress against the plan.

Separating Legitimate Changes from Performance Issues

Here's where the fun begins—and the project baseline gets infected with the black plague of the project world, the uncontrolled-scope virus. It doesn't take long for the plan to change. In the initial weeks upon implementation, we often find that:

- We have left things out of the plan.
- We have to change the way that we will do the work.
- Some of the estimates for time, effort, and costs have been challenged.
- The project sponsor or client has requested additions to the scope.

To this, we add performance issues, such as that it is taking longer to do the work, and the estimated costs for materials did not hold up.

How do we contend with all of these perturbations and maintain a valid baseline for EVA? Let's take each of these situations and propose a practical response.

1. **We have left things out of the original plan.** This is to be expected and it is appropriate to adjust the baseline plan early in the project to incorporate the better thinking that is available as the project gets into gear. The project team should establish a reasonable cutoff date for modifications to the baseline, say within five percent of the planned project duration. Caution! Additions should be associated with the approved project scope. These are not scope additions, but rather additions to the list of work items that comprise the approved scope. This is why we try to design a contingency into the project budget (see earlier discussion on Managing Contingency).

2. **We have to change the way that we will do the work.** Ditto! We should also expect changes in project methodology as initial feedback comes in from the project participants. It is foolhardy to automatically resist changes just to preserve an early baseline, which may no longer be valid. Apply same rule as in (1), above.

3. **Some of the estimates for time, effort, and costs have been challenged.** Here, again, we can expect that we will learn more about the work to be performed and its associated timing and costs. We should leave some room, early in the project, to incorporate such changes. Again, apply same rule as in (1), above.

4. **The project sponsor or client has requested additions to the scope.** Additions to the workscope should require justification, planning, and approval. Such additions should be accompanied by an increase in funding or the contract price. Before these additions are placed into the baseline plan, the work items should be identified and the work should be scheduled and budgeted. An audit trail should be maintained, so that any workscope additions can be traced back to the originator and the funding source.

5. **The planned work is taking longer than expected and costs have exceeded estimates.** Now, here's where we draw the line. The very reason that we are employing EVA techniques is to be aware of schedule and cost overruns. If we were to tinker with the BAC or BCWS for work items just because things are not going as expected, we would destroy the basis for the measurement and lose our ability to evaluate schedule and cost variances. So the rule here is plain and simple. **We do not make changes to the baseline to accommodate poor performance. Rather, we maintain the baseline so that incidences of poor performance are disclosed.**

Maintaining a Valid EVA Baseline

Summarizing the preceding paragraphs, we can adopt this policy.

- A preliminary baseline will be established, containing the project work items and estimates for time, effort, and cost.
- Adjustment will be allowed to the above, early in the project, until the baseline is frozen.
- Additions to the baseline due to additions to project workscope shall be fully identified as to work items, schedule, effort, and cost and will be accepted to the project baseline only after such full definition and after valid authorization.
- No changes shall be made just because the work is not going according to plan.

Having established our baseline plan, we can now look at an example of a pragmatic way to manage scope creep.

Part 3—Managing Scope Creep

Managing Scope Creep

In the previous segment, we list four policies that should be established to maintain a valid baseline. Bulleted item 3 is:

> Additions to the baseline due to additions to project workscope shall be fully identified as to work items, schedule, effort, and cost and will be accepted to the project baseline only after such full definition and after valid authorization.

Here is a recommended procedure for both maintaining control over the workscope and maintaining a valid baseline for EVA.

1. Establish a standard practice for adding to the project workscope.
2. Provide forms, either printed or electronic, to facilitate the practice.
3. Identify roles, including who may originate a scope change and who may approve a scope change.
4. When a scope change is proposed, the work to be performed is to be fully defined, preferably as a list of work items (tasks, activities, whatever) with work breakdown structure IDs, schedule, effort, costs, as applicable to the current methods in place.
5. The source of funding is to be identified. Is the project budget being increased? Is it coming out of a contingency fund? Theoretically, work should not be added to the project database without an adjustment for the added costs.
6. Maintain a record of all scope changes.

Tip By the way, scope changes can be negative. That is, they may involve a scope reduction. This is actually a legitimate means of balancing schedule, cost, quality, and scope requirements, wherein the scope is reduced to meet schedule, cost, and quality objectives. In the case of a scope reduction, the same procedure should be followed. The work items slated for removal should be deleted from the project baseline. Such changes should be fully documented and approved.

Note that this procedure may violate what is often presented as a project control axiom. We are often told that we create a project plan and freeze a baseline. Yet, in this proposed practice, we allow continual updating of this baseline. *It is my belief that a project baseline is managed, rather than frozen.* It should always reflect the plan values for all authorized work. However, the changes to the baseline must adhere to a rigid protocol.

A Simple Change Control Method

In Figure 6.1a (pg. 189), we illustrate a simple spreadsheet-based method for logging changes to project scope. We use this illustration, both for an example of providing an audit trail of such changes, and for registering any changes to the project baseline for EVA purposes.

In this example of a telephone system installation project, we see that it is a commercial, for-profit contract for an outside client. However, the basic approach can be applied to internally funded projects, with some modification. This example also supports my philosophy that divides the contract into three cost segments.

Segment One, the *Task Budget*, includes all the work that has been specifically identified and planned. This task budget is the original baseline for the EVA. If we were employing a traditional CPM system for planning and control, its content would consist of all the work items included in the task budget, including schedule, effort, and cost baselines.

Wouldn't it be grand if we were so wise as to be able to identify every work item at the onset of the project and even enjoy the benefit of foreseeing the future to pre-identify all potential problems? However, we have learned from experience that such is not the case. We somehow manage to omit some items from the original plan. And, sooner or later, a few unplanned problems will pop up. So we learn to allow a contingency for these incidents.

Segment Two, therefore, is what I call *Management Reserve*. It is a contingency amount (in this case 15%) that has been set aside (based on experience) for items that we expect to add to the project workscope, but have not yet been defined (because we don't know what they will be).

It is called management reserve because it is a fund that is to be managed, rather than a bucket of dollars available to any passerby. Funds are moved from management reserve to task budget only when a specific cause is noted and the resulting work is planned. Funds so moved to the task budget become part of the revised EVA baseline.

Segment Three is the *Project Margin* or profit. It is the contract price, less the task budget and the management reserve. At the conclusion of the project, unused management reserve, if any, becomes part of the profit. By the same rule, an overrun of either the task budget or the management reserve will eat into the profit.

Figure 6.1a shows the base dollars and schedule, plus an audit trail of five approved changes. Where the changes were not chargeable to the account of the client (and were not due to performance issues) dollars were moved from the management reserve to the task budget. In each of these (changes 1 & 2) additional work was defined and added to the project plan, and the EVA baseline.

In change 3, the additions were chargeable to the client, and in change 4 the extra work was split with the client. The source of funding is immaterial to the task budgeting process. In each case, the extra work is defined and added to the baseline.

In change 5, we have a deletion from the workscope. The effect on the task budget is similar. Only this time, we identify work to be removed, and the task budget and EVA baseline are reduced.

Changing the Workscope While Maintaining a Valid EVA Baseline

Let's examine what we have gained from employing this simple, spreadsheet-based, change control system.

- We have an audit trail of all changes.
- We maintain control over the management reserve fund, as well as the makeup of the contract dollars.
- We have a negotiated and accepted change in the project completion date.
- We have a valid basis for calculating schedule and cost variances for our EVA system.

Imagine if we did not have such a change control system. What do we use as the project BAC? Is it $100,000 or $115,000? Which is fairer? To answer this, we look at this case further, and assume that the project gets completed at an actual cost of $108,000.

If we use the lower budget figure ($100,000), and the project comes in at $108,000, then we are apt to report that the project had overrun the budget. Yet $10,000 of work had been added to the project. Would it be fair to penalize the project team for the overrun, when it really wasn't such?

If we use the higher budget figure, which includes the management reserve, ($115,000) then we give the team credit for cost performance that was not due to actual project performance but rather to unused contingency.

With our Change Control Log and Management System, we know just what the actual cost performance was. The project team spent $108,000 to do $110,000 of work. *A valid basis for Earned Value measurements was retained.*

Part 4—Managing the Baseline for Phased Projects (i.e., IT/AD Applications)

EVA Baselines: Purposes and Problems

In this chapter on practical applications of Earned Value analysis concepts we have discussed the benefits of establishing a project baseline for the purpose of measuring and analyzing variances from the project plan. We have provided examples of simple methods to manage the baseline and to avoid scope creep.

We declared that paramount to effective utilization of EVA, in any degree of implementation, is the need to establish a valid baseline and to manage the baseline for the inevitable changes without invalidating the baseline. In Parts 2 and 3 of this chapter, we discussed practical approaches to avoiding scope creep and how to incorporate authorized changes into the EVA baseline. In the examples provided, we used a contract-based project model wherein the project was primarily defined at the time of authorization and only minor changes were expected—mostly very early in the project execution.

Obviously, this contract-based model does not apply to a large portion of managed projects, especially those in the Information Technology/Applications Development (IT/AD) arena and other applications where the project scope is defined (or refined) as the project progresses.

Phased Baselining

Human nature dictates that we cannot expect people to participate in a flawed process. In the case of EVA, if the participants realize that the baseline is suspect or invalid, then how can we demand that they diligently manage the project to achieve baseline values? If the project team is experiencing rampant changes in the measurement base, perhaps 20 percent to 50 percent of original values, how can we ask them to then manage the project to stay within, say, 10 percent of the baseline? The process becomes a farce, and support for that process goes down the drain.

With the recognition that such is that nature of many IT/AD and other development projects, does this mean that the EVA process cannot be effectively applied in this environment? The answer is an emphatic NO!

The solution lies in integrating the EVA process with the normal phased approach toward IT/AD projects. What happens in these projects is that as each phase develops, a finer definition of the phases to follow is included as part of its deliverables.

If we develop a work breakdown structure (WBS) based on the project phases, we can create an EVA model that will permit us to have:

- An original EV baseline, based on the estimated scope of the project when it is authorized.
- A modified EV baseline, based on the updated estimate at the completion of each phase.
- A phase-specific baseline based on the latest valid estimates for each phase.

For example, let's use a phased project model that appears in Lois Zell's book *Managing Software Projects* (QED Information Sciences, Inc., 1990).
The phases are:

1. The Kickoff Phase.
2. The Sizing Phase.
3. The Data Gathering Phase.
4. The Implementation Modeling Phase.

5. The Design Phase.
6. The Coding Phase.
7. Testing.

Refining the Baseline

In such a phased project, it would be reasonable to assume that the project estimate and workscope would be refined as we completed each phase. Here is a way that we could deal with this phenomenon to maintain a valid EVA baseline.

1. Develop an Original baseline based on the project workscope as conceived at the time of authorization. This might be developed using one of the traditional estimating methodologies, such as COCOMO or Function Point Analysis. Or it may be derived from a repository of project models, perhaps applying a multiplier. In some cases, it might be a top-down authorization, just to establish a preliminary budget. For instance, the sponsor authorizes a preliminary budget of $150,000, which, based on prior experience and models, is broken down into percentages for each phase, totaling 100 percent for the entire project. At this time, the WBS is only two levels: Project and Phase.

2. Along with this high-level, phase-based cost estimate, there should be a phase-based project milestone schedule. This will define the top-level schedule objectives and constraints at the time of project conception. (See Figure 7.1a.)

3. During the Kickoff Phase, the project review team puts the request or authorization through a vigorous review process. If the project passes review (some projects may not survive this initial screening), it gets placed in the project portfolio. Surviving projects will probably have modifications to scope and budget.

4. Each phase may have some modifications and the next phase (Sizing) should have a detailed plan, schedule, and EV (earned value) estimate. This plan (for the Sizing Phase) should expand the WBS at least two more levels, to include the various work packages that comprise the phase and the measurable components of these work packages (often called Activities and Tasks in traditional IT/AD WBS lingo). Each item in the plan

Figure 7.1a   Project Milestone Schedule

Project Milestone Schedule - Original Baseline

Task Name	Baseline Budget	DUR	Schedule Finish	Required Date
IT/AD Typical Project	$160,000.00	200d	07/06/01	
Project Request	$0.00	0d	10/02/00	
Estb. Prelim. Sched & Budget	$0.00	0d	10/02/00	
Kickoff Phase	$6,000.00	15d	10/20/00	
Proj Assessment & Review	$4,500.00	15d	10/20/00	
Perform Prelim Risk Assessment	$1,000.00	10d	10/13/00	
Prepare Project Charter	$500.00	5d	10/20/00	
Estb. Project Baseline	$0.00	0d	10/20/00	
Proj Approval Milestone	$0.00	0d	10/20/00	10/31/00
Sizing Phase	$12,000.00	20d	11/17/00	
Data Gathering Phase	$15,000.00	20d	12/15/00	
Implementation Modeling Phase	$10,000.00	15d	01/05/01	
Design Phase	$45,000.00	30d	02/16/01	
Coding Phase	$40,000.00	60d	05/11/01	
Installation Phase	$20,000.00	25d	06/15/01	
Testing	$12,000.00	15d	07/06/01	
Conduct Acceptance Test	$12,000.00	15d	07/06/01	
Testing Complete Milestone	$0.00	0d	07/06/01	07/15/01

This first illustration represents a Project Milestone schedule at the initiation of the project. It lists the phases of the project plus a few milestone dates. The initial phase is broken down to include milestones and deliverables. A top-down budget, of $160,000 is apportioned between the seven phases. This will serve as the original baseline, but will most likely undergo several modifications before it becomes a reliable baseline for EVA.

IT/AD Typical Project

should have a budget or an effort estimate (or at least a weight factor). Any one of these three quantification values will allow you to express the relative percentage of the work item against the work package, phase, and project. All key milestones and other deliverables should be identified. (See Figure 7.1b.)

5. If you do not want to push your EVA process down to the task level, you can apply values at the work package level, or you can apply values only to the deliverables. Using the latter method can reduce the number of measurement points, but also provides a coarser analysis of progress and variances. Also, you will have to estimate the percent complete of the deliverable, or wait until the deliverable has been accomplished before recording it as 100 percent complete.

6. The original EV basis should be retained (Original Baseline). This will allow a comparison of progress against the original plan, for historical purposes.

Figure 7.1b Project Milestone Schedule—Revised

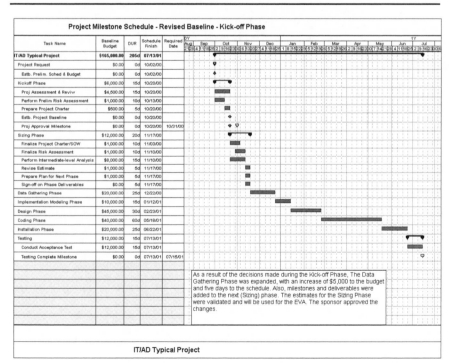

7. The modifications determined during the Kickoff Phase should be documented. What are the modifications? What caused the modifications? What work changes result from the plan modifications? What is the effect of these changes on the original schedule and budget?

8. A new baseline is established for the Sizing Phase. Progress (% Complete and Actual Costs/Hours, if these are tracked) is compared to the new baseline for a valid variance analysis.

9. This stepped process (items 4 through 8) is repeated as each phase is accomplished. Each phase is expanded and the modified scope and budgets are incorporated into the plan for that phase. The original baseline is maintained and a new baseline is created at each phase, for practical variance analysis.

10. Essentially, what you will be doing is setting up a series of subprojects, one for each phase, that will have a reasonably valid baseline. This is so because the baseline is established when information from prior phases allows for the definition of a sound workscope and plan.

11. At the end of each phase, or whenever the modified plan for a future phase is proposed, the new workscope and baseline should be reviewed with the key stakeholders and approved by the sponsor.

12. Remember, the policy of modifying the baseline for each phase is to incorporate reasonable and approved changes based on what you have learned from the preceding development phases. You are not supposed to modify the baseline to reflect poor performance, and to do so would fully negate the purpose and benefits from EVA. Please refer back to Part 2 of this chapter for further discussion on valid and invalid modifications to the baseline.

Benefits and Uses

Getting back to our base case, we were concerned with the practicality of applying Earned Value analysis principles to projects with unstable baselines. On the surface, we might conclude that, when the size, budget, or duration of a project is subject to considerable change during its execution, EVA could not be used effectively. Certainly, we make a case that a stable baseline is a design element of the EVA process.

Nevertheless, we can make a supportable case for an exception to this preference, as long as a structured and managed approach is applied to modifying the baseline as each phase is executed. In this approach, we will have multiple baselines.

There will be an original baseline, for the project and each phase, to be used for reference only. There will be a modified baseline, as each phase is reached, approved by the owner/sponsor and key stakeholders, and used to measure performance.

What we gain is a reasonably valid and up-to-date basis for measuring performance. What we avoid is the appearance of a flawed process—one in which the team is asked to be measured against an invalid baseline. To the contrary, this process actually invites the participants to examine their plan and to maintain its freshness.

In the case of phased projects, where the details of each phase are developed as a product of a preceding phase, this stepped approach toward baselining and EV analysis is our only option.

CHAPTER 7.2

REAL-TIME STATUS VERSUS PERIOD DATA

We want a lot of things from our computer-based project management systems. One of the things that we often ask for is that the data be as current as possible. You need to be cautious about this request. The freshest data is not always the best data. So be careful what you ask for—you may get it.

In the Beginning . . .

In the earliest days of modern project management, handling project data was a batch process—by necessity. Progress data was collected and transferred to coding sheets, and in turn was transferred to punched cards and submitted to the computer operator. Then we would wait for the results, review the output, correct errors, resubmit, and eventually publish the output. This process could often take up to three weeks, by which time much of the data was aged and the ability to react was impaired.

So the industry rejoiced when we matured to real-time statusing and reporting. Now that we are in our fifth decade of automated project planning and control, we have progressed to a point where almost anyone, at any point of time, can get to any data, from anywhere. That data may be so fresh as to have been entered in the system within minutes of retrieval. I once had a department manager describe to me the system that he was looking for. He wanted the ability to access an information database that would let him know what projects were in progress and in the queue, their status, and what everyone in his department was working on. And the data was never to be more than 24 hours old.

Today's Typical Process

Well, today, we can certainly give the gentleman what he asked for. But is that really what he wants? Let's look at a few potential scenarios and unearth a few flaws in such an approach.

First, we start by defining a typical process.

1. The data system is structured, with common project, task, and resource coding, calendars, and preferences.
2. Projects are defined; adding tasks, linking tasks, assigning resources, estimating effort and duration, and calculating schedules.
3. A baseline is established.
4. Progress on tasks is entered.
5. Time spent on tasks is reported.
6. Actual expenses are processed.

Now, at any particular point in time, we can have partially defined projects, and helter-skelter progressing. For instance:

1. Harry, project manager for Alpha Project, enters task status on 4/15.
2. Thomas, project manager for Omega Project, is at an all-day meeting with the project sponsor and can't get his task status in until 4/16.
3. Most of the resources report time spent weekly, with electronic time sheets. These are due on Monday morning, 4/20.
4. Jill, however, will be out that week and enters her data on 4/16, using estimates for Thursday and Friday.
5. Jack is out sick on 4/20 so his time does not get in until 4/22.
6. Janice, in Accounting, downloads expense and invoice data from the corporate finance system and allocates expenses to projects and tasks. This is done every Thursday, based on accounting records as of the previous Friday.

Problems with This Process

If we were to take advantage of our real-time capability, the data would never be synchronized. If we used our executive browser to check on things as of the afternoon of Wednesday, 4/15, we would see task status on Alpha Project as of 4/15, Omega Project as of the previous week, actual hours as of 4/13, and actual expenses as of 4/6. In this example, reported hours and expenses on Alpha Project would be lagging the reported task progress, making performance look better than it really is. Omega Project would also be out of synch.

But this is just the top of the iceberg. On 4/14, Thomas reviews the hours charged to his project for the previous week. He questions charges entered by Mike, who was not assigned to Tom's project. He posts a query to Fran, Mike's manager. Fran, in reviewing Mike's time sheet, has other questions. By 4/16, these are resolved, and they are posted to the database on 4/17. However, this means that the information viewed on 4/15 was incorrect, and has changed.

But the potential problems can get worse. Harry had asked his project team to modify the plan for Alpha Project to reflect design changes. They are going to use a different frabistat, containing four type B gizmo assemblies, rather that two type C gizmos. Tony, the assembly team leader, entered the new task plan and deleted the now obsolete tasks. Just as this was taking place (the new tasks were added—but the old were not yet deleted) Fran is checking the multiproject database to review the project loads on her resources. The system shows a severe overload during the frabistat assembly period. Fran puts in a panic call to Harry, while simultaneously looking into borrowing or outsourcing resources. Harry is perplexed by the unexpected call, not being aware of any overload problems. The problem is quickly resolved, but not before getting several people involved in dealing with a nonexistent problem.

However, while Tony is finalizing the modification to the frabistat plans, he erroneously enters 55 days for a 5-day task, unintentionally adding 10 weeks to this critical path work package. Just as that data was added, Charles, the Executive Vice President, viewed the project summary plan via his browser. Seeing the 10-week slip in this key project, he puts in an urgent call to Harry. "Hey," he says. "You told me that this project was on schedule and wouldn't slip." A flustered Harry doesn't know what to say. He hasn't even seen the information that his boss is reacting to. Now he has to waste valuable time putting out a fire and has lost some credibility with his boss. Yet, Harry hasn't done anything wrong, and, in fact, the so-called problem doesn't even exist.

Nebulous Benefits

So what do we have here as benefits of real-time project processing and immediate access?

1. We have the problem of synchronizing the collection of task progress data, hours charged, and expenses recorded.
2. As a result of this, we diminish the validity of project performance data, often obtaining false indications of schedule and cost variance.
3. We may experience quality problems, as there is no time to analyze and evaluate the data before it is available for publication or viewing.
4. We may cause undue stress and wasted effort when such erroneous data causes other parties to react with shock and alarm.
5. We may, furthermore, precipitate unnecessary responses to problems, which will have to be reversed when the error is discovered.
6. There is a high likelihood of inconsistent information, as various people view the data at different times.
7. Thoughtful and thorough analysis and evaluation of project and resource status is difficult when the data is in an ever-changing state.

A Solution

Perhaps what would be best is a combination of the old batch methods and today's real-time access. Easy, fast access for inputting data from various sources, in diverse locations, if kept under control, can be advantageous. However, there should be a structured method for processing this data before it is available for general viewing and distribution.

In the earlier days of project statusing, we had an *as-of* date. All data was normalized to this *close of data* date. This is still appropriate and essential. In our structured system, all project status is reported as of the close of data date. If Harry inputs on 4/15, and Tom on 4/16, it's okay, as long as the inputs reflect the status as of the data date (let's use 4/10). Time entry must also be as of 4/10, as well as imported expense data.

This might not satisfy that department manager, who wanted the data to never be more than 24 hours old. But let's face it. Would you rather have current (but potentially flawed) data, or good data? You are better off, in most cases, to have good data that is a week old, than to have fresh data that lacks accuracy and consistency, and is therefore unreliable.

Next, in our structured system, there should be a series of quality checks, before the data is published. I have a series of exception queries that I routinely make that helps me to ferret out any unusual data. For instance, if I am doing a biweekly update, I list all the tasks that have slipped more than two weeks since the last update. (I can do this because I capture a temporary baseline of my last published set before further changes are made. Then, I can run a comparison of the 4/10 data to the 3/27 data and list any items with a spread of more than two weeks.) Such occurrences may be legitimate, but some may be the result of erroneous inputs.

Tip Develop an error-checking routine before distributing reports or allowing widespread access to the most recent data update. Compare current data to a recent baseline. Devise exception reports that will list anything that is out of a range of expectations. Then check to see if the exception items are valid.

Now that we have a reliable set of data, what shall we do with it? I, for one, feel that data, by itself, can almost be worse than no data at all. The data should tell a story. The publisher of the data may be fully aware of its meaning. But most of the target audience will need guidance. If there are variances, where are they and what do they mean? What is the impact and what are the recommended corrective actions?

We need to freeze the data at some point in time and stop to analyze it. It is not good enough to just pass the data around, or publish it to a website. The data should be used to generate responses to move the projects ever forward toward their objectives. Reports need to be published for project managers, resource managers, CFOs, other executives, sponsors, and clients. Stories need to be created and told. Meetings and communication need to be initiated around the published data.

Tip Don't leave the data to speak for itself. Provide narratives to go with the data that point the readers to what you want them to see, and help them to understand the message. The data is not the message. The data only provides evidentiary information to back up the message.

We need to be proactive in this endeavor. We can't wait for people to react to raw (sometimes inaccurate) data. If we do that we will end up wasting our time responding to irritating and nonproductive calls, rather than guiding the organization toward project success.

If we do not freeze the data periodically, and pause to analyze and publish clear and informative information, the entire system will drown in data and chaos.

Be Careful What You Ask For

There is an old saying "Be careful what you ask for. You may get it." Recently, many people have been asking for real-time access to project status data. And, today, we can give them what they are asking for. But do they really want it? Do they really want their boss to see the data before they do? Do they really want the client to see the problems before they have had a chance to develop a corrective action plan? Do they want to have all the data out on the street before it has been checked for quality and impact? I would think not.

The answer is to capture and freeze the data periodically, so that it can be checked, analyzed, and reported, complete with informative stories and action plans.

CHAPTER 7.3

AUTOMATIC PROJECT MANAGEMENT: A CLASSIC OXYMORON

We live in the age of automation. The coffee goes on by itself, each morning. The breadmaker does it all: mixing, kneading, rising, baking—just add the ingredients and press Start. I have trouble finding a luxury automobile that does not have an automatic transmission (which I will not drive). Robots and N/C machines make most of our products. And, yes, *there are now some people who think that we want the project management process to be automatic.*

Not that there is a problem in seeking automation. *But not the entire process.* And not for processes that are not completely repetitive and predictable. We have to draw the line somewhere. To qualify this, let's examine the components of a project management support system, and where automation fits in. First of all, there are two basic stages: when we plan the project, and when we progress it.

The Planning Stage

The basic steps here are (1) to identify the overall project goals, milestones, and strategy; (2) to identify the work; (3) to schedule the work; (4) to assign resources to the work; (5) to reschedule considering resources; and (optionally) (6) to establish a project budget. Most of us choose to use critical path scheduling software, which has been designed to support many of these steps.

The software itself has several components. It provides a mechanism for inputting and viewing data. It provides a data storage and management capability. And it provides several algorithms for calculating schedules, resource loads, costs, and variances. While several vendors appear to concentrate primarily on the first two sets of capabilities, it is the latter set of functions that will determine how supportive the software is for generating accurate and useful plans.

I have been an outspoken supporter of critical path software for several decades. However, that support comes with a caveat, regarding both the software and the way that it is used. First, the software must allow the user to create an accurate and discrete model of the work and the resources involved in the project. Secondly, the user must be willing to invest the time and effort to effect a usable solution.

The software must allow the user to define just how the work is to be executed, and not force the user to create some artificial plan, just because the tool is too limited to allow finer definition. A few tools allow finite definition of schedule and resource assignment conditions. For example, the Distribution Spreadsheet Mode, in Scitor's PS8, allows the user to define exactly how resources are applied to tasks. (Tools from Advanced Management Solutions and from ABT, acquired by Niku, provide similar capabilities.) Additional features support discontinuous application of resources (determined during the resource leveling execution), and assignment to multiple tasks.

If this is how people work on tasks, then the tool must allow the user to define such conditions, and the user must be willing to take the time to do such. We cannot throw raw data into the machine and allow the computer to come up with an optimal plan. Such a plan can be achieved only through the interaction between a capable software program and an enlightened team of project planners. It is an iterative process that cannot be handed off to a dumb machine.

The Progressing Stage

As we conduct the project, all the above applies, as we have to be able to replan and adjust to react to execution situations. To this, we must add the ability to input what has taken place and to analyze the impact of performance to date. Here, we can fully appreciate the advances made in database management and multisource, remote access. But none of this would be of value if we did not have the tool capabilities discussed above, as well as the dedicated involvement of the project team.

Anyone who says that this function (project statusing) can be automated, to the extent of eliminating or minimizing the involvement of the project team, neither recognizes nor respects the importance of such man-machine interaction in creating and maintaining usable plans.

Concepts and Approaches That Should Be Avoided (or Approached with Caution)

After four decades of involvement with traditional critical path scheduling software, I still strongly support this approach for most applications. There are other work flow based concepts, both old and new, such as Line of Balance and Critical Chain, which have their places. These are not discussed in this chapter. What we do discuss are some practices and alternative tool approaches that suggest that the process can be highly automated, and executed without being managed by a project team.

Trap   Proceed with caution. The application of such practices as described below might appear to be alternative project management techniques. But these are merely an illusion of such, failing to support generally accepted project management practices.

Auto Actuals

It started more than a decade ago, when several of our project management products were designed to give users an easy way of entering actual costs for tasks and resources. They offered an *auto actuals* option, wherein the system calculated the *actual cost* by multiplying the percent complete by the budget. Of course, this meant that the actual costs would always match the planned cost. The cost variance would always be zero. Doesn't this defeat the purpose of project cost management? Of course it does. And many project managers rejected systems that offered this feature.

Automatic Resource Leveling

Automatic resource leveling comes under the caution heading, rather than avoidance. It is a capability that is very important to good scheduling and an expected component of a critical path software package. We must look to our software tools to provide support for resource scheduling, as it is too complicated to do by hand (for the typical project). However, we must draw a line between allowing the computer to create an undirected, unmanaged resource schedule, as opposed to one that is based on directed conditions and management interaction (see Section 4).

It is not that difficult to obtain usable results from resource leveling. But it does require reasonable assistance from a well-designed software package, together with intelligent interaction by the user. For instance:

- People should not be reluctant to model all the conditions that would be required to support intelligent, automated resource allocation.
- The project management software must allow the creation of a discrete assignment model.
- The resource allocation algorithms must be sophisticated enough to provide acceptable results.
- The user must interact with the results to fine-tune the solution.

Personal Information Managers (PIMs)

Recognizing that traditional project management software is not for everyone, the industry has given rise to alternative approaches toward task and resource planning and management, which are not based on critical path scheduling and serial-mode resource leveling. One of these is the Personal Information Manager (PIM) type of software. Some of these are simple calendar-oriented notebooks— sort of an electronic Day-Timer. The more sophisticated versions attempt to provide a project orientation to the data in the system. A more recent, and powerful entry into this classification was Team Manager 97, from Microsoft. Yet, it is interesting to note that, despite the excellent design of this product (Team Manager), it has failed to gain any strong acceptance in the marketplace. The project management community has almost totally ignored it (opting instead for traditional PM software), and the rest of the potential market for PIM type software continues to be soft. I submit the following reasons for this result:

- For the most part, PIMs are tools that people use for their own information base, rather than as collaborative tools. I guess that's why they call them personal information managers. To be used in a project environment, such tools must be standardized, and their use controlled under the direction of an appointed leader. It is not enough to pass information around using such tools. It must be managed.
- Task information cannot just be changed at will. Changes must be analyzed and either accepted or rejected by the person in charge.
- Individuals cannot always decide what tasks they will work on and when they will work on them. Even with the move to self-directed, multidiscipline teams, we still need to look to the line managers to be involved in staff assignments.

In the past two decades, I have seen several PIM-type products brought to the marketplace, which were supposedly optimized for project team applications. None have been successful.

Resource Requestor/Allocator Software

In addition to the PIM nature of Team Manager, a major feature is a designed capability that is supposed to assist in the assignment of resources to tasks. This is a category that I call Resource Request and Allocation Software. The concept is that someone needing work to be done (for instance, a project manager) will populate the database with a list of tasks. These will be communicated to resource owners (presumably the line managers) who will assign resources to the tasks. Here, too, we have an interesting concept, which has been tried several times before, and has failed to catch fire. It would be interesting to evaluate the failure of previous attempts to address this resource assignment and modeling need. For instance, why did the Artemis Team product (late 1980s) never get off the ground? Why has the latest Artemis effort in this area, Artemis ResourceView, failed to be accepted in the United States (and been removed from the market)? Why has there been less than a stampede toward Team Manager? Why did Sagacity (Assignment Modeling Method and Software), from Erudite (1990) fall from the face of the Earth? Why has adRem's Project Toolbox, based on an advanced resource allocation method, lacked real success?

I think that the reasons are similar to the PIM situation. In using such tools, we lack a strong project-centric focus on the work, and fail to set up standardized practices under the direction of responsible project and functional leaders. There is no one to evaluate the schedules and assignments and to address issues and conflicts.

Our experience with such tools and concepts tends to reinforce the evidence that traditional critical path techniques, supported by well-designed software and organized project teams, is the best way to go.

A Utopian System

A few years ago, I came across a patent for an *Automated, Electronic, Network Based, Project Management Server System, for Managing Multiple Work-Groups*. I love that title. It contains all the popular buzzwords that should get the attention of today's senior managers. The PM equivalent of a low-fat, high-energy, skin-smoothing, muscle-toning, cholesterol-lowering, anticarcinogen, virility-stimulating soft drink. Heck, you just can't lose with this!

Such a computer system (according to selected wording of the patent application) would have these attributes:

- Central database.
- Connected to electronic network.
- Using two-way electronic messaging system.
- Storing and accessing data from a multiproject database.
- Automatic in nature.
- With built-in triggers.
- Based on nature and status of said data.
- *Without need for manual project management coordination.*
- Involves all steps of the PM cycle.
- Identifies owner of received message.
- Identifies nature of received message.
- Setup database—saves messages (according to nature of said received message).
- Receiving project plans and compiling project plans and saving project plans into database.
- Checking plans for resource requests against resource availability and reallocating resources if necessary, based on interproject priorities.
- Recalculating project plans and sending back said plans based on resource allocations.
- Sending project status reports and reminders to organization work group team members based on status of triggers.
- Receiving project updates and status changes and updating said database.
- Repeating periodically.

Wow! Not a bad set of attributes. Wouldn't we all want something like this? Perhaps—until we notice the magic phrase *"without need for manual project management coordination."* This system would have us eliminate project managers or even project coordinators. Heck, in the attempt to have flatter organizations, maybe we can do away with resource managers, as well. Project plans would somehow find their way into this database, automatically. Then, the system would communicate work commitments and work status, and would be continually updated via electronic messaging. The system would automatically resolve all conflicts—without requiring human intervention.

And here I thought that I would never find a utopian project management environment in my lifetime. Beam me up, Scotty!

Hey, I don't want to knock the objectives of such automation. It's just that we can't fantasize about removing the human element. Computer systems cannot manage projects or work groups. They can only offer aid to the people charged with the responsibility to deliver project and operational results. We need sophisticated tools that will make it easier to plan and track work, to evaluate the impact of new work, to evaluate the progress of existing work, and to help with the assignment of scarce and shared resources.

Trap Be careful not to fall for a promise of easy-to-use project management software that virtually eliminates effort and involvement by the project participants. Such a premise is a fantasy.

New products will continually appear that will appeal to those who wish that this could be accomplished without dedicated managers and organizations. These products will be rejected because they don't work. These products will be rejected because they support a fallacious dream of work being managed and conflicts being resolved by a computer. The result will always be a nightmare, instead. I have an entire room full of such products, most of which are no longer being sold.

SECTION 8

PERFORMANCE MEASUREMENT

There are many reasons why we should implement some type of performance measurement routines as part of our project management practices. First of all, there is the obvious justification. That is, to find out how well we are doing. We can add to that another fairly visible (and dubious) gain—the ability to monitor who is performing well and who is not.

But there is so much more. Performance measurement practices, implemented early in the project, can provide an early warning of things that have gone amiss—in time for effective corrective action, at the least cost. Performance measurement data can support progress billing that is based on actual accomplishment, rather than a schedule of planned effort. These are just a few of the benefits.

Performance measurement is a key component of maintaining the plan. Therefore, in Section 7, we presented some illustrations of practical applications of the Earned Value analysis concept. In Section 8, we continue to address common issues and misunderstandings about EVA and provide additional examples of very simple and practical uses of this extremely valuable tool.

Performance measurement, utilizing EVA concepts, has been a common requirement on many projects under the sponsorship of the Departments of Energy and Defense. This has led to a misconception that EVA is used only in big, government-directed projects, and only when absolutely required by the client. I beg to differ with this belief. The basic concepts of EVA, which act as the foundation of a very structured application of DOE/DOD performance measurement protocols, can be easily and effectively utilized on any projects, regardless of size or application area.

Trap Don't be misled to think that EVA is an all-or-nothing protocol. It is possible to use just part of the EVA capabilities, applying them where they are most practical and useful. You can use schedule variance without cost variance, and vice versa. We can apply EVA to just milestones or to parts of the plan. We can use simple EVA practices for accurate progress billing.

In Chapter 8.1, we discuss four common issues and concerns regarding Measuring the Value of Work Accomplishment. *Accomplishment value* is a generic term that I prefer to use for earned value or BCWP (Budgeted Cost of Work Performed). First, we talk about maintaining fidelity in measuring accomplishment value. How do we develop and maintain a valid basis for measuring earned value and calculating EVA measurements? Then we address the question: Can I use EVA if I don't collect actual cost data? The answer, by the way, is YES.

Another frequent and valid question is: What if the workscope changes? Does it invalidate the EVA? We mention this query in Part 3, referring you to detailed coverage in Chapter 7.1. Finally, what do we do when (as is the case in many information technology and other development projects) each phase tends to expand and modify the project baseline? No problem! We have a solution for this common situation, as well.

CHAPTER 8.1

Measuring the Value of Work Accomplishment

Issue 1: Fidelity in Measuring Accomplishment Value

Among the most frequently asked questions about project status are:

- When will the job be finished?
- What will be the final cost of the job?
- Where do we stand on the job today? (What percent complete are we?)

In my 40 years of being involved with projects, it is this third query that most frequently generates challenges to the fidelity of the data. Without a structured way of developing measurements of completeness, the reporter of such data is left with full discretion in computing and communicating this status.

This situation has given way to the classic comment about project progress: "The project quickly reaches 98 percent complete and then sits there forever while the remaining work (and costs) accumulate." This condition creates several problems, among which are:

- A false sense of accomplishment is generated, leading management to erroneously believe that the project performance is better than it really is.
- Along with this is the erroneous belief that the cost performance is better

than it really is (because the costs are measured against a higher %C than the true figure.

- Subcontractors are paid for more work that has really been performed.
- Plans to phase out the project and to release resources are made prematurely.
- There is no way to evaluate performance or to accurately forecast key dates and costs.
- There is no basis for the key decisions that must be made from time to time relative to project expenditures, resource allocations, technical alternatives, and such.

Earned Value Analysis

As noted in Chapter 7.1, the advent of computer-based project management systems, and the interest of such U.S. government agencies as the Department of Energy and Department of Defense, spurred a formal approach toward the analysis of schedule and cost variance, which we commonly refer to as *Earned Value analysis*. This would include DOE's *Performance Measurement System* and DOD's *Cost/Schedule Control Systems Criteria*.

We also noted that EVA systems are not just for major government-type contracts. A key element of any EVA system is a method of measuring the work accomplishment. Such EV measurements are essential for any kind of project, if the project manager is to maintain control of the project, make practical decisions based on knowing what is going on, and avoid surprises when the project is late and overexpended. This would apply to any size project as well as any type of project in any industry. It would also apply to internal projects as well as projects being performed for an external client.

In this chapter we address some of the common issues and misconceptions regarding the application of earned value analysis, and suggest some simple, practical ways to use this most important project control process. We promise a pragmatic treatment of this often intimidating and misunderstood subject.

Measuring Accomplishment Value

Accomplishment value is my generic term for that which we often refer to as *earned value or budgeted cost of work performed (BCWP)*. I use it because it says exactly what it is—the value of the work that has been performed. I like earned value, too—much better than BCWP. In fact, in a system that I developed at the General Electric Company, I chose to coin the term Earned Value of the Work Performed (EVWP), rather than BCWP, because that says exactly what it is.

However, jargon aside, a major issue is maintaining the fidelity of these EV measurements. How do we make sure that the people who are reporting the accomplishment values are using genuine figures and not pulling the wool over our eyes? The one thing that is worse than not having any accomplishment value measurement at all is to have values that are false. In this latter case, we are led to believe that there is validity to the distorted data. Under the guise of a structured system, we have merely produced a very precise error, made further harmful by the misconception of infallibility by having been produced by the computer.

This concern, regarding the means of obtaining objective measurements rather than subjective measurements, was raised in an e-mail that I received a while ago. I would like to share that query with you as well as my response to the question.

A Query

A French student, working on his dissertation on project management at a university in England, sent me a query on earned value. In his note, he said:

> If I want my system to calculate the budgeted cost of work performed, once I have the BAC, I need the actual percent of work complete. Where from do the managers get that figure? Will it be crazy and far from reality if in my system the manager inputs that figure? Therefore I have to assume that he is accurate as far as this datum is not revealed by the system. Which sources does he use to get that information? What I mean is if the % complete is exogenous in my system . . . will it be wrong?

The student is already proving himself to be a good project manager by raising these perceptive concerns. He is correct in the basic equation, which requires both %C (percent complete) and BAC (budget at completion) to calculate the BCWP (budgeted cost of work performed, or earned value). And, of course, if the %C is erroneous, or picked out of thin air, then the EV is also wrong.

He asks:

> How do we minimize the possibility of such errors (deliberate or otherwise). Can the data be trusted if it comes from outside of the project control system (from sources that might arbitrarily pick %C values).

Solutions

First, if people want to deceive the system, they can always find a way. However, there are a few ways that we can either make it easier to calculate %C or make it more difficult to falsify %C. These are all aimed at moving the source of the EV data closer to the internal system (which addresses his stated concern).

1. Use weight factors. For instance, if the task is to produce an engineering drawing, then you could say that the drawing is 25%C when the backgrounds are complete, 70%C when issued for approval, 90%C when issued with approval, and 100%C when all holds are removed.
2. Use milestones. This is similar to the above. Tasks that involve multiple steps are given a fixed %C when an interim milestone is reached.
3. Use the 0%C–100%C method. A task is considered to be 0%C until it is finished. This will always produce a lower EV than actual, but motivates the task owner to complete the task (or lie about completion) to get credit for the BCWP.
4. An alternate to the above is the 0–50–100 method. A task is 0%C until started. Then it is 50%C until completed. This makes things simple. There are three task states: not started, in progress, and completed. Each state has a set %C. No calculation or estimate is necessary. This method is practical only for short tasks.
5. The problem with all the above methods is that there can be a lag in calculated earned value over the real amount of the work accomplished. To counter this problem, we can apply a method that uses a subjective stipulation of %C combined with stepped limits. In this method, we specify fixed %C values associated with specific stages (or phases, gates, milestones, etc.) of the task or work package. We then allow the voluntary reporting of %C up to the specified limit of that stage. This allows some partial credit for accomplishment but prevents abuse of the system by overly optimistic (or deceptive) managers.
6. Use the measured (quantified) progress method. This can be applied to tasks that contain quantifiable results. It might be feet of pipe, miles of road, tons of concrete, lines of code, meters of cable, and so on. If a task (or work package) consists of stringing 5 sets of telephone cable a distance of 500 meters, and the current status is 1 cable completed and 1 cable strung 250 meters, then you could say that the task is 30%C.
7. Base %C on percent of applied hours used. There are two conditions that complicate this approach. First, you must be periodically updating the esti-

mated hours so that the BAC hours are the sum of the hours spent plus an up-to-date estimate-to-complete (ETC). Second, this will cause the ACWP (actual cost) to be equal to the BCWP, thus preventing an accurate calculation of cost variance (unless your system can hold two BACs—baseline and current). So you can see that this is certainly not a preferred method, but is better than nothing when you are having trouble getting good %C figures. The equation is BCWP = Hours Spent / Hours Spent + ETC. Also note that we violate the rule that the BAC is fixed. In this case, we update the BAC every time the sum of the Hours Spent + ETC changes. Here is an example: A task is budgeted at 200 hours. After spending 80 hours (40% of the original estimate) the worker estimates that it will take another 160 hours to complete it. The new BAC is 80 + 160 = 240 hours. The %C is 80/240 or 33%. Recognizing that 80 hours have been spent, we can note that 40 percent of the budgeted cost has been spent to do 33 percent of the re-estimated work.

Level of Detail

A key to obtaining good EV figures is to push the collection of %C data down to the lowest levels. This does not necessarily mean that actual cost data need also to be collected at the lowest level. Let me explain. An EVA system is almost always built upon a Work Breakdown Structure (WBS). The WBS will subdivide the project into smaller and smaller segments, based on a logical grouping of project elements. Eventually, the WBS will arrive at a group of tasks associated with a project deliverable, belonging to an accountable function. The most common term given to this juncture is *cost account*, although we will also see *control point* or *work package*. It is at this point that we most often compare BCWS, BCWP, and ACWP for schedule and cost variance (earned value analysis).

The issue is that these cost accounts will consist of several tasks, each with their own weight (based on budgeted cost or hours). In order to obtain an accurate, weighted %C, it is necessary to determine the %C on a task-by-task basis, or to create fixed %C values based on accomplishment of specific tasks within the cost account.

This may sound like a lot of detail work, but it is not. It is easier (and more accurate) to get down to this detail, and it is easier to actually do it than it is to describe the process. In fact, when utilizing any of the popular project management software packages, you will find that they are designed to input data at the most detailed (task) level, and then to roll up the data to any of the parent levels.

More EVA Issues

Now that we have addressed the issue of obtaining valid measurements of the work actually accomplished, we can move on to three frequently asked questions regarding the effective use of EVA. These are:

1. Can I use EVA if I don't collect actual cost data?
2. What if the project workscope changes? Does it invalidate the EVA?
3. How do I manage the baseline for projects where the baseline changes with each phase of the project?

Further Reading

For a good review of the workings and application of EVA, try *Earned Value Project Management*, Quentin W. Fleming and Joel M. Koppelman, Project Management Institute, 1996. For an in-depth coverage of this topic, see *Cost/Schedule Control Systems Criteria: The Management Guide to C/SCSC*, Quentin W. Fleming, Probus Publishing Co., 1988.

Issue 2: Can I Use EVA If I Don't Collect Actual Cost Data?

There are three popular misconceptions about the application of Earned Value analysis. We need to shoot them down right now, as they are clearly inappropriate. These misconceptions are:

1. EVA is meant to be used on government or aerospace/defense type of projects, only.
2. EVA is a cost-based performance measurement system. If I do not collect cost data, then EVA is of no use to me.
3. EVA is a very sophisticated process, requiring a laborious implementation by dedicated project management experts.

   Each one of these common beliefs is wrong, and I can prove it from my own experiences during the past 40 years. Perhaps the best way to dispel these erroneous beliefs is to describe a successful project that I worked on in the early 1980s. On this project, we had several challenges to maintaining control over the work effort. First of all, about 90 percent of the work was to be performed by a subcontractor. Also, we would not have a critical path schedule and there would not be any measurement of project costs (within the subcontract portion). Rather than submit to the inevitable and just hope for the best, the lack of these planning and control vehicles motivated the team to seek an alternative method of monitoring project progress.

A Project Example

The project involved the installation of a new telephone system at a plastics processing plant. The company (through their internal Telecommunications Division—my employer) was installing a main switch and redoing its 5,000-line voice and data system. The company (we'll call it Plastico) had contracted with a phone system installer to do most of the work. The subcontractor (we'll call them FoneCo) agreed to a fixed-fee contract and a firm cut-over date. Plastico notified the local telephone company (telco) that the plant would be moving over to its own main switching system on the cut-over date. As the start of the contract work approached, the plant manager suddenly got nervous. Here we were, in the hands of a fixed-price subcontractor (resisting giving any information about how the job was planned or priced), and if the work was not done as scheduled the plant could end up without telephone service. This was critical not only for general communications, but also for safety, as the emergency alarm systems were tied into the telephone lines and switch.

After initial resistance, we worked out a reasonable compromise with FoneCo. Together, we identified all the work and put a weight factor on each work item. The weight factor was based on the approximate effort for each item, so that, in effect, the weight factor served as a budget for each work item. The sub refused to prepare a critical path schedule, and we agreed that the nature of the work was that the order of execution was too flexible to be cast in concrete. Instead, they agreed that work would be accomplished at an even pace over the 20-week project, essentially progressing at about 5 percent per week.

Setting Up a Simplified Work Accomplishment Monitoring System

When FoneCo showed up to start the job, we were concerned that they did not have sufficient manpower to execute the work on time. But they retorted that this was not a matter for our concern. They reminded us that they had a firm price and that it was up to them to manage the work as they saw fit. We reminded them that they had also committed to a firm date and that it was our business to make sure that the date was met.

While each party was protective of their contractual obligations, the Plastico project manager and the subcontractor's PM had developed a cordial relationship and wished to work together to have a successful project. So they agreed to walk the plant each Friday afternoon, and to note the progress for each work item on the task list that had been prepared earlier. Some tasks were marked as complete, getting credit for 100 percent of the budget (weight factor). Other tasks were noted as in progress, getting credit for a percentage of their BAC (Budget at Completion—in this case, the task weight factor). After completing the tour, they added up the various BCWPs (the Budgeted Cost of Work Performed) and arrived at a project earned value. In this case, the BCWP did not involve cost (despite the nomenclature) but represented the product of the percent complete times the weight factor (Earned Value [BCWP] = %C × Weight Factor [BAC]). For example, let's look at a task, having a weight factor (BAC) of 20, and consisting of making 500 splices at a splice box. If 200 splices had been completed that Friday, then the BCWP or earned value is $200/500 \times 20 = 8$.

Traditional Earned Value Computation Process

I pause here for a moment to describe the traditional EVA process, although what we used in the Plastico job was even simpler. For example: Let's say that there were four items on the list, which were scheduled for effort during the first week. The BCWS values are calculated by multiplying the BAC by the planned %C.

Task 1	BAC = 1,000	%C_p = 100	BCWS = 1,000
Task 2	BAC = 1,000	%C_p = 75	BCWS = 750
Task 3	BAC = 1,500	%C_p = 67	BCWS = 1,000
Task 4	BAC = 500	%C_p = 25	BCWS = 125

Remember, the BCWS (Budgeted Cost of Work Scheduled) is the value of the effort that was scheduled to be completed as of the end of the measurement period. We can use this to compare the actual work accomplished to the planned accomplishment.

When we take the actual %C as of the end of the measurement period and multiply it by the BAC, we get the earned value (BCWP).

Task 1	BAC = 1,000	BCWS = 1,000	$\%C_a = 100$	BCWP = 1,000
Task 2	BAC = 1,000	BCWS = 750	$\%C_a = 50$	BCWP = 500
Task 3	BAC = 1,500	BCWS = 1,000	$\%C_a = 50$	BCWP = 750
Task 4	BAC = 500	BCWS = 125	$\%C_a = 40$	BCWP = 200

If we sum these numbers, we get a BCWS (the planned accomplishment) of $2,875, and a BCWP (the actual accomplishment or earned value) of $2,450. In this example, you can see that work is proceeding at about 85 percent of the plan. Note that the actual %C may be greater than the planned %C, as well as smaller. Another way to look at these results (for the group of four tasks) is as follows. The planned accomplishment was 71.875 percent (BCWS/BAC) and the actual accomplishment is 61.25 percent (BCWP/BAC).

A Slow Start

Getting back to the telco project, at the end of the first week, the composite BCWP totaled 3 percent, as against the 5 percent target. When confronted with the bad news, FoneCo admitted that they were a bit slow to start, but promised that they were now up to speed. At the end of week 2, the project BCWP was 6.5 percent, against a target of 10 percent. Our facilities manager suggested that the crew size be increased, but, again, the subcontractor resisted. This time he cited a problem with some tooling, which had been corrected. "Not to worry" was the reply.

But on week 3, the actual accomplishment totaled only 10 percent (against the target of 15 percent) and it was obvious that the subcontractor was losing ground. At the weekly review session, the FoneCo manager still protested the claim that he did not have sufficient manpower on the job, but agreed that he would take corrective action if the next week's measurement didn't show an upturn.

Facing Reality

At the end of week 4, the earned value came to 13.5 percent, indicating a fairly constant rate of accomplishment that was only 70 percent of plan (3.5% per week vs. 5% per week). At the next weekly review, the subcontractor walked into the meeting and quickly reported that an additional crew was on the way. With the additional people on the job, the ongoing measurements showed an upturn to about 5.25 percent to 5.5 percent actual accomplishment per week, and the project was soon back on target for the cut-over date. (See Figure 8.1a.)

I am fully convinced that, without the simple planned accomplishment vs. actual accomplishment routine that was worked out by the two parties, the project would have gone into panic mode toward the end and would have missed the end date. This was a most rudimentary use of the earned value concept. It did not even require any use of cost measurements, and in no way compromised the subcontractor's wish to maintain control over the effort and silence over detailed costs.

A Simplified, Value-based Accomplishment Index

All that was required was a list of the work to be done and a weight factor for each item. If a task schedule has been prepared, the system will compute the planned effort (BCWS). But, as you can see from the example, we were able to use the EVA practice without an item-by-item schedule, substituting a planned rate of overall accomplishment. With the weighted task list, all that was needed was a periodic statusing of percent complete. Computers will do the rest. A traditional CPM program will have all the EVA capabilities built in. But if you don't use one, any spreadsheet program can easily be set up to do the job.

Figure 8.1a   Tracking Earned Value on Telco Project

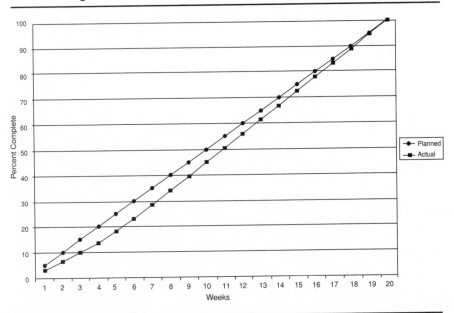

Tool Tip Scitor Corporation has recognized the practicality and validity of this simplified accomplishment value technique. They have added new capabilities to their PS8 and PC-Objectives software packages, building in a unique *Value Performance Index (VPI)* method, which provides a means of entering weight factors for EVA (instead of using costs or hours). The VPI can also be applied to selected work items or milestones (rather than to every line item).

Basing Progress Payments on Actual Accomplishment

There is another advantage to what was done on the telco job that is worth mentioning. Making a weekly earned value measurement provided the data for an accurate and equitable progress payment. Rather than paying the subcontractor a fixed periodic payment, we were able to pay only for what was actually accomplished, based on the weekly BCWP, and the sub couldn't argue with the amount because they participated in the measurement.

Tip The measured Earned Value represents the value of the work that has actually been performed. Many companies have actually started writing contracts that call for progress payments based on measured earned value.

Debunking EVA Misconceptions

This experience should serve to support my hypothesis that:

- EVA can be used effectively on other than government or aerospace/defense projects.
- EVA can be used effectively even if you do not collect cost data.
- EVA applications can be ridiculously simple and do not require the employment of dedicated project management experts.

The benefits of EVA are available to a wide population for a broad spectrum of applications. Such benefits include monitoring project progress toward key completion dates, and more accurate progress payments.

Issue 3: What If the Project Workscope Changes? Does It Invalidate the EVA?

We have already discussed at length the issues associated with change control and scope management. Wherever we have mentioned EVA, we talked about the importance of maintaining a valid baseline. We talk about freezing the baseline. Then we give multiple illustrations of when and how it is okay to modify these data.

Before you accuse us of being inconsistent and confusing, we need to review a few points that were made earlier. These were:

- There must be a baseline plan for the EVA methods to work.
- There are legitimate conditions under which the baseline can be changed.
- No changes to the baseline should be made without a reason for the change, a set of details about the change, and an audit trail for all changes.
- There must be a formal, structured, and heeded system for change control and scope management.

Which all lead us to ask: If the project workscope changes, does it invalidate the EVA? The simple answer is no, it does not. However, in order to maintain a valid baseline for EVA, we need to integrate the change control practices with the EVA practices. All that you need to know to do this was discussed in Chapter 7.1. Rather than repeat these illustrations here, we direct your attention to Chapter 7.1, Part 3.

Issue 4: How Do I Manage the Baseline for Projects Where the Baseline Changes with Each Phase of the Project?

We continue now to look at one more issue regarding maintaining a valid baseline for EVA when the defined workscope keeps changing. In this instance, we address the common situation of a progressively expanding definition of the work at each phase of a development project. We described such projects in Part 4 of Chapter 7.1. We direct your attention to that material to see how it is possible to maintain an EVA baseline as each phase further defines the work and schedule.

This is indeed a challenging situation. But it is one that can be fully addressed and dealt with in such a way as to support the EVA process.

SECTION 9

PROJECT PORTFOLIO MANAGEMENT

Have you noticed that there is a new bandwagon to hop upon? It's called Project Portfolio Management. There are lots of people talking about this new management theme, even if they can't really define what it is. It certainly has a nice ring to it. Actually, if we can figure out just what project portfolio management is, and how we can effectively work it into our overall management practices, we may very well find that it is an important element of the management of the enterprise.

In this section on Project Portfolio Management (PPM), we present three chapters that will explore the world of PPM, including exposing its virtues and its foibles. First, we note the emergence of a special set of needs related to the management of projects within the enterprise. Then we explore the impact of these needs on the way that we normally do project management and on the tools that we use for that purpose. We question the use of the terms *value* and *impact* relative to projects in the portfolio. We initiate a discussion on project risk, and its role in PPM. We make some suggestions about organizing for PPM and present a list of capabilities needed to implement a project portfolio management practice in the firm. This is all covered in Chapter 9.1, Defining and Implementing Project Portfolio Management.

Project Portfolio Management calls for the integration of two important functions within the firm. These are the Operations function and the Projects function. In Chapter 9.2, we discuss Bridging the Gap between Operations Management and Projects Management. We expose the weaknesses and inefficiencies that exist when there is a gap between these two functions, and propose a way to bridge the gap. We also introduce a set of software that has been developed specifically to support our proposed solution.

When covering the topic of risk and contingency in Section 6, we indicated that we would say more about risk in Section 9. This is because risk management is an essential part of PPM. There should be a relationship between Project Selection and Risk, as we note in Chapter 9.3. But, risk is often ignored. Denial reigns supreme, often leading otherwise sage senior managers into accepting and approving risky projects because they have been led to believe that there is no potential downside.

Project Portfolio Management is an important approach toward bringing projects and operations together so that the investments in projects are fully aligned with the strategy and goals of the firm. It is quite easy to accomplish, but it requires an effort to bridge the gap that traditionally exists between the operations and projects disciplines. It requires some cultural change and a few new practices. It also will benefit from integration of the tools used for both disciplines. All of this is discussed here in Section 9.

CHAPTER 9.1

DEFINING AND IMPLEMENTING PROJECT PORTFOLIO MANAGEMENT

Do traditional measures of project success miss the true business objectives? Are scope, time, cost, and quality independent measures of success, or are they only selected components of the objective? What do these popular project management criteria have to do with meeting the overall business strategic objects? Are these measurements (scope, time, cost, quality) what the senior operational managers really watch?

Perhaps this is blasphemous, but I am about to shoot holes in the gospel of project management. Not that what we are preaching is wrong. But it confuses the means to an end with the end itself.

Read the PMBOK® (Project Management Body of Knowledge). Read just about anything else on measurements of project success. They will all dwell on the four pillars of success: scope, time, cost, and quality. We are taught to identify the goals for success in each of these areas and then to create plans that balance these objectives. Then we implement practices and utilize computer-based tools to measure how well we are accomplishing these objectives.

But talk to almost any executive in the firm and they will not be interested in this area of measurement. What do they talk about? They respond to measurements of profitability, return on investment, delivery of content, and taking advantage of windows of opportunity. We used to say that executives are interested in just two things about projects: when will they be finished and what will they cost. Not any more. Now they ask: *"What mix of potential projects will provide the best utilization of human and cash resources to maximize long-range growth and ROI for the firm?"*

Perhaps this is an oversimplification. However, if we start with this premise and examine its meaning, we can begin to realize the tremendous impact of this observation on the way that we conduct project management and especially in the way that we select and implement project management tools.

The Emergence of Project Portfolio Management

Certainly, it is not news to anyone that the basic concept of project management has evolved to what we call *enterprise project management*. At first, we thought that this shift was more of a way of aggrandizing project management—sort of a pompous raising of project management to a higher level of importance. Later, we came to realize that enterprise project management was a reflection of the importance of consolidating and integrating all the firm's projects—for universal access and evaluation. Now, we come to find that enterprise project management entails consideration of potential projects as well as approved projects. We also find that the emphasis has shifted from traditional project-centric objectives to higher-level operational objectives.

Executives have come to realize that *projects* are the basis for future profitability of the firm. Hence, there is a growing interest on the part of executives in how projects are managed. They are precipitating an increased demand for more standardization and automation of project management. But what they are asking for is different from the requests from traditional project management sources.

And what they are calling this emerging project management protocol has also changed. It is no longer just project management, or even enterprise project management. It is now called Project Portfolio Management.

But is Project Portfolio Management for real? Or is it just a nice sounding phrase, without real substance? I get the idea that it's just a lingering melody—a song without words. It's a pretty tune, and, with the right lyrics, it might be a big hit. But for the moment, I don't see a consensus as to how this emerging concept will play out.

But don't mistake my skepticism for a lack of support for the concept. My concern is not whether Project Portfolio Management is worthwhile. It is how to integrate the concepts of Project Portfolio Management with traditional project management that requires attention.

Effect on Tool Selection

We can trace the shifting project management emphasis on the patterns of project management tools. First, there were the project-oriented tools. These provided support for detailed planning and control of individual projects. With the shift to enterprise project management, we saw a change in the project management tools to support multiple projects and multiple users. In some cases, these tools were designed to allow use of the traditional desktop, single project products, by providing a repository-based, client/server environment that consolidated individual projects and added multiproject, multiuser time entry, cross-project resource loading and analysis, and cross-project rollup and reporting. In parallel with that trend, we saw the development of full-featured enterprise project management tools, using built-in multiproject scheduling engines and time entry capabilities.

For Project Portfolio Management, additional attributes are required. The ability to add or extract projects for *what-if* analyses is important. Executives also want to place some value criteria on the projects, so that they can evaluate the relative benefits of adding a project to the mix. Resource and cost impacts of projects will have to be defined at higher than normal levels (because the details might not yet be available or practical to define). Somehow, these executives will expect that the new Project Portfolio Management systems will be able to support ROI calculations (but I don't think that they have yet defined how this would be done).

Tool Tip Software support for Project Portfolio Management requires capabilities and features that extend beyond those in traditional PM systems. Key extensions include: improved multiproject capabilities, adding and removal of projects from portfolios, association with strategic plans, workforce impact analysis, and integration with some of the Operations tools.

The ability to slice and dice large repositories of project information becomes paramount in these systems. The data must be able to be rolled up and expanded, and must be able to be viewed from several perspectives. As the volume of data increases, we will need more sophisticated ways of manipulating the data, so that we don't have to wait for the analyses. Expanded coding capabilities are essential to enabling effective summarization and data extraction.

Misconceptions and Conceptual Gaps

While the overall concept of Project Portfolio Management makes a lot of sense, there remains a tremendous gap between perceived applications and practical realities. I know of at least one instance where senior management expressed a desire to implement a Project Portfolio Management capability (and backed it up with funding). Yet they had little interest in project management itself. It was as if the firm's project mix could be managed and manipulated without management of the projects themselves. Is this possible?

There is an increasing interest in knowing where the firm's resources are committed and what the firm is getting for their resource investment. Again, I have to ask How can this be satisfied without knowing to what work the resources have been assigned and how well that work is going? We might, at the higher level, have built a plan that models resource allocation versus time. But if 40 percent of the way into the project, only 20 percent of the work has been accomplished, then that situation has to be factored into the portfolio analysis. Wouldn't it be absurd to assume that all the work in the portfolio is proceeding exactly as planned?

One of the ways to do this is to use the Earned Value Analysis (EVA) capabilities of our project management software. This simple and effective protocol can provide important schedule and cost variance data. This is important not only as a way of remodeling the resource demand for the project(s), but also as a measurement of how well the project is meeting its objectives. Yet, when we mention EVA to the very people who are asking for Project Portfolio Management, they shudder at the mention of that subject. It is assumed to be too technical for the high-level view that they seek.

Nothing can be further from the truth. I don't see how a Project Portfolio Management system can be put in place without using EVA as part of the performance analysis approach. The resource and cost commitments may have been reasonable (as measured against the expected gains) but there has to be a point where deteriorating performance (increasing investment or time-to-market) crosses the profitability line. More on this in Chapter 9.3.

What Is the Value of a Project?

Another thing that puzzles me, about the emerging concepts of Project Portfolio Management, is how to fix a value on the project. For instance, I have seen requests for the following types of information, under the concept of Project Portfolio Management:

- Find out which proposed projects have the highest value to the organization and therefore should receive priority in resource allocation.
- Evaluate proposed projects in terms of their impact on the overall portfolio, specifically with regard to resource availability and the performance of other projects.
- Identify which projects are 25 percent or more behind schedule, and analyze the impact to the overall portfolio of canceling those projects, again in terms of resource availability and performance of other projects.

These queries seem to be a bit vague to me. How is *value* being defined? How is *impact* being defined? I understand the importance of being able to get answers to these queries. But has anyone thought about just what data is required to answer these questions?

Project Portfolio Management and Strategic Planning

We have fought a battle for years to convince senior management that they can't implement a project management capability by just bringing in project management tools. This holds true for Project Portfolio Management as well. The tools process information. They don't generate knowledge that isn't there. If management cannot describe the aspects of *value*, or define to conditions of *impact*, the system will not know what to do.

This brings us to the realization that the true strategic value of a proposed project must be determined and quantified before it can be placed into the project mix. And this step cannot be executed by the supporting enterprise project management software.

I would hate to think that Project Portfolio Management would be used as an excuse for lack of good strategic thinking. The fact is that Project Portfolio Management *is* part of the normal strategic planning process. We wouldn't have the problem of so many failed and aborted projects if the people who authorized these projects were more organized and diligent about their decisions to proceed. How many times have you seen a business case presented, with a most likely scenario, a best case scenario, and a worst case scenario? Then the presenter says that "the downside will never happen" and the execs buy it? No wonder projects fail. How many times have you seen a project authorized and work initiated, only to learn later that the project scope and objectives (if they were actually defined) do not fit with the firm's overall business strategies and objectives?

Practical Project Portfolio Management and Risk Assessment

So, in order for this modern Project Portfolio Management to work, we need to get back to the sound basics of identifying a range of satisfactory performance parameters for any project. We have to have a predetermination of acceptable performance, so we can set alarms and alerts within the Project Portfolio Management system to advise us of out-of-tolerance conditions. The ROI analysis can't assume just a single result. It must consider a spread of possible scope, time, cost, and quality conditions and identify what values (limits) reduce the ROI to an unacceptable number.

- When does an increase in time-to-market make the project significantly less attractive?
- How much of a cost overrun can be tolerated before it blows the projected profit?
- When does a reduction in scope reduce the expected benefits of the project?

We must consider if the project is worth the risk. This means conducting a thorough risk assessment, identifying both the potential for risk and the impact of risk events. We must consider risk mitigation actions. And then we must evaluate whether the project is still worthwhile after factoring in the costs of risk mitigation. After we have considered the risks, does this project still support the higher-level objectives and strategy?

The New Project Portfolio Team

To make this whole thing work, we have to have specialists who are responsible for evaluating and communicating these essential business/project data. We are already getting management to accept the necessity of the Project Office. Next, we have to expand this to include people who will be responsible for portfolio and risk management. Why not a Chief Risk Officer (CRO)? How about a Project Portfolio Manager (PPM)? And, with the increased concern for resource availability and utilization, perhaps a Chief Human Resources Officer (CHRO) could be justified.

In this enlightened environment, no project should be considered without review by the CRO. No resources should be allocated without review by the CHRO. And no project should be added or removed from the portfolio without review by the PPM. I can see an advisory committee, made up of these three managers, plus the CPO, the Chief Project Officer (or head of the Project Office) and the CFO, to decide on project viability and management of the portfolio. It is these leaders who would use and support the tools that would provide essential information and analyses in support of the projects.

Implementing Project Portfolio Management

I am convinced that Project Portfolio Management is the way to go. I am equally convinced that the success of a Project Portfolio Management initiative is dependent on how the organization develops and supports an environment for Project Portfolio Management, rather than just on tool selection. However, once the decision is made to implement Project Portfolio Management, and once the support structure is in place, the team will want to find tools that adequately support their new way of life. This tool set should include most of the following capabilities and features, over and above traditional project management software functions:

- Electronic time sheets, supporting the collection of actual time spent on project tasks and auxiliary work. These must allow the posting of time to all projects in the system, and should support various means of remote entry. These tools should also provide for management review and control of time reporting. In some environments, the time entry tools must also support progressing of the work, including revised estimate-to-complete data.
- Posting and retention of project data in an open, SQL-type database. This database acts as a repository for the data produced by various PM tools, as well as connectivity to other data of the enterprise.
- (For some applications) integration with corporate accounting systems. For seamless integration, look for Projects modules provided by ERP vendors as part of their financial packages, coupled with integration engines provided by your project management software vendor. (See Section 10.)
- When projects and operations data is integrated it often becomes voluminous. In order to interrogate the data and reduce it to meaningful information, look for OLAP-based slice-and-dice analysis engines, or other means of prearranging the data for rapid access. Also, for the slice-and-dice capabilities, the enterprise project management software must have robust project classification systems (coding) with support for hierarchical structures.
- Earned value computation to support schedule and cost variance analysis.
- Mid- and high-level resource loading and budgeting, with discrete spreading capabilities, to allow analysis of proposed projects without requiring planning at the detailed level.
- Risk assessment, including ranking of project risks, determination of risk possibility, and impact of the risk event. Good risk management practice

supports the inclusion of proposed mitigation plans and the appraisal of the cost effect of taking mitigation action as opposed to experiencing the effect of the risk event.

- The capability to define, display, and communicate the enterprise objectives and goals, and to relate them to the supporting projects.
- A system of feedback from the project monitoring subsystem to the objectives monitoring subsystem, complete with alerts and alarms to warn of endangered objectives.
- An operating environment that encourages access by a wide variety of personnel, from dispersed locations, via networked and web-based protocols. The design of the various screens must facilitate ease of comprehension by a wide range of individuals, using popular metaphors.

Project Portfolio Management is the bridge between traditional operations management and project management. For organizations that will be depending on project success for success of the overall enterprise, a well-structured bridge, built on a good foundation, is the preferred way to overcome the traditional gap between operations and projects management.

CHAPTER 9.2

Bridging the Gap between Operations Management and Projects Management

The Important Role of Project Portfolio Management

One of the hot topics in the management of the enterprise is Project Portfolio Management. In Project Portfolio Management, it is assumed that the enterprise, via the selection and execution of projects, positions itself for increased strength and profitability as well as assuring that the firm continues to thrive in a world of constant change and the threat of competition.

The basic elements of Project Portfolio Management are not new. Nor is the environment in which it is applied. However, before the emergence of Project Portfolio Management as a defined discipline, these elements were the responsibility of two distinct groups: Operations Management and Projects Management. Each group had its specific role, as noted in this table.

Operations Management	*Projects Management*
Objectives	Schedule/Time
Goals	Project Cost
Strategies	Performance
Project Selection & Mix	Stakeholder Satisfaction
Cash Flow	Scope/Change Control

The Traditional Organization

In the traditional organization, responsibility for determining and achieving the firm's goals are assigned to the Operations function. Senior managers, having titles such as COO, CTO, CFO, or Strategic Planner, establish objectives and goals, and develop strategies to achieve these. If there are projects associated with these goals, these senior managers are expected to select from a menu of proposed and pending projects—with the objective of creating the mix of projects most likely to support the achievement of the firm's goals, within the preferred strategies, and within the firm's resource (people and funding) constraints.

When the execution of projects is a normal part of the firm's business, it is expected that the firm will establish, in parallel with the Operations function, a function to manage the projects. This would normally include a Central Project Office, and specialized personnel to manage projects. The Project Office, under a Chief Project Officer (or similar title) will develop standards and practices directed at the effective execution of projects and the attainment of schedule, cost, scope, and quality objectives. In doing so, a project management planning and information system is put in place, and periodic measurements of project progress and performance are conducted.

A problem, common to many firms, is that there is no connection between the Operations and Projects functions, nor is there a structured, consistent, and meaningful flow of information between these two groups. The firm's objectives (enterprise-level goals) are hardly ever communicated to the Project Office, and the periodic measurements, made by the projects group, cannot be related to these objectives.

What a waste! Everyone is off in their own little world—working their butts off to do the best that they can, but not knowing if their efforts are really being effective or efficient. Are the projects that are being worked on (assuming that they were properly selected in the first place) still the best ones to support the objectives? How well are they supporting the objectives? Are there performance issues associated with meeting the objectives? How would the Operations people know?

And over in the Project Office, when the project performance data is evaluated, what knowledge is available to influence the corrective action decisions? If the individual project objectives are in danger, what should the project manager know to work on balancing schedule, cost, scope, and quality parameters? Can this be effectively done in the absence of Operations inputs?

A Simple Solution

While the inability to address these issues can be extremely costly, an easy solution is available. Let's start by isolating the particular problem that we are trying to solve. Most of the published literature on Project Portfolio Management is concentrated on project selection and decision analysis techniques. Some address issues of project termination. But what about project and portfolio assessment? Is a project a static item or a dynamic system?

If a project is dynamic in nature (that is, the project scope, timing, and cost are subject to change), then what effect does this have on the project portfolio? The typical project has a range of possible outcomes and costs. There is the base case and potential upside and downside. If the project was selected on the basis of a set of assumptions (stated in the base case), does that project still belong in the portfolio when its attributes change? We need to periodically review the project to test assumptions, update givens, and monitor progress. We need to periodically examine alternatives (without alternatives, there is no Project Portfolio Management) and consider remodeling the portfolio.

Trap   These three potential weaknesses can obstruct the implementation of Project Portfolio Management:

1. The firm's objectives and goals, as supported by the project portfolio, are not communicated to the people responsible for project performance.
2. The project performance, as monitored by the project managers, is not communicated to the portfolio managers, strategic planners, and senior managers.
3. The gap that exists between these two groups, both in communication and in available information, prevents active management of the portfolio, based on the current, changing status of the component projects.

What is so obviously needed is a basis for addressing project selection issues, deciding on project termination, facilitating reallocation of resources, changing of priorities, and evaluation of alternatives. And without this capability, there is no Project Portfolio Management.

It is my objective, in this book, to address issues associated with effective project management, independent of any of the support tools offered by any particular vendor. However, occasionally a project management software developer comes out with something worthy of special note. In this case, I cannot complete this discussion of bridging the gap between Operations Management and Project Management without mentioning a special set of tools that have been developed to address these needs. In 1999, as I was preparing a series of articles on this subject, Scitor Corporation was also addressing the issues associated with Project

Portfolio Management. This led to the release of Project Communicator 3, which included the new PC-Objectives system. Because this product fully and effectively (and uniquely) supports the needs outlined in this chapter, the best way for me to detail my preferred solution to the problem is to describe the approach supported by Scitor's PC-Objectives.

PC-Objectives Design Concepts

I'll start by lifting an excerpt from Scitor's own whitepaper on PC-Objectives.

> With PC-Objectives, you can define all of your organization's objectives in a top-down manner using your browser. As the originator of an objective, you negotiate the objective with producers to define the objective and its time and budget constraints. A top-level objective can spawn lower level objectives so that all of your organization's project work can be linked at the appropriate level to objectives. In this way, every project's "what we are delivering" is linked to an objective's "why we are doing it."
>
> Measurements answer the "how is it going?" question. A measurement has a target value and performance threshold values for status display. For example, a measurement would go from green to yellow and then to red when it exceeded its yellow and red threshold values respectively. Each objective can have multiple measurements. Measurement values can be linked to project cost and schedule data in a PS8 project database or they can be manually entered. Importantly, PC-Objectives keeps a history of all reported measurement values. You can easily spot trends in status by viewing graphs of your measurements.
>
> Using PC-Objectives, authorized stakeholders can view the organization's objectives in a familiar and flexible outline display. Each objective shows the rolled up measurement status using graphical status indicators. Outline controls are used to navigate from top-level objectives to lower level objectives and measurements. Details on selected objectives are available for review. A complete history log of all objective note transactions is maintained for reference.

What We Achieve via This Process

As you can see, this capability, as described above, perfectly responds to the needs discussed earlier. PC-Objectives fully supports the Operations function's need to have a structured means to:

- Define the firm's objectives.
- Communicate the objectives.
- Negotiate with functional and projects leaders on how best to meet the objectives.
- Set measurements, for time, costs, quantities, accomplishments.
- Define thresholds to advise of danger of missing objectives.
- Communicate measurement and threshold values.
- Link project performance monitoring data to the defined objectives measurements.
- Visually display status against these measurements.
- Use color-coded indicators to alert managers of exceeded thresholds.
- Provide trend analysis of support for objectives.
- Support top-level analysis with selective drill down.
- Provide a common communication vehicle for integrated operations and projects data.
- Provide a basis for cooperative resolution of problems and evaluation of alternatives.
- Maintain an audit trail of objectives, changes, and performance.

All the above can be accomplished either by using PC-Objectives with PS8 (Scitor's traditional critical path scheduling and control program) or with PC-Objectives by itself. Normally, if the project has been planned in detail, using PS8, then it would be efficient to incorporate the objectives in PS8, and then feed the status data from PS8 into PC-Objectives. However, a detailed, critical path plan is not necessary to employ PC-Objectives and gain the full benefits of its objectives monitoring capabilities.

Hopefully, by the time you are reading this, several other software developers will have discovered this need for integrating the operations and projects functions through innovative tools. This is exciting. Here we have a simple process, which can be used by all Operations and Projects stakeholders, to support Project Portfolio Management as it was meant to be. Now we can bridge the traditional gap that exists between the Operations and Projects groups. Now we can actually monitor project performance and relate that performance to the objectives of the enterprise. Now we can have an informational basis for dynamic adjustment of the portfolio, and an early warning system to alert responsible managers of imminent danger. Now we can actually do Project Portfolio Management.

CHAPTER 9.3

PROJECT SELECTION AND RISK

Risk Management Is an Essential Part of Project Portfolio Management

A popular subject for the start of the new millennium is *Project Selection*. As we move toward the management of multiple projects within the enterprise, we are often faced with insufficient capital and human resources to engage in every project opportunity. So a process is put in place to govern the selection of projects for the portfolio. Yet, much to my disappointment, a key component of this selection process is often missing. The selection team fails to consider *risk*.

As a practitioner and proselytizer of project management for 40 years, I have been puzzled by this above all others. Why is *risk management* virtually ignored as an integral part of the project selection and management process? We all recognize that risk is an important part of all projects. If we thought about it, we would all acknowledge that the management of risk could be the most critical factor in project success. Yet as I look at the practices that have been put in place in most firms, and at the tools that are being used to support these practices, risk analysis and management are most often missing.

It's not as if the processes and tools were not available, but more of a major lack of interest in the process. I can provide two stories that might help to explain the perilous avoidance of this essential practice.

The Downside Won't Happen

A company decided to enter into a new business segment. As was standard practice for this well-managed conglomerate, a business analysis plan was prepared to evaluate the potential profitability of the new venture. As a normal part of the business plan procedure, three business cases were analyzed: the most probable case, a potential upside case, and a potential downside case. This is all consistent with good business practice. But then, the general manager, when presenting the business plan to the board, said, "Here is the most likely scenario, a potential upside and a potential downside. However, we can ignore the downside case because it will never happen."

The company went ahead with the new venture (assuming that it couldn't lose), as the most likely and upside scenarios predicted a reasonable profit in a reasonable amount of time. Needless to say, the downside did materialize and the venture failed within two years.

Denial Is Our Biggest Enemy

This true incident can be explained, in part, by the message that was presented by James Taylor, Senior Vice President of Gateway 2000, in his keynote address to the Project Management Institute, in Long Beach, CA (10/12/98). His theme was Denial Is Our Biggest Enemy. Digging deeper, we will find that there are several dimensions to this denial. Perhaps, in the company illustration above, the GM deliberately devalued the weight of the potential downside because "he couldn't sell the venture if he admitted the risk." Another dimension is our eternal optimism—preferring to look at the bright side. Unfortunately, wishing that bad things won't happen is almost a sure way of establishing an atmosphere that will breed unwanted events.

Furthermore, an atmosphere of fear (fear of the truth) brings on such denial. The success-minded manager must remove the emotional elements from the business evaluation and promote methods that require objective analyses of the entire business case. To do otherwise puts the liar, the bully, and the myopic at an unfair advantage. The result, understandably, is the improper selection of business opportunities and a deleterious effect on the corporate bottom line.

Trap The failure to select the best business opportunities may eventually cause the business to lose its market position and eventually cause a fatal collapse of the firm.

So why, knowing all of this, do we fail to require the objective analysis and management of risk? It can't be because the process is difficult. Actually there are many approaches and processes for risk evaluation. All are simple and valid, except for the pain of admitting that something can go wrong (that denial thing, again). The key thing to realize is that all the available approaches are simple, down-to-earth methods, certainly not in the realm of rocket science. We discuss these methods in Section 6.

The solution must consist of a total risk management system. Such a system, as part of a project portfolio management system, must contain all the necessary elements that we would have in our PM system. This includes a risk management process, tools to support the risk management process, training in the process and use of the tools, and clear support for the process at all levels of management. An enlightened, risk management-aware senior management must demand to see the entire picture (rather than just the good stuff) and must play the role of the devil's advocate until the entire picture is presented. Yet, in my experience, executives have done just the opposite. They often give the impression that they don't want to know the potential downside or that if they do learn the true risks that they will squash the proposal (which in many cases would be the proper action).

Trap We must discourage the common environment where we tend to kill the messenger of bad news. Under this deleterious environment, we reward those that ignore or hide the truth and penalize those that are diligent about risk analysis and honest about potential project risk exposure.

Project Portfolio Management

One of the emerging themes for the new decade is Project Portfolio Management. Senior management is paying closer attention to the strategic management of a portfolio of projects, requiring the merging of project and operations management and all the tools and practices associated with both disciplines. Risk management is one of these practices. Yet, there is one aspect of risk assessment that I have not seen, either in the literature or in practice. This is *the effect of risk on "payback time."*

Can we assume that our typical business analysis case will contain a cash flow analysis (CFA)? This CFA will show the outflow of money as the project is executed, and the inflow of money (or the projected cost savings) once the benefits of the project start to be realized. At some point in time, the cumulative curve will cross from negative territory (having recouped the investment plus the time-value cost of that money) to where the expected payback starts to accumulate. Usually, this payback analysis is a key component of the decision to proceed with the project.

Now, consider this. Let's say that a project was to cost $10,000 per month, with expected completion in two years. Let's also say that the cost of money is 8 percent per year and that the project will generate an income (or savings) of $10,000 per month, starting immediately upon completion. The projected payback time would be about 50 months (from project initiation).

What do you think would happen to the payback time if the project ran just 4 months over, at a cost overrun of 15 percent per month? Did you correctly calculate that the payback time is extended by a whopping 18 months? If a truthful risk analysis indicated that there was a high probability of this extension to the payback time, might this be enough to sour the executives on the value of this project?

Let's further consider that this project was the average IT/AD project that was surveyed by the Standish Group, several years ago. That 1998 survey noted that the average IT/AD project ran 50 percent longer than planned at a cost overrun of 186 percent. If we apply this to our subject project, it would make it a three-year job, at a cost of $686,000 (not including the time value of the investment). In this case, the payback time would be 99 months. I wonder how many executives would approve the project, if the risk assessment showed a good probability that the payback time would be 99 months, rather than 50 months?

The *effect on payback time* concept is so simple that it can be done on the proverbial back of the envelope. I created a simple example in an Excel spreadsheet, in less than an hour. I am amazed that I rarely see anyone evaluating the effect of delays and cost overruns on return on investment. Yet, if we use the Standish data, such an evaluation would show that the typical project would, based on such performance, extend the payback time to more than twice the original plan. Of course, this is another example of downside potential. And in today's business environment, such bad news is more likely to be swept under the rug, rather than to have the project rejected because of the risk. It's that denial thing, again. Unfortunately, hiding the risk does not prevent it from happening.

Organizing for Managing Project Risk

Executives have come to realize that *projects* are the basis for future profitability of the firm. Hence, there is increased interest on the part of executives in how projects are selected and managed. They are precipitating a growing demand for more standardization and automation of project management. But I do not see the stipulation of a structured approach toward risk management. There has been some success in getting organizations to recognize the importance of having some kind of Project Office (among pockets of resistance). There has been a flood of articles promoting the importance of the project office (also called: project support office, central project office, project management competency center, program office, etc.). I, for one, have not only preached this gospel at every opportunity, but have gone as far as to suggest that the firm have a position of Chief Project Officer. With CEOs, COOs, and CFOs, why not a CPO?

Furthermore, in an environment of project portfolio management, why not a Chief Risk Officer? The CRO would be responsible for establishing standards for risk analysis and management, and for implementing a system of risk practices and tools. The input of the CRO would be required before a proposed project is accepted into the portfolio. A Risk Analysis and Mitigation Plan would be an essential part of the process. A series of gates would be identified for periodic re-evaluation of the Risk Analysis and Mitigation Plan. This would be part of a periodic go/no-go analysis to consider continuation, termination, or adjustment of the project.

A Series of Closing Doors

As a youth group adviser, a few decades ago, I listened to a colleague tell a group of high school kids that life was a series of closing doors. They had all kinds of opportunities under their control. The decisions that they made and the actions that they took (or didn't take) could allow some of those doors to become closed to them.

In a similar vein, Dr. Taylor suggests that a project is a series of closing doors. By the decisions that we make and the actions that we take (or postpone), we tend to shut some of these doors. As we move further and further through a project, there are fewer alternatives available to address problems. This is a natural condition, which cannot be overcome by even the best management practices. But what we can do is to minimize the problems and minimize the deleterious effect of the eventual problems, by organizing properly for projects (with a CPO and a CRO), by implementing a solid risk management program, and by fostering proactive management for early recognition and rectification of such problems.

SECTION 10

PROJECT MANAGEMENT, ENTERPRISE PROJECT MANAGEMENT, AND ENTERPRISE RESOURCE PLANNING

For the first eight sections of this book, we focused on project management. We treated this topic as if project management were the center of the universe. In fact, we treated project management as if it were alone in the universe. Well, it shouldn't come as a surprise that it's not.

True, during the first eight sections, we acknowledged that we had to expand our range of vision beyond that of the individual project. And we went so far as to talk about Enterprise Project Management.

In Section 9, we began to expand our horizons further. We recognized that projects often are a means to an end, rather than the end itself. We looked at the projects function as a partner with the operations function in achieving the overall goals and success of the firm.

In Section 10, we continue to look outward to the larger system of which project management is a part. We start off with a review of the concepts of Enterprise Project Management (Chapter 10.1). But this is only to set up our discussion of a much larger universe—one that includes enterprise resource management solutions and integrates them with project management.

Whether a firm is involved in projects or not, it will surely require the management of its assets, especially its financial and human resource assets. Thus, while we have been looking at the tools and systems that are available to support the projects function, we also have to consider the tools and systems that may be in

281

place to support the finance and human resources functions, as they relate to project activity.

During the past decade a specific group of tools has emerged to provide such support. It is called Enterprise Resource Planning (ERP) software, and it is available from several very prominent software developers, such as Oracle, PeopleSoft, SAP, Baan, and J.D. Edwards. These vendors have sold multimillion-dollar systems to many of the world's largest firms, and are now also offering scaled-down systems to the rest of the businesses of the world.

The people who use these systems are usually outside the project environment. However, they often share quite a bit of information with the people involved in projects. Until about a half-dozen years ago, there was little interest in developing an effective means of data sharing. Each discipline went its own way and the shared data had to be duplicated. Not only was this a waste of effort, but it also allowed for inconsistencies in the data.

Recognizing this inefficiency and gap in communications, many firms began to develop in-house connectivity between their projects, financial, and human resources data systems. Then, the ERP industry discovered the world of projects and reached out to connect with its data.

The integration of project management and enterprise resource planning tools is gaining interest and support. In doing so, it is moving from a custom application, developed by the end user, to a market basket of generic interface modules, developed by PM software vendors. In this section, we provide examples of some of these applications. We expand our horizons to enterprise-wide project management (Chapter 10.1) and discuss what is involved in using ERP applications with project management applications (Chapter 10.2).

After completing this section, you will most likely want to go on to Section 11. There we explore the next phase of the ever-expanding world of project management. Commonly called Professional Services Automation, PSA is being embraced by PM solution providers, ERP solution providers, and best-of-breed PSA providers. The accomplishments, failures, and potential are discussed in Section 11.

CHAPTER 10.1

THE SEARCH FOR AUTOMATED, INTEGRATED, ENTERPRISE-WIDE PROJECT MANAGEMENT

Minnesota Smith and the Temple of Unrealized Dreams

For quite some time (for articles that I have written), I have been following the adventures of Minnesota Smith. When I last saw her, Minnie was rummaging through the Temple of Unrealized Dreams, in search of *automated, integrated, Enterprise-wide Project Management (EPM)*. I was moved to question whether the concept of EPM was a fantasy. Was our adventurous heroine, Minnie, off on a wild goose chase? Was EPM a dream of a utopian, all-inclusive system—one that would tie all project-oriented data together in one integrated process?

What Is EPM?

Actually, the true utopian, all-inclusive system would even reach out to include nonproject data. The system would be robust enough to support vast numbers of users and oodles (a highly technical term) of projects. It would be open, yet secure, satisfying the Corporate Information Office (CIO). On the other hand, it would be so user-friendly that casual, infrequent users, with limited project management and/or computer savvy, would have no difficulty. Such an all-inclusive system would serve the financial and business managers with a full-featured accounting tool and would serve the human resources departments, helping them to manage their human capital. And, somehow, it would also support the needs of project managers (I would hope).

If this is the dream, what is the reality? Are we chasing after rainbows? Or is practical EPM just around the corner? Just how far have we come toward realizing this elusive goal and where is our search taking us?

Early Observations

During the past 40 years, I have been through the entire spectrum of computer environments for project management: punched cards on a mainframe, and several minicomputer and timesharing computer configurations. All of this was endured with trepidation, as I could only be a computer user—the control of the system was by others (on the other side of a formidable barrier). After a 20-year nightmare of overnight runs, massive core dumps, and 2-week turnaround times, the personal computer burst onto the scene, and with it, the promise of user-friendly, user controlled, and fast processing. And this promise was delivered. But did it deliver what we really needed?

Perhaps not. What we did was to optimize the desktop environment, but not the enterprise environment. Individual desktop machines, even when networked, do not satisfy the corporate need. As a result, those people charged with providing an enterprise solution had shied away from desktop systems. They were too hard to administer. The data ended up all over the place. The individual applications were isolated (as well as much of the data).

Could we have our cake and eat it, too? Could the maze of desktop computers be incorporated into a full-featured, integrated system? Could the CIO move away from expensive and cumbersome legacy systems without giving up the control, security, and connectivity that is required? About five years ago, I saw a move in this direction but did not see any strong, commercially available solutions. From my own observations, and feedback from others, even the best single application package did not come close to meeting the enterprise user's specifications. Even the numerous add-ons and consolidators were falling short of meeting the needs.

The Enterprise PM Environment

One of the key elements of the EPM environment is the vast extension of the user universe. The users are in greater number, they are very diversified in interest, and they are geographically separated. These factors have enormous impact on the EPM solution.

Consider the different roles that are involved in EPM. These may include: the CEO or executive level, the Resource Manager or Functional/Line Manager, the CFO or Accounting/Finance, the CIO or Corporate Information Systems function, Project Managers, Project Office or Project Administrators, and the simple user or end user (people working on projects). Notice that this extends well beyond the traditional PM community, bringing in operations people, finance people, and senior management.

How could we expect a single, desktop solution to respond to the needs of such a diverse community? Without a doubt, the planners and project managers still need a robust scheduling tool. But this serves only part of the user community (and could be expected to be used effectively by only a small part of that community).

Needs: Traditional Project Management

For starters, here's where we need a robust time and resource planning tool. It must support critical path scheduling, resource planning, and cost management. We expect such tools to include support for:

- WBS type structures, both for tasks and for resources.
- Critical path computation algorithms.
- Definition of available resources.
- Allocation of resources to tasks.
- Automatic leveling of resource demands.
- Alternate Critical Path and Resource Scheduling Modes (such as Critical Chain and Spreadsheet Resource Assignment).
- Budgeting.
- Progressing of schedule, resources, and costs.
- Earned value measurements and analysis.
- Flexible reporting and communication.

Needs: Enterprise Project Management

Early project management tools were designed for individual projects. Today, we rarely find projects that stand or get managed alone. Multiple projects are the norm in today's firms and the sharing of resources across multiple projects adds new requirements to our project management tool set. Furthermore, the vast amount of project information that is developed in the course of planning and executing the work need not be isolated from the other vital data of the enterprise. So for support of EPM, we should look for

- Electronic time sheets, supporting the collection of actual time spent on project tasks and auxiliary work. These must allow the posting of time to all projects in the system, and should support various means of remote entry. These tools should also provide for management review and control of time reporting.

- Expanded costing, accounting, and cash flow functions.
- Posting and retention of project data in an open, SQL-type database. This database acts as a repository for the data produced by various PM tools, as well as connectivity to other data of the enterprise.

Needs: Communication and Access

The database is an element of the solution, but is worthless unless we can get timely information to it and disseminate appropriate information to all the project stakeholders. In an enterprise-wide system, this two-way flow of information will come from and go to many individuals in several locations. Therefore, these systems must support diverse methods of access. Networked and web-enabled systems are essential. Reports should be composed to meet the needs of each individual involved, customized for each as required to provide a clear picture of the project and to prompt corrective action as needed.

Needs: Operations Management

Section 9 discussed issues associated with project portfolio management. We saw PPM as a means of bridging the gap that often exists between the Projects and Operations functions within the enterprise. Therefore, our EPM system must provide for the needs of the Operations community as well as the Projects community, and must integrate the data systems so that the effort is not duplicated and so that the data is consistent. Decisions that need to be made on the Operations side should be based on up-to-date knowledge of the Projects situation. They need to know what projects are in the pipeline, how these projects are doing (relative to stated objectives), and how the project work is impacting on the firm's resources, cash flow, and strategic initiatives.

Impact on PM Tools

We can divide the description of an EPM supportive tool set into two parts. First, we define the capabilities that the tool set must support. Next, we define the operating environment for this tool set. We already listed capabilities that are desired to support traditional project planning and tracking.

For *EPM*, we add remote inputting of time spent and task status.

To integrate with *Operations*, we add the ability to define objectives, at high and detailed levels, and to coordinate these objectives with the projects data.

To integrate with *Financial* and other business data, we add the ability to coordinate with Enterprise Resource Planning systems, such as SAP and Oracle.

To support the diversified and dispersed user base, we want a system that offers the appropriate operating environment for each. For planning and control, traditional desktop systems, optimized for client/server platforms, are preferred. For the nonproject specialist, web-based modes are preferred, both for remote access and for less intimidating screen forms. All reports should be able to be produced in both traditional and web formats. However, for comprehensive review and analysis, supporting project portfolio management, the data should be available in such modes that allow for easy drill-down and interrogation.

Where in the World Is Minnesota Smith?

Gosh! While getting carried away with writing this chapter, I forgot about our friend Minnie. I just learned that she has found her way out of the Temple of Unrealized Dreams. While searching through the temple rubble, she came across a set of mysterious tablets. Working with experts to decode the markings, she discovered that the tablets contained maps of Northern California, Colorado, Germany, and Holland. Hoping that it would lead her to her quest for automated, integrated, Enterprise-wide Project Management, she was last seen heading for the airport. We look into what she found in the next chapter.

CHAPTER 10.2

INTEGRATING PM AND ERP

Enterprise Resource Planning (ERP) vendors have jumped on the projects bandwagon with new integrative releases that allow operations and projects to find common ground.

It was only about five years ago when I noticed an increased level of activity between vendors of project management software (PMS) and the developers of enterprise resource planning (ERP) systems. My first impulse was This is getting too complex. It's hard enough to keep up to speed with all the PMS products and associated issues. Now, I need to know about several ancillary (and complex) applications and their associated products. Maybe it's time to retire, I thought.

But, as often happens, a common theme keeps on reappearing. And repeatedly, this issue of connecting PMS to these ERP products appeared on the radar screen. It just couldn't be ignored. I had to find out what was going on. Was there a real need? By whom? For what? Ever the skeptic, I had to find out. Was this integration of PMS and ERP really paying dividends or was this merely a great concept with unfulfilled potential?

What Is ERP?

Before I started looking into this topic, I had a better idea of *who* is providing so-called Enterprise Resource Planning solutions than of what it really is. Vendors claiming to offer ERP solutions include SAP, Baan, PeopleSoft, Oracle, J.D. Edwards, and Lawson. One of these vendors presented the solution as follows:

> The business world is moving increasingly toward a projects orientation of operation to measure the true costs and profitability of any business endeavor. As this paradigm takes root even in industries not traditionally identified as project-driven, the need for a complete activity management solution, integrated to a company's core financial systems, has become more critical. With leaner staff and more demand for performance, every activity must add value.
>
> You need, therefore, to be able to measure the true costs and added value of any activity. And in tracking these factors, there can be no disparity between the line manager's data and the corporate finance numbers, because time spent reconciling this data adds no value. To allow for maximum productivity, this data must be collected with a minimum of administrative burden.
>
> Oracle Projects is the bridge between Operations and Corporate Finance, maintaining the central repository of project information while sharing it with other systems and varied users in the format that serves each best. (Oracle Applications for Projects)

So what do we have here? We have more people jumping on the projects bandwagon—realizing the need for and profitability in support for the projects paradigm. And this should come as no surprise. The information in the projects database must be able to flow freely, securely, and accurately to the corporate accounting systems, and back.

The statement by Oracle seems to hit the nail on the head. It recognizes the increased awareness of projects in the enterprise, and the value of measuring the impact of projects on the overall operations. It further recognizes the necessity for data consistency and integrity.

Frankly, this is not such a new theme. I personally was involved in promoting connectivity and integration of projects and accounting data, more than a quarter century ago, but was rebuffed by the (understandable) skepticism of the financial analysts (the bean counters, we called them) that the projects people couldn't be counted on to contribute timely, consistent data. In the past 15 years, as a consultant, connectivity and integration of projects and accounting data were frequent requirements on a client's system wish lists. But still, the question of how to achieve timely, reliable, consistent data integration, together with the question of who owns and controls the data, stands in the way of achievement of this worthwhile goal.

> **Tip** In many cases, the implementation of an ERP system represents more than just a new tool or system, but rather the opportunity to reengineer key business practices and to benefit from the adoption of recognized best business practices.

Why Integrate?

Let's get back to the basic recognition that the management of projects and the management of operations are essentially different. They are different in both the way that performance and success are measured and in the type of personnel and skills involved in the measurements and management. As noted previously, we rarely see the operations people, with their emphasis on period-by-period business operations and financial measurements, involved in the analysis of project performance. On the other hand, how often do we see project managers evaluating the effect of their projects on the current and future success of the enterprise?

Yet the raw truth is that the two are inseparable. Enterprise-level planning, analysis of results, and decisions for the future require that the total picture be available. The data supporting this total picture must be current, integrated, and able to be analyzed from several perspectives.

Once we recognize the need for such data integration, we can also realize the benefits of single entry of data and consistency of such data. Without this integration, we not only lose efficiency by necessitating redundant data entry, but also face the risk of conflicting data.

> **Trap** Many operations people, and software providers supporting business operations, have been attempting to bridge this gap with so-called project accounting systems. However, for the most part, these tools address little, if any, of the needs of project management. They tend to emphasize historical performance and financial controls, at a summary level, ignoring forecasting and performance analysis, and limiting the ability to apply the data to project details.

Examples of Projects/ERP Integration

I decided to take a closer look at some of the ERP-based solutions, starting with the one offered by Oracle. It appears to deliver the capabilities advertised in their statement. Looking specifically at the role of a suite of products (sold under the umbrella label of Oracle Projects), we do find a bridge between projects-oriented data and the corporate operations data. Oracle Projects is their doorway into Oracle Financials and other Oracle components, as shown in Figure 10.2a. By partnering with PMS vendors, they create a second doorway, which allows continuity between projects and accounting data, with single entry. This is what people are asking for when they talk about enterprise PM systems.

Tool Tip The discussion here on ERP/PM integration focuses on a solution offered by two vendors, Oracle and Artemis. This is only one of several offerings from many of the popular PM and ERP vendors, and is used solely as a means to illustrate the types of solutions that are available in this area. The mention of any of these offerings does not constitute a vendor choice by the author.

Figure 10.2a   Oracle Projects Integration

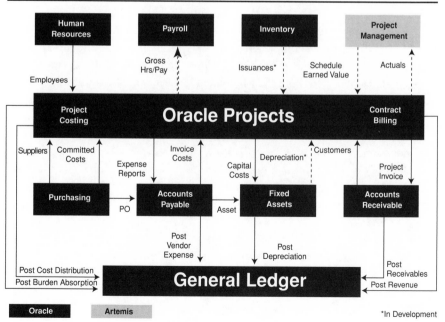

Oracle has developed partnership agreements with several PM vendors, including Artemis, Primavera, Welcom, and Mantix, and is adding new partners every year. The role of the partners is to develop, market, and support an interface product, which will facilitate two-way transfer of data between the project management program and the Oracle Projects Activity Management Gateway module.

For instance, Primavera has developed a set of Application Programming Interfaces (APIs) which enable rapid data access between applications. In addition to linking Primavera Project Planner (P3) to Oracle Projects, an interface can provide access to Project System, from SAP. This facilitates integration with the SAP R/3 system. Primavera also has interfaces to PeopleSoft and J.D. Edwards. All of these interfaces will work with the full range of Primavera's project tools: SureTrak, P3, P3e, Team Play, and Expedition.

Welcom has developed links between Open Plan and Cobra (their PM and Earned Value products) and two ERP products: SAP/R3 and Baan (IV & 5).

Artemis has developed their ArtemisViews/Oracle Projects interface to link ProjectView, TrackView, and CostView with Oracle Projects, as shown in Figure 10.2b. The ProjectView/Oracle Projects interface facilitates the transfer of system-level data, such as organizational structure, calendars, and resource data from Oracle Projects to ProjectView. Project templates stored in Oracle Projects can also be used to open a standardized project in ProjectView. Once the project is established, via either transfer or development in ProjectView, the project data can be sent to Oracle Projects. This might include work breakdown structures, activities, resource requirements and budgets, performance, and earned value data. During project implementation, accounting data, such as charged hours and invoiced costs, can be entered directly into Oracle, and passed down to the scheduling system, as well as on to Oracle Financials.

Artemis' CostView software manages the extensive cost data usually associated with government projects (C/SCSC). With the CostView/Oracle Projects interface, these cost data can be transferred between both products. The interface provides three window tabs, for Actuals, Budgets, and Earned Value.

Artemis has also joined SAP's Complementary Solution Program, for integration with SAP R/3.

In addition to the three partnership agreements between Oracle and Artemis/Primavera/Mantix, Oracle has determined that an interface is needed to integrate with Microsoft Projects. In this case, rather than development and sales of the interface tool by the project management software vendor (Microsoft), the tool (Project Connect) is provided by Oracle.

Figure 10.2b   ArtemisViews/Oracle Projects Interface

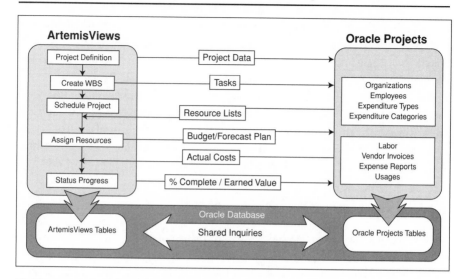

What's Different?

The ability to transfer data between applications is certainly neither new nor unique. If fact, even some of the vendors discussed above have accessory packages to facilitate such connectivity. Primavera's DataStore allows the saving of P3 data in native Oracle formats, as do several other programs. Artemis' ProjectView has long used Oracle as one of its file formats. Furthermore, most programs support ODBC protocols to allow exchange of SQL-formatted data. Artemis also markets GlobalView, an OLAP-based tool to facilitate the multifaceted analysis of project data generated by their other Views products.

Where we gain from the ArtemisViews/Oracle Projects modules, and other similar capabilities, is improved automation and control. Working within the Oracle Projects modules, we can define process workflows and rules. Oracle Workflow is one of the tools available to define such things as required approvals for changing project status or budgets, as well as defining the notification process.

The Oracle Projects Activity Management Gateway (AMG) is the mechanism used for connectivity to project management software packages, to other Oracle systems, such as Financial Accounting, and to a data warehouse. The AMG module also provides for security and standards by defining the rules for data exchange and updating. An AutoAccounting function automatically generates financial accounting transactions and posts them to General Ledger.

Individual contributors use the Oracle Personal Time and Expense module to record their time and expenses. An option, for online posting, via the Web, is available in the Oracle Project Costing module. These modules are also integrated with Oracle Projects Billing, which is further integrated with Oracle Receivables.

For enterprise-wide, multiproject, multidimensional analysis, the industry direction is to bring data from selected modules into a data warehouse, utilizing online transactional processing. For example, the Oracle Data Analysis Collection Pack facilitates interrogation of all the project data of the enterprise. The multidimensional views allow you to slice and dice the data, at varied levels of detail.

State-of-the-Art

This is a fairly new set of technology. Most of the products just discussed were officially introduced during the past four years. The development of project-centric data handling structures, by the leading ERP and data management companies, together with tools that facilitate the integration of these products with traditional project management software, is a natural move toward more inclusive, better integrated systems, that will also provide improved security and rules standardization. The trend is toward greater use of web-based capabilities, which is also bringing about rapid changes in the names of the products.

Firms seeking to manage all of their projects in an enterprise-wide mode, while minimizing duplication of data entry and maximizing connectivity to the corporate financial and data systems, will want to take a good look at these new offerings. The CFO will appreciate the ability to analyze the impact of projects on the business. The CIO, using the data warehouse, will appreciate the improved data security and consistency. Both will appreciate the rules-based flow of data within the greater system. The CPO (Chief Projects Officer) will appreciate the automated link to time and cost data, and the single point of entry. The CEO will finally gain the long-awaited objective of fully integrated analysis and forecasting of all the firm's business.

Trap   While putting an interfaced PM/ERP system in place can go a long way toward providing the CEO, CFO, CIO, and Projects Team the tools that they need to manage both operations and projects, we must not forget that a strong, structured project management function is still a prerequisite for project success.

Issues

Some issues have come up in my readings and discussions that should be explored. One is some concern that these ERP systems can require considerable consulting support before they are fully implemented. Another concern is the total cost for acquisition and implementation of an ERP system.

ERP systems are not off-the-shelf software. The cost of taking the packaged software and turning it into an operating solution can often exceed the base cost of the bare software itself. Even the task of determining your needs, envisioning a solution, and designing the solution may exceed the skills of your internal organization. This may motivate you to seek consulting support from the many firms that specialize in this discipline. This is another source of considerable cost of a PM/ERP solution.

Trap Software acquisition or licensing is but a small part of the cost of ERP/PM systems. The larger segment, by far, is consulting. But this may also be the key to successful system design and implementation.

The Bottom Line

As noted earlier in this chapter, the integration of project management and project accounting tools and databases, by independent systems integrators, is neither a new objective nor a new process. So we wondered what impact the emergence of these new vendor-integrated, partnered systems would have on the market for enterprise-wide system integrations. Perhaps the best answer comes from an e-mail that I received from a consultant who had been earning his bread from working on custom enterprise solutions. We quote:

> As far as I am concerned the Oracle Project/Artemis API integration is the future for Integrated Enterprise Project Management Systems—anyone who continues to pursue internal development in this area will be selling themselves and their Company short.

We can probably substitute several names for the project management and ERP software vendors mentioned in this chapter. The successful providers will be companies who understand both the projects and operations side of the enterprise—and who can work closely and enthusiastically to serve this emerging market.

SECTION 11

PROJECT MANAGEMENT AND PROFESSIONAL SERVICES AUTOMATION

Markets change. And as the needs that are represented by these markets are identified, new business models, and tools to support these models, emerge to respond to these needs. Some tools come from new vendors who, seeing the opportunity, either develop software capabilities specifically to meet the needs, or acquire tools to create a best-of-breed solution. Other tools come from existing vendors who switch gears either by changing the emphasis of their solutions or by teaming with other developers to widen their response. Mergers and acquisitions become almost daily events as the aspiring vendors maneuver to gain position in the emerging (and not yet well-defined) market.

In 2001, all of this activity is centered on the relatively new Professional Services Automation (PSA) market. Even as this chapter is being written, the vendors change, merge and acquire companies, products, and skills, and sometimes even discard the ones that they picked up last year.

This emerging market lies almost entirely within the Information Technology (IT) sector. But this is such an enormous sector, especially where issues of project management and delivery are concerned, as to warrant significant attention and activity.

In this section, we describe the PSA market and discuss the issues associated with this market. We will look at the various sources of solutions and present an overview of what these sources are providing. But first, let's look at who the target beneficiaries of PSA solutions are. Primarily, they are divided into two groups:

1. Professional Services Organizations (PSOs).
2. Internal Information Systems Organizations (ISOs).

The PSOs are also called ESPs (External Service Providers). These are businesses that are involved in consulting, advertising, system integration, and so on. They will benefit from automated support to help them manage activities, account for time and expenses, and forecast possible sell time. They are primarily concerned with:

- Opportunity management.
- Resource management.
- Program/Project management.
- Time and Expense management (T&E).
- Document management.
- Knowledge/Practice management.
- Invoicing and Billing (Financials).
- Reporting and analysis.
- Customer Relations management (CRM)—Contact Management—Client Management.

The ISOs are not that different. They will be managing similar work as the PSOs, except that they are not involved in selling their skilled resources to the external market. Consequently, they are primarily concerned with:

- Resource management.
- Program/Project management.
- Time and Expense management (T&E).
- Document management.
- Knowledge/Practice management.
- Project Accounting and Chargebacks (Financials).
- Reporting and analysis.

In addition to PSA, you will find similar services being offered under different names, such as:

- Service Chain Automation (SCA).
- Enterprise Service Automation (ESA).
- Enterprise Workforce management.
- Workforce Automation Solutions.
- Service Delivery Management Solutions.
- Services Process Optimization (SPO).

In this section on Professional Services Automation, we first define the PSA market (Chapter 11.1). We then look into what kind of solutions are being offered and where they are coming from (Chapter 11.2).

CHAPTER 11.1

DEFINING THE **PSA** MARKET

In the introduction to this section, we started to define PSA and the market that it serves. Let's move on to look at some of the pertinent questions in this area. Who are the people served by these solutions? What problems are they trying to solve? What parts of the IT industry are involved? And, perhaps the most important, what conditions have precipitated and influenced the birth and growth of this market?

Gartner Group has been active in defining the PSA market and in following developments in that area. The following are extracted from analyses conducted in 2001.

- Virtually no enterprises can meet all of their IS service requirements internally. E-enabled enterprises' reliance on External Service Providers (ESPs) will continue to grow, to unprecedented levels.
- As internal IS service providers become more profit-minded and value-focused, their business models will begin to mirror ESPs'.
- By 2003, 50 percent of large enterprises will use ESP prime contractors to help manage the complexity of IS contractor services.
- By 2003, most enterprises will use computerized collaborative practices extending beyond the enterprise for RFPs, resourcing and project management, and other administrative functions.

Gartner's market research leads them to conclude that:

- One hundred percent of customers say they cannot meet their IT service needs internally.
- Seventy-five percent of customers say that, within the next 12 months, they plan to conduct some portion of B2B or B2C transactions over the Web.
- Thirty percent are currently using or planning to use an IT utility service.
- Thirty percent of enterprise organizations are planning on becoming virtual companies.
- Fifteen percent of Fortune 1,000 CIOs do not want to own their IT infrastructures.

This creates an environment wherein the current skill sets of External Service Providers will have to grow from Process Management to include Resource Management, Demand Management, and Financial and Business Management. These expanded skill sets will include:

- **Process Management**
  Process Engineering.
  Measurement and Metrics.
  Quality Assurance.
- **Resource Management**
  Strategic Sourcing.
  Capability Management.
  Skills Management.
  Recruitment/Retention.
  Continuous Development.
  Compensation/Rewards.

- **Demand Management**
  Business Development.
  Relationship Management.
  Sales.
  Marketing.
  Communications.
  Market Research.
- **Financial & Business Management**
  Competitive Analysis.
  Financial Management.
  Product Development.
  Product/Service Bundling.
  Pricing Strategies.

To support the needs expressed in the list, above, PSA solutions are being developed to automate a large variety of business functions. According to a report by SPEX, the specific functions supported may consist of any or all of these:

- *Administration*—The tools provided to monitor and optimize the workings of the system. This includes support for automated deployment, the ability to configure alerts, customization of the user interface (UI), support for databases, and so on. There are no clear leaders in terms of administrative functionality, but each solution may approach the same problem differently. This is why we include it as a differentiator.

- *Opportunity Management* (including sales automation and proposal management features)—The ability to manage and track contacts and competitors, perform win/loss analysis, and draft winning proposals, based on specific price margins. Opportunity management helps manage clients, ensuring greater customer intimacy. It also ensures that the most profitable opportunities become engagements. Account4 has greatly improved its CRM functionality recently, which puts it at the top with Evolve and Portera.

- *Human Resources (HR)*—The ability to maintain information on your resources, support for training management, including online training courses, as well as the procurement of external resources from other departments, labor exchanges, partners, or even independent contractors. PeopleSoft has a clear edge here, though Portera has excellent training management functions as well.

- *Resource Management*—The ability to search for resources across multiple pools with weighted (dynamic or static) criteria (e.g., skills, location, availability) and the ability to staff these resources in the most efficient manner possible, ensuring that no resource remains on the bench. We believe Evolve and Novient offer exceptional resource management functionality, though other vendors are beginning to gain ground in this area (e.g., PeopleSoft, Account4, QuickArrow, Changepoint).

- *Program/Project Management*—The ability to track and manage programs and projects, with alerts to make sure projects will be completed on time and that the project end does not impede on profit margins. PlanView clearly offers the deepest PM functionality, though Novient has made tremendous strides, after having integrated WebProject into its PSA solution.

- *Time and Expenses (T&E)*—The ability to enter T&Es with support online and offline, as well as support for multicurrency, multiple projects, and expenses to be applied across projects. PeopleSoft offers deep T&E functionality, as do Evolve and Portera.

- *Workflow Functionality*—The ability to set thresholds and floors, where alerts (visual, audio, and e-mail alerts) are sent to indicate user-defined events. Workflow helps manage and automate process flow within the organization. There is no clear leader in workflow functionality as each package offers certain strengths and limitations.

- *Knowledge Management* (including document management and best practices)—The ability to store, in a central repository, all documents related to employees, opportunities, and projects, with security and then to draw on this information to improve the effectiveness of interactions with clients, and fulfillment of engagements. Novient and Portera offer exceptional capabilities in this area.

- *Reporting Tools*—The ability to generate flexible and detailed reports for individuals throughout the organization (e.g., consultants, project managers, executives, clients), with support for dashboards, OLAP, and import/export. Changepoint continues to have an edge in the creation of reports, but Novient and Evolve both offer solid reporting features as well.
- *Billing*—The ability to create detailed invoices natively that can be sent to clients. It is important to have flexibility in determining the frequency of billing cycles and adjustments that need to be made to T&Es before bills are sent out. PeopleSoft offers the richest billing functions.
- *Financials*—The ability to track A/P, A/R, and GL to know how well the company is performing. Most packages integrate with third-party solutions to offer this functionality, but with the emergence of ERP vendors in this space, it is certainly a critical differentiator. PeopleSoft offers the richest financial functions, but other PSA vendors have solid interfaces to a greater diversity of financials applications. This is important for organizations not already using PeopleSoft for financials, which is at an additional cost. Portera offers seamless integration to a customized version of Oracle Financials.
- *Integration*—The heavy reliance on third-party applications for CRM, HR, PM, and financials makes solid integration a necessity. At the publication of last year's report, most integration involved flat files, but now PSA vendors are offering XML-based APIs and a few are partnering with enterprise application integration (EAI) vendors to offer greatly improved, standard interfaces to commonly used third-party solutions. In terms of APIs, most vendors offer solid XML-based APIs.

(SPEX, division of Meta Group, Inc., 2001)

This is all a far cry from the traditional scope of offerings from the popular PM or ERP vendors. With PSA, we are moving from buying a product, with multiple capabilities, to buying a solution, made up of several products. Unfortunately, as we see in the next chapter, there are many hurdles to clear before these solutions reach maturity.

CHAPTER 11.2

BUILDING PSA SOLUTIONS

PSA is an amalgam of PM and ERP, focusing on resource management (or human capital) like time, knowledge, skills, and business relationships, as opposed to simple task management. Because the solutions are built on several different aspects of project, resource, and business management, we are finding that the purveyors of such solutions are coming from several areas of the industry.

Sources of PSA Solutions

For starters, we can see at least four distinct groups that are providing PSA solutions. These are:

1. Traditional PM Providers—Vendors of traditional project scheduling and management tools, such as PlanView, Account4, Artemis, Primavera, and Business Engine.
2. ERP Providers—The traditional Enterprise Resource Planning vendors, such as Oracle, PeopleSoft, SAP, J.D. Edwards, and Lawson.
3. PSA-specific Providers—New developers, building new solutions to support this newly identified application area. These include vendors such as Niku, Novient, Evolve, Changepoint, and Portera. In many instances, these solutions are not based on new tools, but are rather a best-of-breed creation, made via the acquisition of existing products.

4. B2B Resource Exchange—A newly emerging category. Business-to-business (B2B) tools are aimed at bringing businesses together, electronically, by providing immediate access to needs and supply data. A particularly pertinent (to PSA) aspect of the B2B category is the sites that promote the matching of available resources to defined needs. These would include SkillsVillage and Opus360. For instance, PlanView has alliances with three B2B personnel sites. In general, the concept of the public labor exchange has not gained wide acceptance. However, a more limited model, supporting organizations that have a predefined labor agreement (a private labor exchange), does show more immediate promise.

In all cases, of the four categories described above, the vendors are being forced to extend their capabilities well outside their traditional boundaries. This is being accomplished via acquisitions, mergers, and partnerships. For instance, in the PSA-specific category, Niku acquired project management products from ABT Corporation, and Novient acquired project management capabilities from WebProject.

The other categories are just as active. PeopleSoft (ERP) has acquired Skills Village, while Artemis (PM) has acquired Opus360. More recently, Lawson expanded their ERP focus to acquire one of the PSA leaders, Account4.

The Typical PSA Model

A problem with this emerging category is that there is no typical PSA model. The potential coverage of a PSA suite can include processes and data for a plethora of projects, resources, finances, customer relations, opportunities, and other business operations. Each emerging PSA provider tends to focus on the area in which the firm has built its reputation, slowly expanding that focus and adding new capabilities (often via the merger and acquisition route).

Thus, the traditional PM providers tend to be rich in PM capabilities, whereas the ERP providers may initially emphasize the financial and human resource management functions. To complicate things even further, many early entries into this market are already redefining and redesigning their models. One of the first developers to enter and define the PSA market recently told me that they no longer label their offerings PSA. In other cases, some of the acquisitions that were made to expand product depth have been abandoned.

This obviously is not a well-defined product area. To the potential PSA user, this presents both an opportunity and a risk. On the plus side, the lack of a rigid model means that there will be greater variation and selection available. The user should be able to find a provider that comes from the primary area of interest and shares a common focus with the user. On the other hand, there is little assurance that the products that are offered today will be available and supported a year later.

Trap The immaturity and instability of the emerging PSA line of products poses a risk to the buyer of such services. Utilizing such services on a pay-as-you-go basis (monthly subscription) reduces the potential loss of a large cash investment. However, since the cost of software licensing is a small part of the total cost of implementing such systems, having to abandon the system (or having the vendor abandon the system) reduces but does not eliminate the risk. The buyer should evaluate the risks and take them into consideration when selecting a vendor.

PSA: Now You See It, Now You Don't

The emergence of a new market, PSA, has come at a difficult time. When first conceived, the technology arena, including software development, was in overdrive and investment capital was abundant. The Y2K scare had passed and the entire field was accelerating to full speed. Then the pullback hit and the market went into a holding pattern. (Or I guess a spin would be more accurate.)

Especially hard hit were the PSA-specific vendors. These had not yet established a solid customer base and were working more on investment funding than client income. The more established PM and ERP vendors, although also affected by the pullback, had a sufficient client base and income stream to keep their heads above water.

At the same time, the PSA-specific vendors appear to be redefining their target market and the products to support that market. As a result, the term PSA, which ironically had originated with these firms, is being dropped, in favor of things like Workforce Optimization and Enterprise Services Automation.

The marketing focus is being directed to internal IS operations and the CIO. There is less attention to Professional Service Organizations, partially because these types of organizations are suffering badly from the technical sector recession. The market just isn't there.

PSA Options

If you are looking for PSA type solutions, you still have several viable options. The traditional PM software vendors will continue to branch outward to embrace additional capabilities in support of enterprise-wide services management. Likewise, the leading ERP vendors will also be adding functionality to expand opportunity management, project integration, and collaboration.

While this is all happening, prospective users will be advised to use caution in selecting a solution provider. If the new capabilities are being added via acquisition, it may take some time to achieve effective integration of the expanded functions. If the new capabilities are being added via internal development, it may take some time for the new features to reach maturity and become fully functional.

If you need strong PM functionality, your best bet may be to stick with established PM software providers. Their offerings will usually be the strongest in support of PM requirements. If your needs center more on financial or human resource management, you can expect better support from the ERP vendors, at the expense of weaker PM support.

Almost all PSA offerings will provide support for Microsoft Project. However, at this time, most PM practitioners rate that product as weaker than desired to support enterprise-level project management.

Another area of concern is the actual execution of the PSA capability within the organization. Unless your organization is willing to adapt its practices to match the out-of-the-box solution provided by the software vendor, you can expect to require customization of the application, using third-party providers.

Therefore, you can expect to make a choice among:

- An out-of-the-box solution—accepting the design of the software vendor to drive your practices.
- A biased solution—emphasizing the focus of the vendor, toward either PM functionality or ERP functionality.
- A best-of-breed solution—selecting components from various providers and building a custom application and integration of the tools.

Trap The term *best-of-breed* would lead us to believe that such solutions contain the best components possible. While this is potentially true, the fact is that the capabilities of best-of-breed products can be negated by the lack of seamless integration of the components. This has been a problem for those firms that acquire (or partner with) the best products, but struggle to make them work well together. It usually takes a few generations of system development to smooth out the problems of different characteristics and cultures of the individual components.

SECTION 12

TOOLS OF THE TRADE

Throughout this book, we continually express the position that project management isn't just about using the computer for planning and control. Rather, we have pleaded with you to address the issues of organizing for project management and developing appropriate project management practices and procedures. Only then can we be in a position to select and utilize computerized tools for project management. But now it is time to look at the subject of using the computer to support our project management practices.

The act of specifying, evaluating, and selecting project management software can be intimidating and confusing. Often, we are called upon to initiate this action while under the extreme pressure of dealing with a project in crisis, and under the extreme limitation of not knowing anything about what we really expect these tools to do. Frankly, when I have been asked to advise an organization on the issue of selecting project management software, I try to get the group to sit through a seminar on project management basics prior to initializing the selection process. Unfortunately, as important as this step is, it is not always practical to exercise.

In Chapter 1.4, we illustrated a recommended plan for the implementation of a computer-based project management capability. This consisted of five steps, starting with (1) Methods, (2) Tools, (3) Training. It is essential that this first step, determining your methods of project management, precede the selection of the tools. The tools are required to support your method of project management.

We can easily direct you to a process for specifying, evaluating, and selecting project management software that can take a good part of a year and involve extensive use of resources. However, the name of this book is *Practical Project Management*. So we will compromise by providing a simplified approach to project management software selection, in Chapter 12.1. This process will get you up and running. It is certainly possible that what you come up with will not be perfect (there is no way to expect that even with a very diligent selection process).

But it will put you in position to have automation support for your project management practices, and to learn from the initial experiences so that both the practices and the tools can be improved as your project management capabilities mature.

While you are out looking at the available tools for project management, you will likely run across several new categories of automation support, in addition to the traditional CPM-based products. Some of these are new capabilities and some are rearrangements of older capabilities, with new names. We discuss the emergence of these new tools in Chapter 12.2.

Along with the emergence of the rebadged capabilities is a whole set of new capabilities that build upon the new web-based environment. Collaboration Services, Business-to-Business Services, Gateways and Portals, are all part of the twenty-first century's gift to project management practitioners—providing us with a greater reach to information and knowledge and greatly enhancing and speeding up communication. We discuss the e revolution in Chapter 12.3.

CHAPTER 12.1

A SIMPLIFIED AND BALANCED APPROACH TO PM SOFTWARE SELECTION

Chapter 1.4 outlines the five key steps to implementing a computer-based project management capability. The five components of this process are:

1. Methods.
2. Tools (Software Selection).
3. Training.
4. Implementation Plan.
5. Audit Process.

In that chapter, we deferred detailed discussion of the second component to this section on Tools of the Trade. We start off with a few of the comments that were presented earlier followed by a practical method of selecting the tools that you will need to support your project management initiatives.

Software Selection

It is very easy to go overboard with the PM software selection process. I have seen teams of more than 50 people formed and spend two years in a structured selection process. A selection specification was developed that would dwarf a phone book. Vendors were called in for presentations. Shortlist products were tested. Selection candidates were approved by several levels of management. Perhaps a bit of overkill?

But is the other extreme any better? Should PM software be selected by the edict of a single individual, based on something that he had read, without any knowledge of the product or the application? I guess that I'd rather have the overkill.

I have seen a selection team review dozens of candidates, against an extensive selection specification, and then reject the lot of them in favor of developing an in-house tool. This is not something that I would recommend. The firm's talents can be better put to use for other tasks that would contribute to the firm's mission. The firm's mission is not "to develop project management tools."

Again, on the other extreme, I have seen the selection process completely short-circuited when a complimentary copy of Microsoft Project mysteriously appeared on a desk. "Why bother looking at anything else" was the result.

I cannot recommend any of these approaches. But there is a middle-of-the-road solution that I can prescribe.

A Simplified and Balanced Approach to PM Software Selection

The selection of project management software should be a team effort. Normally, the team would consist of from three to six key players, relying on contributions from all stakeholders. The team needn't find consensus among all the stakeholders. But their inputs should be sought and valued, and they should be made to know that their inputs count.

Trap   It is a basic tenet of human behavior to wish to be included in decisions that affect you. It is usually very difficult to include all such stakeholders in the entire decision process, and it is virtually impossible to satisfy the desires of all the stakeholders. But it is also a general behavioral response that, if contacted and included in the discussions that lead to the decisions, these individuals would be more likely to accept the eventual decision.

Furthermore, this same human behaviorism tends to make people oppose and reject decisions that were made without their inputs or consideration. Therefore, to avoid unnecessary opposition to your PM software selection decisions, you should openly seek wide discussion and communication of the process.

Selection should be made on the basis of the large picture. Consider connectivity to other systems. Consider both current and future needs. Avoid political decisions, such as choosing a product because you would have less risk of criticism if the solution failed. Look for ways to bridge the normal chasm between the projects and the operations functions.

Don't concentrate too much on software cost. Most tool solutions represent but a miniscule part of the costs of doing projects. But do consider life-cycle costs. How much will it cost to operate the system, say for five years, including software, hardware upgrades, and training?

Don't get caught up in little details. Look more at what you need to accomplish with the software, rather than at the feature set. A recent *Dilbert* cartoon, by Scott Adams, pictured someone presenting a desired feature list of several hundred items. When questioned as to the potential effect of such an expansive list on the usability of the software, he responded, "Oh! Let's add ease-of-use to the list."

There will need to be a balance between the expanse of features and ease-of-use. But here are two things to note about this. First, due to differences in product design, some products will be easier to use than others, even when having similar functional attributes. Second, expect all PM software products to be complex. They will not be as easy-to-learn or easy-to-use as word processing or spreadsheet tools because the typical user will have to learn many new things about planning and control in addition to learning the new tool.

Information Overload

Over the past 15 years, I have written, taught, lectured, and consulted on the topic of Specifying, Evaluating, and Selecting Project Management Software. This includes a formal seminar, a book *Project Management Using Microcomputers* (Osborne/McGraw-Hill, 1986), a chapter on that topic in David I. Cleland's *Field Guide to Project Management* (VNR, 1998), and a video produced by IBM's Skill Dynamics.

In my enthusiasm to fully cover the topic, I more often than not got carried away with details. This compulsion to cover every aspect of software selection and use may have been technically sound, but, in retrospect, may have failed to have the desired effect. I may have made my audience more knowledgeable and aware (an important objective), but did I leave them in a better position to make a selection decision (the ultimate goal)?

Looking back, my approach was to use a work breakdown structure to organize the details. There were about a dozen first level subjects, each with several sub-items, making for about 200 total characteristics and features to consider. I fear that my extensive coverage of the topic was as intimidating as it was helpful.

The Simplified, Balanced Approach

In this chapter, we offer a more simplified approach to PM software selection. Recognizing the growing popularity of The Balanced Scorecard philosophy, we reduce the 200 items to just four major categories, and look for comprehensive and balanced support for these four areas.

It is important that the software that is selected will meet the needs of the entire community that is involved in projects, and that it provides complete and quality support for the firm's project management process.

The Four Key Categories

Subject to the possibility that we may be moving from an overly detailed approach to an overly simplified approach, we will consider these four important areas:

1. The User Interface.
2. Data Management.
3. The Scheduling Engine.
4. Multi-user Access and Communication.

Tip If we can satisfy all four categories, we are likely to have a product that we can use effectively as part of a computer-based project management system. If any one of these areas is unduly weak, we can expect failure of the entire system.

The Scheduling Engine

As our software systems get more and more sophisticated, and the user base gets more widespread (and less computer savvy), the software selection process tends to focus more on the User Interface characteristics. As a response, the software developers have placed a special emphasis on making it easy to put the data in and to navigate about the tool.

Likewise, as the user base for the system output expands, the need grows for improved data management and manipulation. Here, too, the vendors have responded with razzle-dazzle features that slice and dice the data from every conceivable angle.

Chances are that these two items (the user interface and data management) are the ones that get most of everyone's attention. Yet it is in the scheduling engine where we see significant differences, and where deficiencies can lead to ineffective computer-based PM applications. So let's look at the scheduling engine criteria first.

Across the board, the available products keep on getting better in these first two areas and the user community has benefited from these improvements. But let's think a bit about why you are using project management software in the first place. Here's a list of typical objectives.

- Store system calendars.
- Store resource pool data.
- Store project key dates and milestones.
- Store the project workscope.
- Store the project work breakdown structure.
- Store time and work estimates, resource assignments, and costs.
- Calculate schedules.
- Assist in assigning resources.
- Resolve resource scheduling conflicts.
- Calculate budgets.
- Plot cash flow curves.
- Collect and calculate applied time (timesheets).
- Collect task status and recalculate schedules.
- Collect actual costs.
- Calculate earned value performance results.

In addition, many users may wish to add the following, either in the basic product or in add-ons:

- Identify risk areas.
- Quantify risk items.
- Calculate risk mitigation options.
- Employ Critical Chain scheduling protocols.
- Store typical plan templates and estimates.
- Integration with ERP products and data.
- Incident tracking.
- Change control.

Trap The simplified selection process discussed herein covers much of the detail that was included in my more extensive earlier methods. The difference is that the newer method places the focus on the use of the tools and the results that they deliver, rather than on a list of specifications. It is easy to get carried away with the detailed specifications list and lose sight of the objectives—which should be to automate your PM practices, based on your preferred PM methodology.

Think about these functions. What kind of data do you need to input, calculate, or output regarding these items? Can the tool that you are considering handle these data, in the manner that you need for your business? Can you create discrete models of your plan in the system? Or do you have to jury-rig them to make them fit the systems limitations?

Are the algorithms in the program sophisticated enough to calculate correct and efficient schedules? Can you repeat the calculations and get the same result each time? Can you preserve defined constraints? Can you define complex assignments?

When you attempt to resolve resource conflicts (via resource leveling), are you left with gaps where resources are available to work but are not assigned to tasks that could be worked on? Are the resource schedules consistent with the task schedules (I have experienced products that could have a task scheduled for two days, but show the resource as working on it for five days)? Are the earned value calculations correct? These are not idle questions. These are all items where I have found deficiencies in some PM software products in the past.

Chances are that you assumed that all products work about the same and will produce similar results. My evaluations of the popular products show that this is not true.

While I chose to use the term *scheduling engine* for this key category, you can see that it goes well beyond basic scheduling. On the one hand, almost all the popular products use the traditional activity-on-the-node critical path scheduling approach, and the serial algorithm for resource leveling. However, each vendor has designed its own characteristics around these two basic calculation models, which may add or detract from the basic capabilities.

In addition to evaluating for fidelity and consistency, for ability to handle your specific needs, and for usability, you will also want to consider other performance characteristics, such as speed of opening files, calculating schedules, leveling resources, saving files, and manipulating data.

And don't forget to examine all of these items from the point of view of multi-project management. Working with multiple projects places extra demands on the system. These may include the ability to handle large amounts of data, the ability to identify and manipulate multiple project data, control of and access to the resource pool, and control over replacing data in individual projects after working in multiproject mode.

All the above may be overlooked when you are evaluating the user interface and data manipulation characteristics of a product. Yet they are at least as important to having a successful system.

Data Management

This category is receiving greater attention every year, as well it should. Here are some of the capabilities that can be supported by advanced data management functions.

1. Data Access and Transfer
   - As we move toward multiproject management and project portfolio management, the data expands exponentially. We also may need to access data from multiple data sources. For instance, additional, nonproject data may be generated by Enterprise Resource Management (ERP) systems. This data may have to be coordinated with the project data.
   - Hence, we are moving away from fully proprietary databases, toward popular, open database systems. Whether utilizing ODBC conventions or storing in Oracle or SQLServer, the process should be close to invisible to the user. The process should also be fast and secure.
   - Where data resides in several locations and in several databases, you may wish to consider data warehousing systems.
2. Slicing and Dicing
   - As the user base expands, different people need to access different information. The general projects database will almost always hold way more data than any one person will need at any one time. We look for a robust data manipulation capability to allow the user to slice and dice the data as needed to support individual knowledge requirements.
   - In days past, we often needed an external repository for the data and had to learn an arcane command language to make data queries. Today, it doesn't matter if the data is internal or external. In the latter case, the link is usually transparent to the user. Also, today's products provide a simplified query process, often menu and/or icon driven. Knowing that these capabilities are now available, why settle for anything less?
   - In larger data systems, the process can be improved by using On-Line Analytical Processing (OLAP) engines. OLAP systems arrange the data into preformatted groups (or cubes) to speed up access.
3. Administration and Customization
   - Individual users should not be required to set up the OLAP cubes or the slice and dice queries. The software should come with an administrator

capability, to facilitate design of the data system, including retrieval and security.

- The administrator should be able to determine the information needs of each user and tailor outputs, queries, spreadsheets, and graphical presentations as appropriate to meet these needs.
- Data must be able to be presented in user-defined, time-phased segments, arranged to system-defined hierarchies. Graphical presentation is very popular.

4. Summarization
- Caution is advised when reviewing the software for summarization capabilities. Most products provide a large variety of data fields, for text, dates, costs, and so on. Today, we are provided with almost unlimited user-defined fields. However, you should be aware that sometimes the data in these fields can only be sorted or filtered, but not summarized. Do not take it for granted that all data fields can be summarized or rolled up to a defined hierarchy. Yet, this capability is essential for advanced data manipulation and reporting.

User Interface

The first thing that anyone notices is the user interface. We all like the graphical user interface style, such as supported by Windows and Macintosh. Here, again, there are some things to look for and some things to avoid.

1. There are several ways that the user interface can facilitate access to the system functions.
- The most popular mode is via graphical icons. I find these to be useful only if there is text along with the icons or there are pop-up tool tips (text appears when cursor is moved over icon).
- Drop-down menus is my preferred mode. This allows me to move through the menus and learn what functions are available.
- Hot-key codes (usually combinations of Ctrl or Alt with F1 through F12) can reduce key strokes and mouse movement, but I usually can't remember the codes.
- Several programs can only call up specified functions by clicking the mouse in a particular place on the screen. The call may require a left-click, or a right-click, or a double-click. Sometimes these will immediately initiate a function and other times it will open a window that presents a selection of functions. This capability is fine—when available in addition to accessing these functions from the menu bar. I find it to be

unacceptable for such functions to be available only via these *hot-spots*, as there is no way to learn that they are there unless you already know.

5. Under this category, I also include those features that help me to input and view my data. These include:
   - Flexible screen arrangement.
   - Drop-down or *pick* lists.
   - In-cell editing.
   - Custom, saved views.

6. The User Interface can be considered to be part of a larger group, called Usability. To this group, we can also add:
   - Ease-of-learning.
   - Ease-of-use.
   - Macros.
   - Context-sensitive Help.
   - Tutorials.

Multi-user Access and Communication

It is more than four decades since critical path scheduling was developed and made available to computers. Initial computer systems assumed that single projects would be managed by a colocated group. Over the next 20 years, mainframe and minicomputer systems changed as the developers recognized that project participants were scattered. The time-sharing systems of the 1970s allowed data input and analysis to take place in multiple locations.

It is about two decades since this technology was ported to microcomputers. Here, too, at first the system design favored the individual user, on single projects. Remember—we called them *personal* computers. But it soon became apparent that the user base was in multiple locations, working on multiple projects. Again, the industry responded. However, they were hampered, somewhat, by technology that was really not designed to optimize multiple, decentralized users.

The initial developments were centered around computer networks. The concept of client/server systems was a key basis of emerging designs for multiuser project management. These eventually developed into multitier client/server systems that maximized the efficiency of the computer equipment while extending the user access and security.

During the past few years, this entire world of multiuser computing was turned upside down by a tornado of sorts—web-based computing. The Web has revolutionized the way that we use the computer and what we can accomplish with it. And if there is any application area that can fully benefit from this new technology, it is project management. The improved access and collaboration capabilities, enabled by Web technology, have totally changed the way that we use project management software, and the things to consider when you are selecting such software.

For many people involved in project management software selection, Web support has moved to the top of the list of key selection criteria. Again, I would advise caution. Web support must be provided on top of solid scheduling capabilities. It should not be given such a weight factor as to allow it to dictate the selection process and subrogate the essential scheduling and calculation capabilities.

When we talk about web-based systems, there are several configurations. These include:

- Web-based services—A web-based application service, hosted by an external vendor. The user pays a usage fee to access the service.
- In-house total web-based system. The user owns the system and places the software on internal hardware.
- A hybrid system, utilizing client/server and web-based components.
- Web-based output (not really a web-based system, but rather web publishing).

Today, you can expect all modern project management systems to embrace the Web to some degree. However, many of the early entries into the totally web-based segment of the market have sacrificed scheduling functionality, as compared to the more established products. The exception to this would be companies that have already established strong client/server systems that are redesigning the system to be fully web-based.

With every new release, web-based functionality increases. As this is being written, I am learning of new web-based products and product updates with new web capabilities. If web-based functionality is important to you, then you must specify these needs and search for products that support that criterion. Today, just about every product configuration is available. We had expected that, as the industry matured, several vendors would fall by the wayside. Surprisingly, the opposite has occurred. We are seeing a growth in vendors and products, and a greater variation in what they have to offer. For you, as a software selector, the greater choice will let you find what you want, but the act of choosing is more difficult.

Final Comments on Software Selection and Implementation

As the user, you have to put all the various benefits and deficiencies in perspective and weigh all the attributes against your specific environmental preferences and needs. Another tradeoff area is track record versus freshness. In general, the newer products are using more of the newer and advanced technologies. You have to weigh the attractiveness of this against the benefits of a more established product, with proven performance. Also, another caveat: Often the newer technology can exhibit more razzle-dazzle than substance. Check it out thoroughly.

Check out the vendors, also. Give them a call. Does someone answer the phone? Do they return phone calls promptly? Are they knowledgeable about project management? Some of the new products may sound exciting. But are these tested, shipping products, backed up by a vendor with an office and qualified staff? Checking this out is part of the software selection process.

We highly recommend that you take a balanced approach toward the selection of project management software. Furthermore, to enhance success with these new tools, we recommend that you adopt a formal, five-step process toward the implementation of your computer-based project management capability. Methods, Tool Selection, Training, Implementation Planning, and Implementation Auditing are all essential elements of the process.

CHAPTER 12.2

NEW NAMES FOR OLD GAMES
Rebadging Sound and Proven PM Concepts

I hate to throw things out. So my closets are chock full of narrow ties and suits sporting inch and a half lapels. "They are passé," my wife would say. "Heck no," I reply. "They'll be back." If you've managed to live through more than five decades of wearing ties, then you know that wide and narrow ties have come and gone and returned again. Likewise with lapel sizes. And if you've labored through four decades of the study and practice of project management, you see similar recycling of earlier concepts.

The same old themes return, time and time again, under new labels. Some are claimed to be "revolutionary." But, frankly, many are re-inventions of the wheel. Not that the wheel is a bad thing. Where would we be without it? But today's wheels do much of the same thing as they did in ancient days.

What we are seeing, most of the time, is a rebadging of an earlier idea or process. Often, in doing so, the application of the rebadged concepts is clarified and improved. The mag wheels on my roadster are certainly an improvement over the spoked wheels on a Conestoga wagon. It is really this enhancement of the concepts that leads us to herald a new paradigm, forgetting that the concepts have been with us for years.

During the past few years, several new models have emerged on the project management scene. Among these are: Project Portfolio Management, Opportunity management, Engagement management, Workforce management, Intellectual Capital management, and Human Capital management. Then there are Critical Chain, Professional Services Automation, Stage/Gate, and Cross-disciplinary teams. These are exciting and valuable concepts. But they are not new.

These so-called new models are, for the most part, a rediscovery of tried and true concepts that have stayed with us through the years because they represent a practical, common sense approach to addressing the needs of the project management community.

Cross-disciplinary Teams

Let's take a look at cross-disciplinary teams and other models of teamocracy. Certainly, we have come to recognize that the rigid bureaucratic structure, with fixed boundaries, is detrimental to prompt and effective resolution of project problems. The team model has emerged as a means of achieving more rapid response and action, as well as promoting wider input into the solution.

But new it is not. Back in the 1960s, a project that I was working on came to a total halt when the design of a major component of a nuclear reactor was found to be faulty. We convened a Task Force comprising all the involved disciplines, for a 13-week program to resolve the critical problem and get the project back on track.

In the early 1970s, I was asked to prepare a strategic plan for an engineering-design group. We convened a temporary, cross-disciplinary strategic planning committee, which developed the required plan.

In the later 1970s, we were asked to develop an entire new process for managing projects at our division. Again, a special team was put together, comprised of six individuals, from various groups concerned with project success. This team worked together for a couple of years, determining needs, developing new processes, training personnel, and implementing the new practices. During that period, we all continued to perform our regular duties, within our individual components, while also executing our special team obligations.

I am happy to report that all of these team situations were very successful. I believe that the results could not have been achieved without going to the team model. So, as you can see, this team model is far from being new.

Tip Teams are an important mechanism for getting things done promptly and for breaking down barriers between disciplines. Organizations that resist the use of the team model to address emergency situations are working at a disadvantage and will often fail at resolving such crises. Teams should not be reserved for critical situations, but should also be used to facilitate better communication and cooperation and accelerated project delivery.

Stage/Gate

This one, also called *phase-gate*, sounds like a Ronald Reagan defense system, but it's a "new" concept for managing projects in the new product development arena. But what is really new? In many projects, especially in new product development (NPD), we proceed in steps, stages, or phases. At each step, decisions are made. These may include: (1) which direction to go in, (2) which option to choose, (3) how much to invest in the next phase, (4) go/no-go decisions, (5) project termination, (6) pause and regroup, (7) add or reduce scope, and so on. Such steps may involve new authorizations or new funding.

Is this anything new? Intelligent use of PM software would have us identify such key points in the project. The software would alert us to such pending milestones (gates) so that we can address these *stage/gates*. I laugh at those vendors who would advertise these as new capabilities. But I applaud them for broadcasting a clear emphasis on this gate process. It is an essential part of the management of NPD projects.

Tip In development projects, it is often valuable to move forward in stages, with a *check-valve* placed between the stages. These are milestones where the progress toward the objectives is evaluated and a decision is made to move on to the next stage. These milestones should be prominently inserted into the project plan and should set alarms to trigger the stage-end evaluations.

Critical Chain

A new name for an old game. Kudos to Eliyahu Goldratt for his delightful discourse on this topic, in his book *Critical Chain*, and for his codifying of the concept of shared contingency. Sorry, Eli, but I wrote about shared contingency several years before your book. And so have others.

But, no doubt, Goldratt has popularized and brought this important concept out into the open and spawned a few supporting computer programs, such as ProChain Project Scheduling and a new component in Scitor's Project Scheduler

8. He has also developed a loyal group of disciples, who extol the virtues of critical chain, shoot down any of its critics, and champion the cause of this "new" scheduling elixir.

Putting any pride of ownership aside, the concepts of critical chain deserve our attention. It makes absolute sense to move the inferred (but undefined) contingency out of individual tasks and to group calculated contingency in a shared buffer. This has always been an option in traditional critical path programs (without the buffer analysis), and does not require the abandoning of such programs just to adopt the shared contingency protocol.

If you were to adopt the full critical chain philosophy and support programs, you would also have to adopt the full set of rules and processes associated with critical chain, and abandon many of the important features of traditional CPM, such as earned value and milestones. So be sure that you want to do this before changing over to the "new" scheduling system. But either way, shared contingency is available to you—under the old badge of CPM or the new badge of Critical Chain.

Tip Avoid the building of excess margin in your time estimates by sharing the time contingency among several tasks within a task group. Shared Contingency is discussed in Chapter 3.2.

Project Portfolio Management

Would a rose by any other name smell as sweet? Is Enterprise Project Management better than Project Management? In essence it is usually the same. It just recognizes that the management of projects usually involves more than one. What about Engagement Management? It's just another label for Project Management. It is primarily used by consulting or service organizations that "engage" in projects.

One of the hot topics in the management of the enterprise is Project Portfolio Management (PPM). In Project Portfolio Management, it is assumed that the enterprise, via the selection and execution of projects, positions itself for increased strength and profitability as well as assuring that the firm continues to thrive in a world of constant change and the threat of competition.

The basic elements of Project Portfolio Management are not new. Nor is the environment in which it is applied. However, before the emergence of Project Portfolio Management, as a defined discipline, these elements were the responsibility of two distinct groups: Operations Management and Projects Management.

Each group had its specific role. On the Operations Management side, attention was given to Objectives, Goals, Strategies, Project Selection and Mix, and Cash Flow. On the Projects Management side, we look at: Schedule/Time, Project Cost, Performance, Stakeholder Satisfaction, and Scope/Change Control.

So what we have here is a rebadging of these two disciplines in an environment that bridges the gap between Operations Management and Project Management. As with any of the other topics in this book, a solution requires the implementation of both the methodologies and the tools to support Project Portfolio Management. To date, there has been more talk on the subject than substance. Look for tools that address enterprise and project objectives and tie them to project planning and control systems. We discuss Project Portfolio Management in greater depth in Section 9.

Trap   Don't be fooled by the label Project Portfolio Management. It may just be a case of pretentious inflation of traditional Project Management. Real PPM would involve integration of project and operations data and concerns. This is different from Project Management, Enterprise Project Management, and Engagement Management.

Professional Services Automation

According to Ted Tzirimis, of SPEX, Professional Services Automation (PSA) is an amalgam of Project Management (PM) and Enterprise Resource Planning (ERP), focusing on resource management (or human capital) like time, knowledge, skills, and business relationships, as opposed to simple task management.

Several years ago, ERP emerged as an enterprise system designed to integrate the finance, human resources, and projects aspects of the business and to improve on the automation of the processes and the flow of information between them. The primary industries to apply these systems were manufacturing and process oriented businesses. The systems were concerned more with applications that dealt with products and inventories as opposed to services.

Tzirimis defines the primary market focus of PSA solutions as Professional Services Organizations (PSOs) and internal IT departments. PSOs are service companies (e.g., consulting, advertising, IT management consultants) that require more detail and specialization than current PM software can accommodate. They not only need to manage activities, but also to make simulations before planning a project so they can forecast possible sell time (what they charge the client), prebilling, and review approval processes.

Not unlike PSOs, internal IT departments are confronted with shrinking resources and demands for increased performance. They differ in that they primarily serve internal constituents and must find ways to manage skills, schedule resources, forecast budgeting and costing, perform quality and risk management, and assess progress at any time during the life cycle.

PSOs The growth of service-oriented companies has created the need for detailed resource management and planning. PSA solutions work to automate as much of the sales cycle as possible. This includes managing leads, managing contacts, drafting proposals and bids, managing projects, and performing win/loss analysis. PSA software allows for the storing of detailed customer information including contact information, competitor bids and proposals, as well as any documents that relate to a given opportunity. The software allows the PSO to know the needs and habits of prospective clients so that it can generate successful bids.

IT Departments Traditionally IT departments turned to PM solutions as they saw tasks to be completed as simple projects. With dwindling resources and increased time and efficiency pressures, IT departments have found needed functionality with PSA solutions. Managers can search across programs and projects and access very detailed information on employees to find the closest desired match in a weighted manner, which is dynamic in certain instances. This includes the ability for parametric (case based reasoning) searches. IT departments have found PSA solutions beneficial in searching for employees, staffing programs and projects, and program management office (PMO) automation (i.e., document management, knowledge management, workflow).

Typical PSA software is a collection of any of the following capabilities: Sales Force Automation (SFA), Opportunity Management, Resource Management, Human Resources, Program/Project Management, Time and Expense Management (T&E), Document Management, Knowledge or Practice Management, Invoicing and Billing (Financials), and Customer Relationship Management.

Through the PSA portals, many PSA systems have partnered with human resource outsourcing companies. The internal PSA system is used to identify resource needs, which are then moved through the portal to search for resource matches from resource suppliers.

So here again, we have a repackaging of existing capabilities, addressing the needs of a newly identified market and bringing to that market a set of seamless, automated solutions specifically designed for their business purposes. Professional Services Automation is discussed in greater detail in Section 11.

More New Terms

The PSA category has conjured up a bunch of new terminology. In the business development area, Proposal management has given way to Opportunity Management. In the resource area, Resource Management has shifted to Workforce Management. And in an attempt to look at the workforce as an asset, we now have Intellectual Capital Management and Human Capital Management.

Rebadging Is Good

So here we have some new and popular protocols: Project Portfolio Management, Critical Chain, Professional Services Automation, Stage/Gate, and cross-disciplinary teams. Do they represent new paradigms? Not really! They are more of a natural outgrowth of earlier thinking and capabilities.

Please don't take my use of the term *rebadging* as a pejorative. On the contrary, the repackaging and rebadging of existing practices and capabilities is usually efficient and effective. Why should people have to use systems that were designed for foreign applications? Why should they have to use tools that employ irrelevant jargon and that are patched together from pieces of systems that were designed for other purposes?

No, these rebadged systems are just what the doctor ordered for today's enterprise management needs. The roots may not be new, but so what? It makes perfect sense to build on what has worked for other applications and enhance and adapt these systems to new environments.

CHAPTER 12.3

THE e REVOLUTION: COLLABORATION SERVICES, B2B, GATEWAYS

I've often wondered what older people must feel when they experience the benefits of today's technology and look at it in the face of what they grew up with. For instance, I'm talking about my 90-year-old mother-in-law, who marveled at being able to face this week's 95-degree temperatures by throwing a switch on her air conditioner. This—by a woman who can remember when she didn't have electricity.

But now I've reached that stage of my career and my life where I marvel at where we have brought communications and computer technology, while feeling a bit threatened by it all.

Punched Cards and Paper

You see, I was introduced to the world of computers back when we communicated to these devices via punched *Hollerith* cards. The computer regurgitated its holdings in boxes of wide, fanfold sheets of paper that had rows of holes on both sides and alternating green and white bars across the sheets. Oh! Those were the days, my friend.

I survived the breakthrough of keying directly to tape. I exalted in moving to time-share computers, with direct input from a keyboard. And in the early 1980s, I was an early convert to personal computers—starting with a trash-80 (TRS-80) from Radio Shack and getting one of the very first IBM PCs, with dual floppies and a green screen monitor.

Now after two decades of networked PCs and four decades of using computers, I am overwhelmed by the e revolution. My computers are still the center of my computing and communication environment. But that environment is rapidly changing and how I use the tools is changing with it. Terms that I laughed about years ago—hypertext, virtual teams, gateways—have graduated from jargon to reality.

Business-to-Business Computing (B2B)

At the crux of the e revolution is the ability to breach the confining walls of the office and factory and to reach into every corner of the world with ease. Business can be conducted anywhere, at any time. There are no boundaries or barriers, except those that are deliberately established to maintain security.

The e revolution has brought significant gains to the world of project management. This is especially noticeable in two industries: construction and information systems. In the architect/engineer/construct (A/E/C) industry, B2B systems are being utilized to ease and speed communication among owners, prime contractors, subcontractors, and suppliers. In information technology/application development (IT/AD), B2B capabilities play an important role in workforce management and outsourcing.

PlanView, Inc., is an important supplier of web-based solutions for project management, professional services automation (PSA), and B2B applications. I prevailed upon Patrick Durbin, CEO of PlanView, to discuss the B2B phenomenon and its impact on PM in general and on IT/AD in particular. Here is the text of our interview.

Briefly, What Is B2B, and What Does It Bring to the PM Practitioner?

In general, B2B for project management is an alternative way to procure goods and services. The use of automation changes the requirements, bidding, selection, and payment processes. For example, on construction projects requiring physical goods, the project is little affected by how the steel is delivered just as long as it's fabricated and shipped.

In IT/AD projects, the key impact of B2B is in the procurement of outsourced services or the outsourcing of projects. In the case of outsourcing an IT/AD project, B2B can act similarly to a general B2B. In other words, the exchange can automate the selection process.

In the past couple of years, there was an expectation of public labor exchanges where work and resumes would be posted and an exchange facilitated. These exchanges have by and large failed due to not taking into account the complexity of skills needed to do IT/AD projects. Even more important, labor exchanges were problematical for IT because it is hard to trust an unknown partner. Now we're seeing a growth in private labor exchanges where organizations deal only with partners whom they know and trust with their work.

What Are the Key Benefits from Applying B2B Practices to IT/AD Projects?

For outsourced labor, it can speed the delivery of services and more deeply integrate the contractor into the internal processes of the buying organization. An example may help. In current conditions, a project or resource manager may be forced through a complex process to get an external resource assigned to their project. Using a private labor exchange, the details of billing should already be in place, and the contracting organization might allow a direct view into the availability of their staff. The project or resource manager can then search the staff database by skill and assign contractors to the project. Then there would be no need for an invoice; payment would be made directly from approved time sheets.

For outsourced projects, the requirement documents can be generated to the contractors meeting predefined criteria, bids can be automatically graded and awards made faster.

How Does Traditional Critical Path Type Software Fit In with B2B Solutions?

For general project management there is little direct effect of the B2B approach to procurement. The durations of the procurement activities will be different and there will be different risks on those activities.

For IT/AD, the critical path will not have much impact, but the resource search and assignment could be very different. If you could imagine a private labor exchange with visibility into availability of the virtual organization, you begin to see how many trade-offs of cost, duration, skills development, and so on might become available to the project manager.

How Is CPM Being Integrated with Other IT/AD Tools? How Successful Is This Integration?

We extend the CPM term to mean project scheduling which includes assigning resources and getting their commitment to do the work. In the broader context, project scheduling is touching IT/AD tools in many ways: (1) using best practices or methodologies to generate the work breakdown structure, estimate durations and effort, and assign skill types or roles to the work. This integration is an important step to improve the quality of the initial schedule; (2) integrating projects with service requests and standard activities. A project schedule is meaningful only if the resource assignments are based on true availability; (3) integration of risk and change management into the scheduling process. Technology projects are inherently risky (much more than bridge or building projects) and acknowledging that risk and managing it is critical; (4) the relationship between project schedules or forecasts and the actual performance both in meeting delivery dates and accounting for the spent or charged resources. Integration of project management and project accounting for both progressing and customer billing is a current reality. Linking project schedules to contracts and customer information is also a reality today; (5) project scheduling and resource assignment are organizational processes that feed data marts or data-mining applications to give management an integrated picture of the business.

I could go on to more integration processes, such as knowledge management or asset management, but the key point is that enterprise project and resource management is an integrated information system in most IT/AD organizations and the integration is critical.

What Is the Impact of B2B on How Firms Are Organized to Manage Projects?

By further reducing the walls separating different organizations, B2B is thereby helping to create the virtual organization. Properly organized, B2B provides workarounds to barriers to trade and creates processes to quickly and easily outsource work.

How Does It Impact on Traditional Roles and Organizational Boundaries?

The organizational barriers need to be handled or defined through formal documents, like a contract. Then once the organizations are a part of a common exchange (typically run/owned by the buyer), they can deal with integrated processes. The role of the project and resource manager can be dramatically impacted by this new approach. The key is who has the obligation to assign work to a resource and what criteria they use.

How Does the Implementation of B2B Practices Impact on the Central Project Office?

In our definition of the *project office*, the CPO (Central Project Office) has responsibility for best practices, policies, and procedures and integrated reporting. Each will be affected by the new extended organization. The best way to look at it is that the approved vendor relationships extend the organization to an extended enterprise and a virtual organization. We believe that the construction of the B2B will be driven by the buying organization.

What Do You See as Some of the Key Issues in the Area of B2B for PM and IT/AD Projects?

- Creating trust in the B2B.
- Developing the policies and procedures for using it.
- Extending best practices to include the virtual organization.
- Training resource and project managers on when to use the B2B.
- Accounting and billing practices in the new environment.
- Maximizing the knowledge management and knowledge transfer.

What Do You See as Some of the Key Trends in the Area of B2B for PM and IT/AD Projects?

- Clearer definition of the buyer/contractor relationship.
- New payment systems that do not include invoices.
- Expanded management information systems.
- Integrated project management, resource management, and time and billing.
- Virtual organization searches for skilled resources.

What Is the Impact on the Computer and Communication Infrastructure to Be Able to Implement B2B Capabilities?

- Internet access.
- Broadband width.
- Security.
- Project management schedules that include subcontracts (subnets) outside the organizational repository.
- Resource management searches that extend across the Internet.

What Is the Relationship of B2B with Other Outreach Practices, Such as PSA and PM/ERP?

We see PSA as generally another term for professional-services-based enterprise project management. Some groups define the integration of CRM, Enterprise Project Management (EPM), and ERP as PSA. We see that product offering is a good match only for the niche of emerging organizations who need to implement all of their enterprise solutions at one time. The fact that a single-source provider for all of these features must necessarily be broad and shallow is not always a problem for these emerging companies. For most established organizations, and those with mature processes in place, full replacement of all systems at one time would be ill advised. They are usually looking for upgrades in specific areas, with the requirement that tools and techniques integrate well with tools and processes they mean to keep.

PM/ERP is an integration point more than a new system. The core competencies of work breakdown structures, relationships, resource assignments, and risk plans are very different from the general ledger accounts, invoices, and accounts payable of the ERP world. Generally, an ERP product would see project/person as being the appropriate level of management detail, while an EPM system deals with the assignment of resources to an activity. The appropriate question is where is the best place to merge these two core competencies? In a single PM/ERP or at a contact point—like project accounting?

Anything Else?

There is a trend causing many IT/AD organizations to reorganize how they manage their resource pools. In the past it was typical to have a functional organization that owned the projects and the resources. Recently, we have seen more matrix organizations that improve resource productivity by sharing resources across multiple projects. Web-based collaboration and virtual project teams are requirements in this environment. As B2B functionality allows for external resources to be viewed as if they were a part of the virtual organization, it will lead to an organizational structure that will probably give the project and resource managers as much control over external resources as they have over internal ones.

B2B in Construction

The B2B capabilities in IT/AD are aimed at facilitating service-type work, especially by matching defined resource needs with available skills. B2B applications are also being developed in the Architect/Engineer/Construct (A/E/C) area, where one of the aims is to facilitate procurement of materials.

Early implementations of B2B in A/E/C are seeing acceptance of new automated processes for collaboration, project control, and project commerce. A popular feature is online progress payment. Data is reviewed by approving parties and sent to owner for payment. However, there is resistance to the automated bidding and procurement capabilities. This feature has not yet been embraced by the A/E/C community.

Tool Tip Primavera Systems, Inc., has broken new ground in the area of B2B services for the A/E/C community with a B2B system called PrimeContract. It is available by subscription, with pricing based on the value of the project.

Collaboration Services

What's in a name? The progeny of the e revolution are available in various forms and are called by many names. Any B2B capability would appear to be a type of collaboration service. But there are other products appearing under this moniker that cover partial B2B or different capabilities. Common capabilities of collaboration tools would include:

- Discussion streams.
- Web forums.
- Document management.
- Document check-out and check-in.
- Version management.

Regardless of the particulars of any so-called collaboration tool, the basic objective will be to allow widespread access to data, standards, knowledge, commentary, news, alarms, and status. How do you tell which collaboration tool is right for you? First of all, it should provide customizable windows for each user so that the user does not have to wander all over the place to access his or her most common features (or filter out what is not needed). Second, the tool should possess the processing functionality that is needed to do your job, or provide a strong, seamless link to such capabilities.

Portals and Gateways

Confused by all these new products and services of the e age? Join the party. Among these new services are websites that are billed as portals or gateways.

These portals are more than vendor websites. They also feature news and white papers on subjects of interest and direct links to many areas of interest, sometimes determined by a user profile. A special feature of some portals is the ability to subscribe to online software on a by-use basis. This option is offered as an alternative to owning or buying a license. Some portals also offer premium services to users who sign up for such on a fee basis.

One could get carried away with all the available portals, leading to extreme redundancy. But a few select portals, configured to serve your defined area of interest, can be a valuable reference tool and a gateway to other needed services.

SECTION 13

MAKING PROJECT MANAGEMENT WORK

Project Management is an ART. Project Management is a SCIENCE. Project Management is a PROCESS. Yes, it is all of these. But, most of all, Project Management is a lot of COMMON SENSE.

Without organizing for project management, and without establishing a set of project management practices and developing a project management culture, project management is likely to fail. Yet all of these are not enough to assure that any project management initiative will be successful. This is because project management cannot be solely an academic subject. Rather, it must be the practical application of the accumulated theory, knowledge, and experience—about organizations, people, operations, and projects.

There is a lot of structure to the art and science of project management. But these are guides to how you might practice the project management craft. It is good to learn all aspects of the craft and to know how to use the tools. But, like a good craftsman, it is just as important to know when and where to use each tool.

So how do we make project management work? Primarily, it takes a commitment and an effort to establish a culture that is supportive of project management. This includes a certain level of training, for everyone who will be involved with or affected by the project management process. Our recommendations for training are presented in Chapter 13.1.

At the core of a successful project management implementation is communication. At the core of most failed projects is a lack of communication. What do we communicate? With whom do we communicate? How do we make the communications most effective? This is what we discuss in Chapter 13.2.

Another cause of failures in implementing project management can be traced back to this simple misconception: that we can take shortcuts with project management—that we can treat it casually and unprofessionally—and still have it work. There is a tendency to treat project management differently from other disciplines. Too many people, especially at senior levels, attempt to respond to current crises with a quickie project management fix that fails to have depth, breadth, structure, or commitment. We discuss why project management implementation programs fail, in Chapter 13.3.

Chapters 13.4 through 13.6 deal with people. All the structure, processes, and tools in the world can't make project management work without the people wanting to and knowing how to make it work. In these chapters we offer a philosophical look at how people can work most effectively within a project management culture. First, we look at the trend toward teams, task forces, and matrix organizations in a project management environment. We also offer some example of successful team experiences. This is followed by a discussion on how to stimulate initiative and innovation within a project management environment—taking a look at the psychological contract. Then we look, briefly, at rewards in the project management environment. If the team is sharing responsibility for project success, shouldn't they also be sharing the rewards? Easier said than done. But definitely possible.

CHAPTER 13.1

IMPLEMENTING PROJECT MANAGEMENT
Commitment and Training Ensure Success

Two Scenarios

The contrast was startling. It was like Mutt and Jeff. Like Reagan and Carter. Like Saddam Hussein and Mother Teresa. Here were two clients, both from the same industry, both in the process of implementing a computer-based project management process. Yet there was a clear difference in how they were going about this implementation. One had undertaken a cohesive plan of action that would help to maximize the potential benefits from this investment. The other had difficulty in putting all the pieces together, and in making the commitment to fully support the new process.

One of these firms was taking a series of well-coordinated actions that would provide them with an excellent chance of success. The other would certainly gain some benefits from their move toward structured, computer-based planning, but would find that these benefits would be scattered and intermittent, negating the potential for enterprise-wide schedule and resource management.

My files are packed with examples of failed project management software implementations, and it is not difficult to point to the reasons for these failures.

The Role of Project Management Software

In my books, videos, and articles, I have frequently addressed the issue of project management software selection. In these, I urge the readers to take a deliberate and structured approach toward software selection, considering their project management methods, their corporate culture, and their specific planning and control requirements. Yet regardless of the diligence that is needed in this area, the selection of a project management software product is *not* the most significant element in the successful implementation of a computer-based project management capability. The project management software is *part* of a process. It is only a tool to aid in this process. It is more important to ensure that everyone understands the process, understands their role in the process, and is fully committed to its success.

Reducing all of this commentary to just two words, they are:

- Commitment.
- Training.

Commitment

A firm that is fully committed to the successful implementation of a computer-based project management capability, like our first example, will embark upon a proactive program consisting of these elements:

- Establish a project management implementation team, with a project manager, responsible to a senior officer of the organization.
- Examine the way the firm is organized to manage projects, and the methods employed to do so.
- Recommend changes, as required, to bring the organization and methodology in line with the project management objectives.
- Obtain support for these recommendations from key stakeholders, especially from top management.
- The employment of project management software in the project management process is often just a part of the system of computer-based functions. The benefits from using such project management software, therefore, can be considerably enhanced by integrating the functions of the project management software with the other automated functions. Common data should be shared between these functions. Redundancy is not only wasteful, but leads to inconsistencies and, eventually, confusion.
- Provide a common data structure for integrating of computer-based functions. Look for common labels and pigeonholes to link the data between subsystems.
- Secure management support by seeking a sponsor, a clear advocate and champion of the new process, supported by some type of corporate direc-

tive announcing that project management, as set up by the new methods and responsibilities, is to be a *way of life* in the company.

- Support this way of life through job descriptions and rewards. Make certain that all project management responsibilities are outlined in the applicable position descriptions. Eliminate old responsibilities that conflict with the new way of life.
- Integrate project management software with all other relevant management systems.

An otherwise good process can be crippled by muddled roles and responsibilities. There is a tendency today to incorporate project functions into traditional functional-type organizations, without delineating the specific roles and responsibilities that are contained in the new functions. It is usually a mistake to just add these responsibilities to those already required of line managers. Therefore:

- Project responsibilities should be clearly delineated and separated from functional responsibilities. Wherever possible, these responsibilities should not be shared by the same individual.
- The roles of a project leader are quite different from those of a functional leader. In clarifying these roles, it is important to emphasize how they are different, complementary, and equally important to attaining project success. Efforts should be made to minimize the perception of threat or power jockeying within each camp.
- In the project environment, much is accomplished by acceptance of the leaders by the project participants. Project direction is often accomplished by *knowledge power* rather than the traditional *position power*. In addition, project leaders often obtain support via their ability to build alliances and via superior communication skills. Keep this in mind when selecting project management personnel.
- Another common characteristic of the project environment is delegation. Many efforts, and even responsibility for results, are delegated to various members of the project team. It is essential that the parties to each delegation action fully understand the extent of that delegation and the expectations of each party.

Training

None of the actions prescribed above can bear fruit without a comprehensive training program. This training goes well beyond the training in the use of the tools (such as the project management software).

There are several basic areas of training that must be provided for the people involved in the project management process, which may include the following.

General Skills for Project Managers (and Key Players)

- Presentation skills.
- Communication skills.
- Team building.
- Decision making.
- Problem solving.
- Leadership skills.
- Stress management.
- Time management.
- Organization and management theory.

Corporate-Specific Practices

- Understanding the organization.
- Operating practices and procedures.
- Specific roles and responsibilities.

General Project Management Knowledge

- Principles and practices of project management.
- What does project management software do.
- Estimating, proposals, and project initiation.
- Techniques for project planning.
- Role of the project manager.

Using the Project Management Software (PMS)

- Basic computer training.
- Basic PMS training.
- Using the PMS for your applications.
- Application-specific formats and procedures.
- System interfaces.

Tip   Training should be designed to meet the specific needs to the trainee. This will require multifaceted, multilevel training sessions, aimed at a target audience. The project management system should be designed to recognize the role of each user, especially in regard to input forms, output forms, and included data. The training sessions should pick up on these specifics and show how the system is designed for each user in the audience, and how it will be used by each.

Are These Really Necessary?

Are all the above recommendations really required for the successful implementation of a computer-based project management capability? It is dangerous to take for granted that your people have any of these skills, or that your objectives will be met without them. Every time I have been called into a company to fix a project management software application, I have found that the majority of the problems were not directly attributed to the software itself. They nearly always fell into the categories listed above: lack of commitment, poorly defined roles and responsibilities, lack of essential skills, and misunderstanding of what the project management software does.

> **Trap** Here is something that I can state with absolute certainty. It is entirely impossible to implement a computer-based project management capability without also implementing a broad, multilevel training program. Even if the computer plays a small role in your project management process, an understanding of the principles of project management and the local practices that have been put in place cannot be taken for granted. A formal training effort is required to prevent failure of the project management initiative.

Do You Really Want Success?

Some time ago, I was called in to help a well-respected NASA component that was experiencing problems with its project management software application. It seems that the plan being presented by the system was not reflecting the actual plan as desired by the project manager. Furthermore, reports being produced by the system were not getting the desired results.

Upon interviewing the participants in this process, I found two underlying problems. First, there was a widespread lack of knowledge about what the system did, and especially of what was done with the plans and data they entered into the system. Second, the framework (work breakdown structure) that was established within the system did not reflect the actual working breakdown used by the people who were planning their work. It wasn't really their fault. No one had bothered to provide an orientation on these principles. So how was anyone to know?

Even if the system had been outputting accurate and consistent planning information, it would have been lost on those who were targeted for the output.

First, the system operators had failed to design good reports. They needed to identify who the project decision makers were, and what kind of information they needed to support that responsibility. Then, they should have designed specific reports for each, containing the records that were appropriate to their action area. The reports should have been sorted in the most effective manner to facilitate analysis of the data and limited to the data elements needed to support their expected response.

No one had bothered to indoctrinate the recipients of these data. You have to tell people how to read the reports and how to interpret the data. They need to know how to identify an out-of-tolerance condition, and what is expected of them in the way of a response.

In the case just illustrated, the situation was completely turned around by presenting two half-day workshops. As a result, the framework was changed, the input data was reconfigured to support the CPM process being employed, and the reports were redesigned to support the needs of the intended recipients. The participants were now able to understand how the process worked and what their role was in the process.

Heading for Success

Getting back to my experience with the company that I felt was proceeding with a worthy program to implement project management, here is what they were doing:

1. An individual was assigned responsibility to lead in the design of the application, including system interfaces and configuration.
2. That individual also set up standards and templates for using the selected project management software product. Although system users get product training, they do not have to design their own reports, forms, tables, or filters.
3. A multifaceted training program was implemented. This included:
   - A two-day series of lectures and workshops on the general skills that are useful in the project environment.
   - A one-day seminar and workshop on the principles and practices of project management, including roles and responsibilities, and project initiation techniques. The workshop was customized for the client by having the consultant precede that effort with a day of interviewing and examining the company's methods and program.
   - A two-day seminar in using the project management software.

It would appear that this firm has demonstrated the level of commitment essential to the successful implementation of the computer-based project management capability. And they have backed it up with a comprehensive indoctrination/training program.

Training and Commitment Make the Difference

The message here is a simple one. If you are going to invest in an improved project management capability, you should back that investment up with the training and commitment that are essential to make that investment pay off. A compromise in this area is very likely to lead to total failure of the effort.

CHAPTER 13.2

MAKING PROJECT COMMUNICATION WORK

Everything You Need to Know
about Project Communication

In real estate, it's "location, location, location." When it comes to project success, the three most important factors are: "communication, communication, communication."

Throughout the entire life cycle of the project, it is communication that enables the flow and transfer of knowledge that is essential to project success. In its earliest stages, it is communication that is the amniotic fluid that sustains the emerging project and brings the project to life. During the sensitive planning stages, it is communication that brings out ideas and builds to consensus. During the project execution phase, it is communication that supports and reports progress, and facilitates corrective action and management decisions as needed. And at the conclusion of the project, it is communication that spreads the word about the success of the project and records the knowledge gained and lessons learned.

Tip When properly handled, good, effective, timely, appropriate communication can have an important role in achieving project success. On the other hand, poor, haphazard, incomplete, untimely, and misdirected communication is a recipe for project failure.

If we review the reasons why we communicate, we should easily see its importance.

Why We Communicate

Discuss Objectives and Strategies

Perhaps this is the most important communication of them all. This is where we collect ideas as to the best ways to achieve the project objectives and to avoid pitfalls. Here is where we start to build project consensus and develop buy-in by the project stakeholders.

Disseminate Project Guidelines

Once the project objectives, constraints, and strategies have been defined, it is important that the project participants all get on the same track. This requires leadership and guidance. It requires that these key data be broadcast to the project participants and that it be made clear that these guidelines are be followed by all.

This can be accomplished by the issuance of a Project Charter. The practice of having Project Charters as the defining guideline is a key factor in achieving successful projects. The Project Charter will have signature approvals by senior managers, as a sign of authorization to proceed and demand for support.

Collect Project Plan Inputs

The Project Charter becomes the basis for building a Project Plan. It is a communication vehicle to collect plan inputs from all the project contributors. Very early in this planning stage, the team should create a Project Milestone Schedule (PMS) and a Work Breakdown Structure (WBS).

The PMS serves as a guideline for building a schedule. It contains the project start and end dates and key interim dates. It notes important milestones, contract commitments, and constraints. It communicates the preferred (or required) periods for each project phase. Ordinarily, if the project contributors can commit their support for work within the defined periods on the PMS, it minimizes the necessity to micromanage the schedule.

The WBS serves as a guideline for defining and organizing the workscope. It provides a checklist for selecting the work items that make up the project. It provides a structure for assigning responsibilities, and its hierarchical form facilitates summarization, selection (filtering), and sorting of the project work items for reporting. The WBS is also used for earned value and performance analysis.

Build Baseline Plan

The Baseline Plan is the convergence of the definition of the workscope, the schedule, the assignment of resources, and the project budget. Achieving objectives in each of these areas often precedes meeting the objectives in other areas. So the establishment of a Baseline Plan may involve negotiation and adjustment to find the best balance in each area. Obviously, this is a major communication event.

Obtain Commitments

Even the best project plan, diligently developed by the project team, will fail unless the team can get widespread buy-in from the participants and a commitment to do whatever is necessary to meet targets and obligations. The team must be sure to have communicated these targets and to have made clear the consequences of deficient support.

Communicate Baseline Plan

Support for the plan cannot be expected if it is not communicated. Communicating the baseline plan means more than circulating a document. The plan and everyone's role in that plan must be fully understood. Responsibilities for managing and performing the work must be clear. A traditional weak spot is the interface where performance or management of work is transferred to other people. These areas should receive special attention to be sure that the people involved will communicate status and transfer data, and that they clearly understand the nature of the interface.

Again, senior management should indicate approval of the baseline plan and approval to move to the project execution phase.

Gather Project Progress Data

Gathering progress information is getting easier and easier with today's advanced computer-based systems. We have the ability to generate automatic notifications of events, changes, and accomplishments. Our systems can now communicate over direct, hardwired links, via facsimile transmission, by e-mail, and so on. Information is now available in real time. We have electronic timesheets, and automated routines for approval or rejection.

There is no excuse for failing to collect timely and accurate progress data. Yet, there is still a great possibility for grossly erroneous data unless the communication of such data has human intervention.

The project team should designate someone to facilitate the dissemination of progress information and the retrieval of progress data from the participants. This individual(s) shall review all progress data and check it for validity. Communication, at this point, is more in the nature of mentoring and providing assistance to participants so that they understand what kind of progress reporting is needed and expected.

Report Project Status

This is an area where a little creative thinking can produce very productive results. We need to discard the old approach, wherein we produced voluminous pages of insipid data, which was distributed to all involved parties. This generally led to the reports accumulating dust in a far corner of the office, or taking up valuable space on the hard drive. It was usually too much data and not enough information.

First of all, the capability exists to customize project status reports so that each participant receives information that is tailored to his or her specific need. The data may be detailed or summarized, depending on need. The data can be selective, providing detail over a narrow band, or at a higher level of detail for a wider span of interest. Data can be restricted to a particular area, such as schedule, cost, or resource utilization. It can focus on accomplishments, performance, and problems.

The key to success in this communication area is to consider each targeted recipient, individually. If we can determine what each person is going to do with the information, we can tailor the reports to serve that purpose. We need to consider what type of decisions are to be made on the basis of the information, and design the communication to provide what is needed, in the format that is needed, and in the detail that is needed.

Trap There is a tendency to employ a one-size-fits-all philosophy when designing input screens and reporting formats. This will encourage resistance to support of the system by the target users, and cannot be justified in light of the capabilities of today's PM tools.

We need to provide more than just data, but real information about the significance of the data. Where corrective action is indicated, we should (where feasible) provide information about effect and alternatives.

The Project Progress Reporting function will also serve to support the following:

- Report out-of-tolerance situations.
- Request or report scope changes.
- Facilitate corrective action.

Keys to Effective Communication

The project manager is at the center of project communications. The project manager must ensure that all communication needs, both formal and informal, are fulfilled. The project manager must always look for and close gaps in understanding and communication, between all participants and interested parties, and between all work items. The project manager is a bridge.

- Communication and measurement bases must be consistent from period to period.
- Schedule, resource, and cost information must be synchronized.

Project Phases and Communications

A lot of information can be processed during the project. These will change as we move through each phase of the project. As a guide, here is an example of items that can be communicated for each phase of the project.

Project Development and Initiation

- Workscope.
- Organization.
- Stakeholder Analysis and Strategy.
- Objectives and Constraints.
- Milestones.
- Budget.

Project Planning

- Task Identification.
- Task Estimates (time and resource).
- Constraints.
- Resource Availability.
- Resource Assignments.
- Baseline Plan (schedule, resource plan, costs).

Project Execution

- Work Status.
- Hours Expended or Charged.
- Actual Costs.
- Performance.
- Scope Changes.
- Corrective Action and Replanning.

Closeout/Termination

- Punch List (What/Who/When).
- Personnel Reports and Recognition Letters.
- Project Historical Data.
- Project Post-mortem Analysis and Report.

Communication Targets

Information should be tailored to maximize the usefulness and impact for each information target. For example, here are some of the categories of people with whom we communicate project information.

- The Project Manager and Project/SubProject Leaders.
- The Functional Managers.
- Individual Contributors.
- Suppliers (Materials and Resources).
- Senior Management.
- The Client/Sponsor/User.

Communication Categories

There are several classifications of project information. Some of this is input data, and some represents the results of processing the inputs. Interest in these various communication categories will differ among the project stakeholders. Some categories are:

- Schedule Information.
- Resource and Cost Information.
- Workscope Information.
- Integrated Information.
- Baseline or Target Plan.

- Progress and Status.
- Performance Evaluation.
- Exceptions (out of acceptance range).
- Turn-around Data (for statusing).

Types of Communication Information

There are also differences in the level of detail and the formats of the information. Again, just which type is appropriate will depend on the role and needs of the target audience. Effective communication will be achieved by limiting the communications to the most appropriate formats, rather than bombarding people with the full warehouse of project data. An advantage of accessing data via computer screen retrievals (today's most popular mode) is that the user can go to the most favored format, but then drill-down or summarize up to see either more details or a wider picture, or a different format. Key traditional information formats include:

- Detailed (inclusive).
- Detailed (by exception—by distribution).
- Summary.
- Narrative Analysis.
- Corrective Action and Replanning.

Information Formats

Whether detailed or summarized, whether inputs or outputs, whether hard copy or screen based, the information will fall into these traditional formats.

Tabular

- Typical: Rows for records; columns for data fields.
- Matrix: Select two sets of data (i.e., Resource/Cost vs. Time).

Graphic

- Gantt Chart Schedule (bar chart).
- Network Diagram (PERT chart).
- Time-scaled Network or Linked Gantt.
- Resource and Cost Histograms—incremental or cumulative.
- Performance Curves (Earned Value).

Narrative

- Usually combined with one or more of the preceding, to discuss progress and issues.

Report Variables

Here are some of the items that should be addressed when we design our reports.

- Subject.
- Purpose.
- Distribution.
- Data Items (fields).
- Selection Criteria (records).
- Sorting Criteria.
- Formats.
- Time Scale and Time Span.
- Summarization Criteria.
- Subtotals.
- What is the reader supposed to be looking for?
- What is the expected response?

Project Portfolio Management and Communication

All the preceding discussion was directed toward communication on a single project. Most of us contribute to or manage multiple projects, which necessitates additional considerations for communication.

Most of the preceding comments can also apply to the multiproject environment. Here are a few additional considerations.

- Resource-oriented data, especially in formats designed to obtain timesheet data, should cover all projects that involve the target personnel.
- Performance data may cover multiple projects so that the performance attributed to groups involved in multiple projects can be fully evaluated.
- Milestone-level data for multiple projects can be tracked in combined formats, for comparative progress and performance analysis.
- Special reports should be developed to address specific concerns involved with managing the portfolio.
- If the firm works on projects that are similar in nature, it might be advantageous to develop a standard Work Breakdown Structure, to be used for all projects in such a group. In this case, the project becomes the second level of the standard WBS, and the project group becomes the senior level. This allows performance analysis and reporting to be performed across projects.

CHAPTER 13.3

WHY PROJECT MANAGEMENT IMPLEMENTATION PROGRAMS FAIL

Trap   The failures in implementing PM can be traced back to this simple misconception: that we can take shortcuts with PM—that we can treat it casually and unprofessionally—and still have it work.

In my experience in working with corporate clients wishing to implement a computer-based PM capability, I have found the satisfaction level to be very low. While we can easily attribute much of this to lack of adequate participation by the user, we can't get off the hook that easily. We need to ask why this participation level is so low and what we can do to improve it.

As in any other business venture, the typical consultant will experience a wide range of success (or failure) in his various engagements. While some of the shortfalls can be attributed, at least in part, to the consultant, there are often major failures on the part of the client. Much of this can be categorized as lack of sound communication and/or inability to have a practical vision.

The purpose of this chapter is not so much to place blame as to share the lessons of these experiences. *"He who fails to learn from his mistakes is doomed to repeat them."* For this chapter, I focus on engagements that involve the objective of implementing a computer-based project management capability in organizations that did not have such a capability or had a very rudimentary system that was deemed inadequate.

Reflecting on personal consulting experience in working with corporate clients wishing to implement a computer-based PM capability, I often find the following typical sequence.

1. Client expresses desire/need to know what is going on—when work is to be done—what people are working on—what the impact of new projects are on the firm's resources, and so on.

2. Client wants to get people to plan their work, communicate the deliverable dates and other project info, and control the effort (somewhere in line with the published plans).

3. Client does not have a PM methodology in place and resists the imposition of too much structure. Simple front-end practices, such as a project charter, do not exist.

4. Client is unwilling to integrate key components, such as Operations, Finance, Human Resources, Projects, and Line Management.

5. Client comes up with extensive list of selection criteria for sophisticated tool support of nonexistent practices. Makes major effort to review candidate products, via purchase of reports, extensive staff research, and/or use of consultants. Invites sales presentations and proposals from several tool vendors.

6. Client will not establish a Project Office or designate personnel as responsible for PM. Client will not establish PM as a *way of life* in the firm, or make support of PM a *condition of employment*. Reference to PM responsibilities does not exist in anyone's position guide.

7. Client terminates program to implement a computer-based PM capability. Or if client does buy a product, fails to educate users and otherwise support the process.

8. Client determines that the failure to accomplish the goal is due to the demanding nature of PM and PM tools—requiring a structure and level of effort exceeding that considered to be reasonable.

In all fairness, we must admit that there is some truth in the last item. Project Management, although based entirely on a set of common sense approaches, is structured and demanding. And even the best-of-breed in PM tools will require some education and compliance with designed processes in order to produce usable results. However, I do not find these demands to be unreasonable. As in most other things, there is an investment required if one is to gain the desired payoff.

With this in mind, let's expand the above list to see what we can do to make the implementation of a computer-based project management capability a positive and rewarding experience.

1. Client expresses desire/need to know what is going on—when work is to be done—what people are working on—what the impact of new projects are on the firm's resources, and so on.
2. Client wants to get people to plan their work, communicate the deliverable dates and other project info, and control the effort (somewhere in line with the published plans).
   - These two items represent the identification of the *need* for a computer-based project management capability. There is recognition that something is either missing or inadequate. What is important is that the wish list be kept practical. It must be consistent with the ability to realistically support the desired result and it must recognize the organizational culture. True, a strong leader can bring about changes in the culture, but I have found it to be rare for top management to go to the wall to institute major change for the purposes of implementing modern project management.
   - Change, even simple change, should be deliberate, as part of a strategy.
3. Client does not have a PM methodology in place and resists the imposition of too much structure. Simple front-end practices, such as a project charter, do not exist.
   - The implementation of a computer-based project management capability has two major components. *The first is the identification of a project management methodology.* The automation of that methodology comes next, but only after the first has been accomplished.
4. Client is unwilling to integrate key components, such as Operations, Finance, Human Resources, Projects, and Line Management.
   - Managing projects is a subset of managing the business. The strategies that drive the projects and the conditions that impact upon the projects involve other components of the enterprise. Success cannot be achieved without full participation and cooperation of these business components.
5. Client comes up with extensive list of selection criteria for sophisticated tool support of nonexistent practices. Makes major effort to review candidate products, via purchase of reports, extensive staff research, and/or use of consultants. Invites sales presentations and proposals from several tool vendors.

- We all know that the purchase of a violin does not turn a layman into a musician. Then how can anyone believe that the acquisition of a PM tool would automatically position that organization to be fully PM competent, complete with practices, policies, and procedures? No! The PM tool is acquired to automate a set of PM practices. While the tool can be helpful in clarifying the PM structure and practices, it does not actually create them.

6. Client will not establish a Project Office or designate personnel as responsible for PM. Client will not establish PM as a *way of life* in the firm, or make support of PM a *condition of employment*. Reference to PM responsibilities does not exist in anyone's position guide.

   - The establishment of a PM capability starts with top-down direction and requires the full diligence and support of senior management. In sponsoring and taking command of the PM implementation, the CEO creates an environment where PM is thoroughly integrated and ingrained into the organization, and the staff understands their requirement to support PM.

   - PM is a special discipline. Many people can participate in PM, but only specially trained and experienced people can be experts. PM cannot be successful unless a central component is established and staffed with such experts. The PM Office is a single point of policy direction and PM mentoring. Its leadership and expertise help to make PM a successful endeavor.

7. Client terminates program to implement a computer-based PM capability. Or if client does buy a product, fails to educate users and otherwise support the process.

   - By this time, the sponsors of the PM initiative realize the full scope and requirements of the program. If they haven't yet made the commitment, they often decide that they are not willing to make the investment in organization, policy, manpower, and procedures—as well as in tools and training.

   - If the purchase has been made, they fail to follow up with all the things that are needed to make it work—and the initiative fails.

   - A successful program to implement computer-based project management starts with a realistic set of objectives, which are consistent with the firm's needs, culture, and strategies, and winds up with a supportable commitment at all levels.

8. Client determines that the failure to accomplish the goal is due to the demanding nature of PM and PM tools—requiring a structure and level of effort exceeding that considered to be reasonable.

- This is a self-fulfilling prophecy. It is not the tools that require this structure and level of effort. It is the entire program of project management that calls for this. It is no different from any other professional discipline. Whether it be engineering, finance, R&D, or manufacturing, we expect that there will be leadership, organization, policies and practices, and expertise. We should expect no less for PM.
- The failures in implementing PM can be traced back to this misconception: that we can take shortcuts with PM—that we can treat it casually and unprofessionally—and still have it work.

CHAPTER 13.4

TEAMS, TASK FORCES, AND BUREAUCRATS

Ever since people discovered structured ways of getting work done, we have dabbled in defining better ways to organize to do work and to lead the work-force. All through the twentieth century, we listened to arguments about central-ization vs. decentralization. We heard discourses and criticism of the bureaucratic form of organization, and discussion on exploitative authoritarian leadership, vs. benevolent authoritarian leadership, vs. consultative, vs. participative.

However, even in the most structured organizations, it didn't take long to rec-ognize that there were certain situations that were better addressed outside the formal, fixed structure. Yet there are always diehards, who will resist exceptions to the very end. Take this situation, for example.

The Bureaucrats

A few years ago, I was called in by a company, an HMO, that had just been handed a virtually unachievable deadline. The HMO had recently received gov-ernment approval to start a new service and was in the early stages of a four-month program to implement the new offering. Coincident to this, this HMO announced the acquisition of another HMO agency, which was already approved and committed to offer the new service. As a consequence, the federal program that was approved to start in four months was now required to be operating in six weeks. This deadline, under the best possible circumstances, would appear to be an impossible task.

However, this HMO did not have the best possible circumstances. They operated under very rigid boundaries, within a traditional hierarchy. Each discipline within the organization had its own director, and all practices required going through the directors for action. The boundaries were like stone walls.

With at least four months of work to be accomplished in this six-week period, I asked if the company had set up an emergency team, with representatives of each stakeholder group. I was told that this company did not believe in any type of task force arrangement, under any circumstances. When I asked how each of the stakeholder groups communicated and coordinated their efforts in support of this high priority program, I was told that the *directors* of each group met *monthly*. My pressing for an exception in this instance met with total resistance.

The Task Force

I have no intention here to get into a discussion on the advantages or disadvantages of a highly structured, rigid organization. But I do want to press for the acceptance of exceptions to such formal structures, when a situation such as the one just described arises. In the example, surely a task force approach is almost mandatory. In this case, I would have had the Manager of Senior Services (the critical stakeholder) head a team of representatives of each contributing department. These representatives would be authorized to make decisions for their discipline (following procedures that were set up by the director of each department). They would be dedicated to the special project to whatever level of effort was required to accomplish the goal.

The task force would meet frequently (at least once a week) to communicate results and resolve outstanding concerns. The task force members would communicate with other contributors from their discipline and coordinate their efforts. At the initial task force meeting, the team would develop a project plan and would disseminate the plan and obtain supporting commitments from members of their department. The task force leader would be able to communicate freely with the task force members and establish commitments and program results without having to go through the department directors, or to wait for a monthly meeting.

Although this is a significant deviation from the rigid structure that was in place in this organization, the use of a task force in this situation should not be looked at as an attack on the establishment. It is a temporary organization, formed for a specific objective. When the goal has been met, everything returns to normal.

Trap Rigid organizational structures can prevent the firm from a prompt and appropriate response to a crisis or critical deadline. All organizations must be able to establish temporary teams or task forces to respond to such situations.

Success Stories

The task force model can work for the most varied situations. Here are three case histories where the task force or special team approach proved to be very successful.

Case 1—Design Crisis

As a designer of nuclear propulsion systems for the United States Navy, this organization was involved in overseeing the design and manufacture of the core for a shipboard nuclear reactor. This element was one of thousands of critical components being built for a prototype vessel, to a tight schedule. Suddenly, the manufacturing contractor discovered that the intended method for welding the fuel elements was not going to work, putting the entire program on hold for this critical component.

Immediately, a task force was established, with representatives of all the concerned groups within the organization. The task force leader—a department head—called the team together and led in the development of a 13-week schedule to resolve the problem. Weekly meetings were held—not to hear any excuses of delays or failure—but only to communicate results. The schedule was refined only once, during the first week, and was then frozen. Everyone shared the sense of commitment and produced as was expected and required. At the end of the 13 weeks, the desired remedy was achieved and the program moved forward.

It is doubtful that this kind of commitment, cooperation, and execution would have been achieved within the normal, day-to-day operations of the organization. In this task force mode, the team was able to focus on the critical problem, somewhat free of conflicts with other obligations. The high priority of the task force assignment was clear and effective.

Case 2—Strategic Plan

An Engineering–Design organization was asked to develop a strategic plan. The organization was to: (1) identify areas of expertise and opportunity; (2) identify what was needed to build expertise to position the organization as first or second (in business performance) in five selected capability areas; and (3) to develop a plan to prioritize and excel in these five selected areas.

A strategic planning team was called together for this purpose. Although the primary membership in this team was engineering and design managers, the team leader was actually a much lower statused individual, but one with strategic and management planning expertise. As an example of today's tendency to recognize knowledge power as equal or superior to position power, the managers willingly followed the lead of this individual as he guided the team to the successful development of the strategic plan.

In this instance, borders were crossed and the traditional hierarchy was inverted. And everyone was pleased with the results. The objective was achieved, by a group of people who had not previously been involved in developing a strategic plan. The establishment of a temporary team, with a common objective, helped to break down any of the traditional territorial defenses.

Case 3—Developing New Practices and Systems

In this case, the firm was a leader in the power generation and power delivery equipment industry and had built a growing business in delivering turnkey power generation solutions. However, the firm was not entirely satisfied with the results (financial and other) of these projects. Senior management decided that the entire method of managing such projects needed to be evaluated and, if found wanting, should be replaced with improved methods.

A task force was established, made up of six individuals with expertise in the areas associated with developing new practices and systems to support project management. These included PM experts, finance experts, systems developers, and training professionals. The team set out first to determine what methods were desired to manage the turnkey projects. Having gained consensus and approval of the proposed methods, they then defined and developed the computer systems to support the new methods. The team continued to operate as they led in the development and execution of training programs, to indoctrinate the organization in the new methods and systems. Finally, selected members of the original task force were engaged to audit the implementation of the new practices, and to assist in mentoring individuals in support of the program.

The task force activities were executed over about a two-year period. All task force members carried out other, normal activities in addition to their special obligations to this program. For their normal activities, they reported to and took direction from their direct managers. For the task force activities, they were directed by a manager who was assigned to oversee the work of the task force and to facilitate reaching organization-wide consensus and approvals. Because the work of the task force continued over a long period of time, this manager was invited to contribute to the periodic employee evaluations for the task force members.

The full set of objectives for the program was achieved, and a major part of the organization was trained in the application of the practices and tools. Several decades later (with some upgrading) the basic set of practices and systems was still in use.

Teams, Task Forces, and Bureaucrats

In the 1990s, the concept of teams reached a high level of acceptance. It has led to a newer organization style, coined *Teamocracy* by David Cleland. Teams for everything. Teams for Concurrent Engineering. Self-managed Production Teams. Teams for Reengineering. Teams for the current crisis. Teams for projects.

The concept of the task force goes back much further, and for most organizations was recognized as a practical way of breaking down provincial barriers, expediting critical work, and bringing about faster, better solutions for special situations. It would seem that, with the acknowledged success of teams in the past decade, it would not be necessary to build a case for the task force method. But the experience mentioned at the start of this chapter reminds us that sometimes even the most accepted practices have to be sold to the few diehard defenders of rigid hierarchical structures. We hope that the illustrations of success, in these three very different situations, will help to convince them otherwise.

In today's business environment, teams and task forces may become the norm, rather than the exception. There is serious evidence, from David Cleland, Tom Peters, Robert Waterman, Rosabeth Moss Kanter, and many others, to support these operational modes. My own personal experiences fully support this premise.

CHAPTER 13.5

THE PSYCHOLOGICAL CONTRACT
How to Stimulate Initiative and Innovation in Any Organization

Through the years, arguments have persisted relative to the philosophy of people in organizations. Knowledgeable and perceptive experts in behavioral science repeatedly offer analyses of the ills in organizations and propose remedies by the hundreds. These are usually fascinating dissertations. Based on formal studies in this discipline, and extensive, personal field experience and observation, I offer some of my own thoughts on this topic.

Behavioral Studies

What a treasure trove of discoveries and prescriptions we have in the literature of the past century. Reaching back to Frederick Taylor's breakthrough treatise on productivity and efficiency of men and machines, through Joseph Scanlon's provocative concepts of group rewards, continuing with behavioral observations by Abraham Maslow, Frederick Herzberg, George Odiorne, Douglas MacGregor, Henry Mintzberg, Herbert Simon, Chester Barnard, James March, Rensis Likert, Elton Mayo, Henri Fayol, Theodore Levitt, Chris Argyris, and Warren Bennis, and more recently, writings on leadership by Tom Peters, W. Edwards Deming, Peter Drucker, and Rosabeth Moss Kanter, we are the beneficiaries of years and years of research, reduced by these experts to a few hundred books on organizational behavior.

Many of these are from what I call the Timex School, addressing what makes people tick (and how to make them tick better). Many address issues regarding the design of the organization (theoretically to promote better support by people of the organization's mission). Many of them treat people as chattel, as if the only thing of importance is the organization's mission (which is usually to increase the return to the stockholder). Essentially, these writings fall into one of three stages of behavioral discovery.

- *Production Efficiency:* Getting the most out of people while having little regard for the people themselves.
- *Human Behavior:* Motivation, needs, and the nature of man.
- *Leadership:* How to use what we know about people to lead them to greater productivity and happiness through individual performance and initiative.

In addition to the treatise on individual behavior, we are exposed to arguments about centralization vs. decentralization. (Have you ever noticed that if a consultant is called in to look at a centralized organization, he will recommend decentralizing? But if called in to look at a decentralized organization, he will recommend centralization.) We get discourses and criticism of the bureaucratic form of organization, and discussion on exploitative authoritarian leadership, vs. benevolent authoritarian leadership, vs. consultative, vs. participative. We divide aspects of the workplace into motivators and satisfiers. We have advocates of the bureaucracy, challenged by advocates of adhocracies, questioned by advocates of teamocracy. And all the time, I get the feeling that we are looking at laboratory rats, rather than human individuals.

Choosing among Organizational Alternatives

"A time for everything under heaven"   (Ecclesiastes)

My library is replete with eloquent, supportable arguments for every organizational style under the sun. We have the classic bureaucracy, which has been described as both implicitly efficient and patently inefficient. Within bureaucracies, we have exploitative leadership styles, as well as benevolent, consultative, and participative. We have adhocracies, with a shift in power and purpose. The adhocracy style has been supported by such recognized experts as Warren Bennis, Alvin Toffler, Henry Mintzberg, Robert Graham, and Robert Waterman. It has been adopted to allow individuals and groups to operate more freely across the traditional organizational boundaries. It has created new conditions for power and communication. It has led to the *Teamocracy* organization style.

It is not the purpose of this chapter to argue the various virtues of these organizational styles, but rather to discuss certain conditions that apply to all of them. There are two maxims that I would like to explore here.

The first refers to the quote from Ecclesiastes. Rather than to blindly support a particular organizational or managerial style, we must be aware and appreciative of many styles, and be prepared to apply the right style at the right time.

Even in the most conservative and rigidly structured organization, there must be times when the barriers are allowed to come down (if only for a short time and a single purpose) to meet a challenge for which the bureaucracy would not otherwise be able to adequately respond. On the other hand, even adhocracies and teamocracies must operate within an underlying, formal structure, lest there be anarchy.

The second maxim to explore is the relationships between people within the organization, respective to goals, measurements, and rewards. Here we have at least two issues. The first is to address the way that people work and lead in a traditional hierarchical organization. The second is how we take what we have learned about human behavior in the workplace, and about leadership, and apply it to more flexible and informal organizations.

Stimulating Innovation, Enterprise, and Initiative

In the introduction to her critically acclaimed book *The Change Masters*, Rosabeth Moss Kanter, in visiting with corporate executives across America, says *"I have been struck by an ever-louder echo of the same question: how to stimulate more innovation, enterprise, and initiative from their people."* She then proceeds to describe the environment that breeds such a lack of innovation, enterprise, and initiative, and provides illustrations of companies that have created a new environment to overcome this malady.

It is powerful and worthwhile reading. But I pondered her lead-in question and chose to phrase it differently. The issue is: How can I take advantage of the natural innovation, enterprise, and initiative that is present in most of the people in the organization?

Contrary to the thinking of many of our most revered organizational psychologists, stimulation and motivation are not the key issues. Rather the issue is how does senior management avoid *stifling* initiative. In my experience in corporate America, a significant number of self-motivated employees sit in frustration while their bosses utilize just a teeny-weeny amount of what they have to offer. They are treated like children, "to be seen but not heard." Management tells them to stuff 95 percent of their knowledge in the desk drawer and to limit their contribution to only what they are told to do. And then these managers have the audacity to ask what they can do to stimulate and motivate initiative? Balderdash!

Where the problem exists, the root of the problem, I believe, lies with these managers themselves. We can point to two types of behavior that permeate the (nonstimulating) manager personality.

First is the necessity to "be the boss." "I'll tell you just what to do and what not to do. And you will do as I say because I am the boss and I can hurt you if you challenge me." It's the power thing.

The other debilitating behavioral trait is sort of the opposite. It is fear. In times past, many managers rose through the ranks because of their apparent ability to direct others to perform the work (coupled sometimes with cronyism and office politics). But they may not have had the greatest technical strength in the areas in which they manage. Some of these managers, those that are not psychologically healthy, live in constant fear of their underlings, who may show them up. They lack confidence in themselves and are afraid that their people might exhibit greater knowledge than theirs. It often becomes a control issue. The manager limits the reach of the subordinate in order to keep things from getting out of a range that can be controlled.

So, because of these two behavioral traits, we often find managers who prevent initiative rather than stimulate it. Under such an environment, there is also the tendency to be risk averse. Hence, innovation is likely to be suspect rather than encouraged.

I can provide an illustration of just such a risk averse situation. A company wanted to supplement their primary project management software capability with a low-end package. They narrowed the choice down to two products. One was clearly the better technological solution. However, the second one was from a source that furnished the current tool set. It was decided that the latter would be selected, because no one would question that choice (it was a risk-free decision).

If we are to have psychologically healthy managers, we must look for behavior that is different from what I just described.

We need to replace the parent-child relationship with a peer-to-peer relationship. The manager may be boss because of the bureaucratic structure of the organization, and because there has to be someone to be responsible to the next level of management. But that doesn't mean that the subordinate must be treated as an underling. That doesn't mean that the subordinate should not be respected equally to anyone else.

The model that I prefer is nicely defined by Edgar Schein, as the Psychological Contract.

Schein and Kanter

The field of Organizational Psychology has grown in the past four decades, as organizational research has provided more insight into the nature of the organization and the people in it. But the nature of human behavior has not changed so much as to totally nullify earlier findings. Rather, we have to examine these findings in light of our newer understanding of the problems of the enterprise and the nature of the workforce.

What has changed drastically in the past couple of decades is the unwillingness of newer people in the workforce to blindly accept leadership solely on the basis of placement in the hierarchy. This new breed of worker tends to respect knowledge power over position power. This has had an extreme effect on the traditional system of rewards and punishments.

Even as early as 1965, Schein wrote: *"an organization has within it many groups which generate their own norms of what is right and proper behavior, and that such norms extend to the amount and type of work to be performed."* Today, that is more applicable than ever. Schein continues: *"the organization is a complex social system which must be studied as a total system if individual behavior within it is to be totally understood."*

The questions that Schein raises are not unlike those of Rosabeth Moss Kanter. *"How can an internal environment be created for members of the organization which will enable them to grow in their own unique capacities?"* *"How can organizations be designed to create optimum relationships between various subgroups which tend to develop within them?"*

So it is that the same questions raised in the 1960s and in the 1980s are still being addressed today. The fact is, however, that these questions have been answered and that several reasonable and rational solutions have been offered. In instances in which these proposed solutions have been adopted, there are measurable results (see Kanter, *The Change Masters*). Yet, in many other areas, the old, inbred managerial and organizational behavior has resisted change. So we continue to write about the subject and propose solutions.

Kanter talks about *trust* as a part of the solution. She also mentions the tendency for older style organizations to be *risk-averse*. And everyone talks about the bureaucratic structures as impeding a solution because it segments the organization. My experience has been that the degree of centralization or decentralization is not the issue. There is no evidence that I know of that shows that flatter organizations always perform better than hierarchical organizations. It is reasonable to expect a correlation between risk taking and innovation. As Kanter says: *"a quarterly financial statement is not a good measure of economic health."* Again, my experience shows that by concentrating on umpteen consecutive quarters of revenue growth, a company will usually hurt its future by minimizing investment and risk to assure current year, bottom line results. But of all of these, it is *trust* that stands out as the key factor in bringing out the best that employees have to offer. And it is trust and respect that are at the core of Edgar Schein's Psychological Contract.

Trap Initiative and innovation are often stifled by organizational segmentation, the absence of trust, and the unwillingness to take risks. When any of these three conditions exist, it is difficult for talented individuals to flourish and to contribute all that they are capable of. This is a lose–lose situation, as the individuals feel frustrated and unappreciated and the firm fails to obtain the full measure of each individual's potential contribution.

There are some basic tenets regarding *authority* in the organization that influence the Psychological Contract concept. One is the aforementioned *knowledge power*. As we move from the traditional bureaucratic organizational structure to a less structured *adhocracy*, we move from a model based on *position power* to one based on *expert power*. A person's job title may have less standing (at least in the informal organization that underlies every printed organization chart) than a person's applicable knowledge. Authority, according to Schein (re-stating a view postulated by Barnard and Simon), implies the willingness on the part of a subordinate to obey because he consents, that is, he grants to the person in authority the right to dictate to him.

Schein goes on to claim that *"an organization cannot function unless the members consent to the operating authority system, and that this consent hinges upon the upholding of the psychological contract between the organization and the member."* While we may have questioned this position on authority 20 years ago, we certainly can see that it has become more of the norm as we enter the twenty-first century.

Before we get to a description of the Psychological Contract concept, let's explore some common theories about human behavior in the organization. While we cannot apply these theories to everyone in the workforce, we hold these attributes to be characteristic of today's psychologically healthy and productive individuals.

- These people have an inherent need to use their capacities and skills in a mature and productive way.
- They seek to make their work more interesting, challenging, and meaningful.
- They thirst for a sense of pride and self-esteem.

The Psychological Contract

According to Schein, for these individuals to achieve these goals in the workplace, and to obtain satisfaction from their work, depends to a large measure on two conditions.

1. The degree in which their own expectations of what the organization will provide them and what they owe the organization match what the organization's expectations are of what it will give and get.
2. (Assuming that there is an agreement on expectations) what is actually exchanged—money in exchange for time at work; social-need satisfaction and security in exchange for work and loyalty; opportunities for self-actualization and challenging work in exchange for high productivity, quality work, and creative effort in the service of organizational goals; or various combinations of these.

So here we have the essence of a Psychological Contract. And I can tell you from experience that it works. I remember a time, back in the 1970s, when I was requested to accept a new assignment, at the General Electric Company. My new manager (someone whom I had known professionally and respected) invited me to sit down with him and discuss our needs and expectations. He presented his needs from my new position and what he expected. And he told me what he had to offer for my fulfillment of these needs. He asked me what I felt that I had to offer in this position and what I expected to get out of it. We negotiated a working relationship that extended to me a greater than usual autonomy in return for my acceptance of a new and challenging assignment. The relationship was based on immediate trust and confidence in each one's being able to deliver the goods—to meet needs and expectations that were mutually agreed to. For me, it was the best 2 years out of the 24 that I had at GE. For him, he knew that I would do whatever it took to support the goals. Although he was my manager, it felt more like we were partners.

Would this approach—the Psychological Contract—work today? Absolutely! In today's environment of greater respect for expert power and a period of low unemployment, it is those managers that embrace this Psychological Contract concept that will gain the trust and unreserved support of their subordinates. It won't matter if the nature of the organization is a bureaucracy or an adhocracy, or even a teamocracy. There will always be those who will be responsible for motivating the contributions of others to support the goals of the enterprise.

Tip Leaders, whether formal managers or temporary leaders or even those to whom we voluntarily grant authority, who offer to negotiate a Psychological Contract stand the best chance of providing a stimulating environment for all involved.

Admittedly, the diverse organizational styles of today's corporations do make the concept of the Psychological Contract much more complex. If a typical firm operates under a basic hierarchical structure, further broken down into cross-functional teams or matrix forms, it is likely that most of the people will be working under the direction of multiple leaders. These may include the formal manager, a long-term project manager, a shorter-term task force leader, and the elected leader of a temporary team. While it would be a stretch to assume that a Psychological Contract would be negotiated in every one of these relationships, it is a logical assumption to recognize that these teams will work better when there is a reasonable match between expectations and contributions among the team members.

In order to do this, we need to instill two behavioral protocols into the organization.

1. There must be a culture, supported at the very top of the organization, which believes in this approach and shares this belief with the rest of the company.
2. The human resources function must reinforce this culture, by maintaining an awareness of the individuality of each worker and including that information in the skills inventory.

Tip In the twenty-first century, maintaining a cadre of knowledgeable, skilled, motivated workers will be a major component of the true assets of a company. Being able to pull workers from this store, based on matching skills and assignment preferences to the need, will be of paramount importance to success.

Machiavelli in the Twentieth Century

In my readings on organizational behavior and leadership, I was amused by the frequency of quotations from Machiavelli. While we are quick to reject Machiavelli's ways, we surely recognize the pervasiveness of such reasoning in the organization. It must be embarrassing to realize that in the not too distant past, we selected and rewarded managers for exactly the traits and philosophy expounded by Machiavelli. However, this will not stand the test of the new century. There are better alternatives in leadership structure and style that will work better with today's psychologically healthy and productive individuals.

CHAPTER 13.6

SHARED REWARDS

Regardless of the type of organizational or management style, we all operate on some basis of measurements and rewards. These are usually tied to some set of expectations, objectives, or responsibilities. In the classic organization, management sets the objectives parameters, creates a set of measurements, and doles out the rewards. Rewards come in all shapes and sizes. They may include money, position, opportunity for advancement, a corner office, security, greater challenge or autonomy, and any collection of perks. They may be based solely on the expectations of the boss, or (in the case of the Psychological Contract) they may be based on a negotiated set of objectives.

What is common to almost all of these situations is that the measurements and rewards are based on individual performance. So how do we adapt such individualistic measurement and reward systems to the newer environments of matrix management and teams? If there is shared responsibility, shouldn't there be shared measurements and shared rewards?

Trap In the traditional system, we give individuals responsibility and a list of expectations. We then measure performance and distribute rewards. We expect the rewards to motivate performance. When there is shared responsibility and expectations, such as may exist in the projects environment, we often

371

maintain the individual measurement and rewards system. This promotes individual performance over team performance.

Shared rewards is not a new idea. The Scanlon Plan, a good half century ago, allowed for incentives for production teams, well before the concept of teams was even recognized. But this was applied under a much less complex set of conditions. First of all, the entire team reported to the same supervisor. Second, they were dedicated to a single program. And, third, the measurements were quite simple. As productivity objectives were met, the group shared in the rewards. In essence, it was an early type of profit-sharing plan.

So perhaps we can't apply the Scanlon Plan verbatim to project teams. But, what about the concept of sharing rewards? Can't we make that work to our advantage?

Much has been written about teams, but little about how to reward teams. There are several issues here. In the case where a team has been established specifically to achieve a goal, rewards can be related to the results. However, more often, an individual's time and effort may be split between a direct, line responsibility and partial support of multiple team efforts. This gets more complicated.

The key, of course, is to recognize that the old, individual measurement and reward process may no longer be suitable for the current work environment. If rewards are part of a motivation system, this system must be modified to suit the current environment and to promote the desired results. If the objective of teams is to achieve improved results from shared contribution and responsibility, then we need to establish incentives and rewards that foster such behavior.

Trap　　The reward system, even when designed to recognize the accomplishment of teams, must never forget that each member of the team is an individual. Each person requires recognition as an individual as well as a team member, and each person will have reward needs based on that person's specific needs and expectations. While the shared rewards should recognize shared results, they need not be cookie-cutter rewards, but rather provide for equal rewards based on individual preferences.

Caution is advised when we are introducing any changes to the reward system. Studies of human behavior have shown that people do not want to give up anything that they have gained, as far as compensation and recognition are concerned. Being a member of a team does not relieve most people of their need to guard their position in the pecking order. Therefore, it is likely that any approaches to shared measurements and rewards will have to be installed on top of existing practices, rather than in place of them.

What this means is that existing practices for individual measurements and rewards will stay in place, and new practices will be added to recognize team performance and results. There can be some changes to the individual measurement practices, however, such as involving peers in the performance appraisal. This affords team members the opportunity to recognize the contribution of other team members and to influence their rewards.

Some Shared Rewards Concepts

We can't get into actual shared rewards designs at this time. First of all, they must be developed to support the specific projects environment within each firm. Second, they need to be addressed by competent human resources specialists, which I am not.

However, I can venture forth with a few ideas that may serve to guide the specific developments.

- The measurements system should be balanced. That is, it should cover a wide range of desired results, both individual and team oriented, pertaining to both projects and technical performance, recognizing contributions to both projects and operations goals, and comprising both short-range and long-range objectives.
- The performance review should be based on inputs from a wide range of associates. These would include both functional and project managers and specialists, on both a supervisory and peer level. The team leader, where there is one, should be able to coordinate and influence such reviews. Also, where there is a team leader, the members of the team should participate in that leader's review.
- The reward pool should be available for equal sharing among the team participants. If there is a formal measurement and ranking of individual contributions to the project's success, then it might be feasible and proper to modify the individual rewards on the basis of results of the performance review. This should be exercised with caution, as such individual rating and reward practices can just as well act as a point of contention rather than as a motivator.
- Equal rewards does not necessarily mean identical rewards. What we are looking for is equal reward value. However, the specific reward can be tailored to the individual, based on that person's preferences (see Psychological Contract, in Chapter 13.5).

- If a team has been assembled to respond to an immediate crisis, then prompt team recognition should be given to the team members for pulling the firm through the crisis.
- If the team has been assembled to re-engineer systems and practices toward a goal of reducing costs, then it would be appropriate to design a team reward based on the savings achieved by the team.
- If the team is involved in a profit-based venture, then it would be appropriate to design a team reward that is based on achievement and preservation of the planned profit.
- Be prepared to abandon some of the old reward protocols. In today's professional environment, where leadership is being recognized on the basis of knowledge, rather than position, the concept of rewards is also changing. However, make such changes carefully so that the appearance that something is being taken away is avoided.
- Recognizing this changing environment suggests that we also take a fresh look at some of the traditional views of human behavior in business. For instance, Frederick Herzberg's theories on motivators and satisfiers, in his 1966 book *Work and the Nature of Man* (World Publishing Company), submits that five areas: achievement, recognition, the work itself, responsibility, and advancement constitute motivational factors. There were other items that he grouped under the label of *hygiene factors*. These lower-level needs had to be recognized, but were not considered incentives. The underlying philosophy behind Herzberg's findings of 35 years ago is probably even more applicable in today's environment, but needs to be re-examined in light of the psychology of today's professionals and the utilization of such personnel in team and matrix configurations.
- For members of teams working to achieve project success, it would appear to be logical to base much of the added rewards on how well project success was actually achieved. This would further suggest that a survey of customer and stakeholder satisfaction be taken both during and at the conclusion of the project. (Frankly, such surveys should be executed to aid in achieving stakeholder satisfaction, regardless of the impact on performance evaluation.)

Remember: the objectives in a shared rewards system are to stimulate improved performance of individuals working on teams, and to maximize their contribution to project success. Anything that works toward these goals, while fully respecting the individual team member, should be considered.

Index